D1108526

THE MOVIES OF THE EIGHTIES

Canadian Cataloguing in Publication Data

Base, Ron, 1948–
The movies of the eighties

Includes bibliographical references.
ISBN 0-9694786-0-7

1. Motion pictures. I. Haslam, David, 1944–
II. Title.

PN1993.5.A1B37 1990 791.43'75 C90-095175-3
Marquee Communications Incorporated
77 Mowat Avenue
Suite 621
Toronto, Ontario
Canada M6K 3E3
Printed and bound in the United States of America

For Joel and Erin Ruddy
who helped make
going to the movies of the
eighties so much fun.

For my parents
Gordon and Mary Haslam
who introduced me to the
joy of movies and in
memory of my friend
Barry Carnon who
introduced me to the
business of movies.

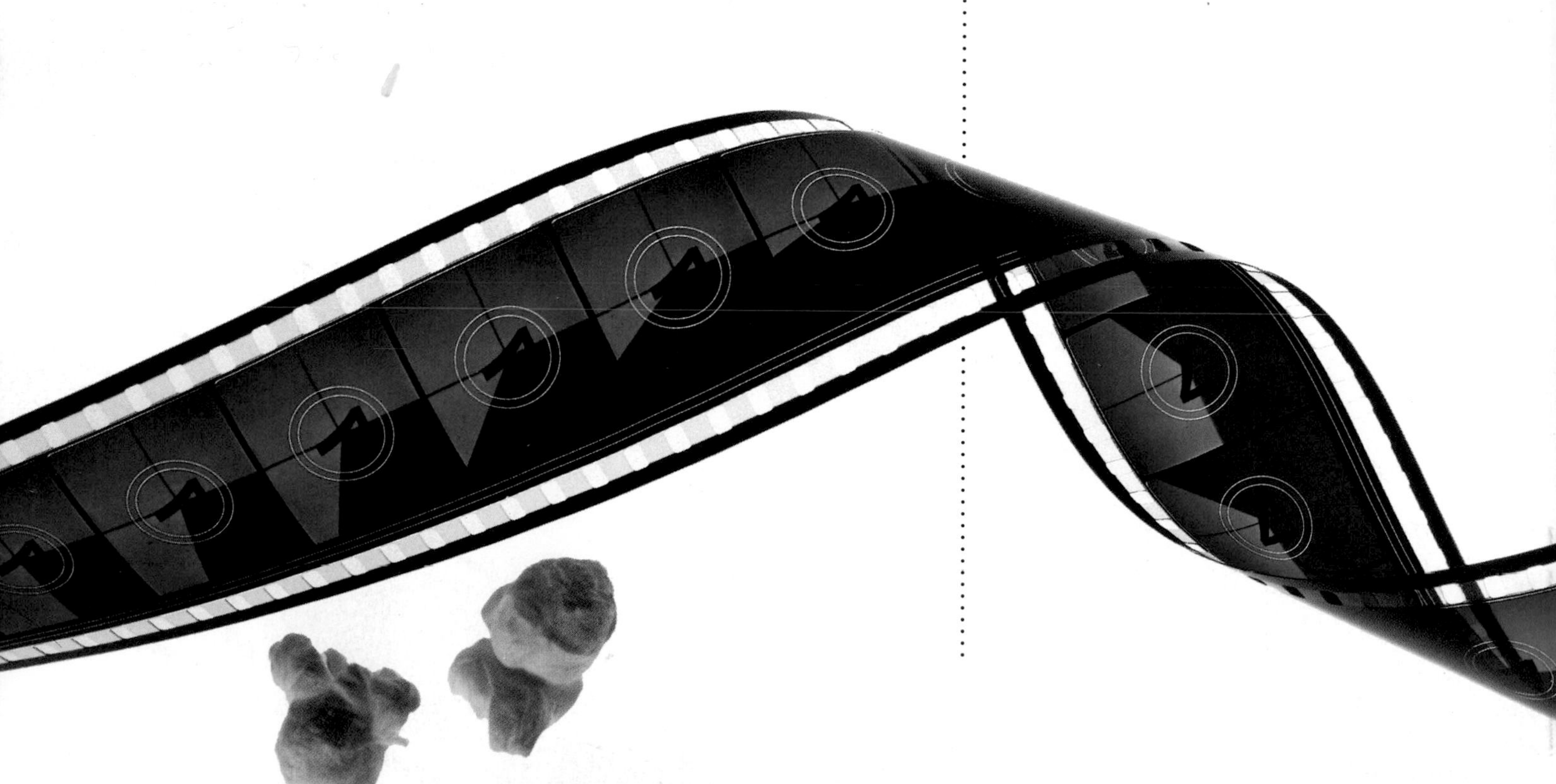

THE MOVIES OF THE EIGHTIES

BY RON BASE AND DAVID HASLAM

A MARQUEE PUBLICATION
A MARQUEE PUBLICATION

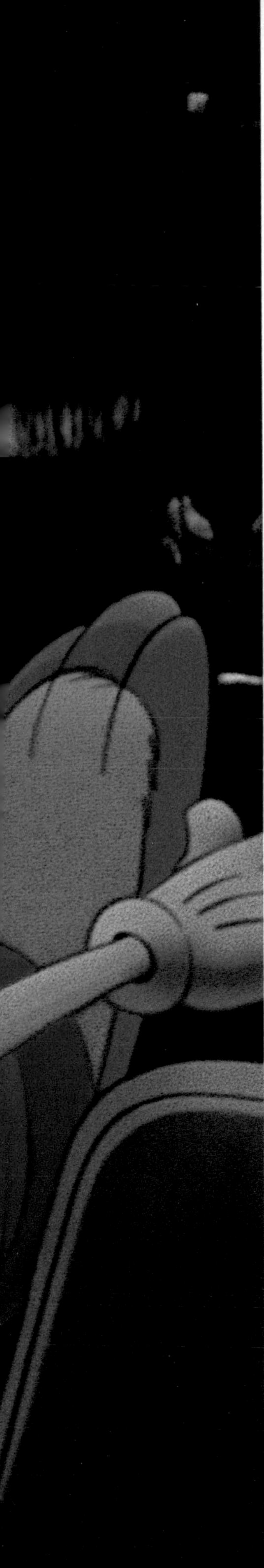

CONTENTS

E.T. PHONES HOME

AN INTRODUCTION TO THE MOVIES OF THE EIGHTIES

E.T. — The Extra-Terrestrial **was first released in May of 1982 and became the biggest box office hit of all time, grossing $700 million. No other film came close to matching its popularity during the eighties, despite the increasing obsession with megaprofits. Even so, *E.T.* has a way to go to overtake the longevity of *Gone with the Wind,* which remained the largest-grossing movie in history from 1940 until *The Sound of Music* replaced it as the box office champ in August 1966.**

Hollywood in the eighties rediscovered the movies. It moved into the future, staring at itself in a rear-view mirror. Old formulas were used again and again to remake the kinds of movies Hollywood always liked: the bigger-than-big, glossier-than-glossy, more-stars-than-in-the-heavens kind of extravaganzas. Ronald Reagan was in the White House, fantasy and escapism were the order of the day, and Hollywood was right there to provide it on the big screen. There was a great deal of grumbling about commercialism and greed during the eighties, about continually reworking the same formulas, but in fact the love affair with movies, renewed around the world during the decade, helped to create a surprising amount of diversity. What follows is the story of an era in movies the like of which has not been seen since the halcyon days of the thirties and forties, the story of the most fascinating and commercially successful decade in the history of the movies, told through the voices of the stars and directors and producers who made the movies of the eighties. It's a story that begins, for our purposes, at a French seaside resort, with a young director preparing to unveil his new movie . . .

The phenomenal success of *E.T.* spawned all sorts of imitations throughout the eighties. The most successful of them was *Cocoon* (1985), about aliens who arrive in Florida to retrieve their stranded brethren. They inadvertently make a group of elderly people young again. This aliens-and-the-fountain-of-youth story revived the film careers of veterans Jessica Tandy, Hume Cronyn, and particularly Don Ameche. The former Dominici Felix Amici had been one of the most popular stars at Twentieth Century-Fox in the mid-thirties and forties, but he had not worked for years when director Ron Howard signed him to the cast, and he won an Oscar for best supporting actor.

ON THE SORT OF BRIGHT CLOUDLESS MORNING in May that the tourists flock to the French Riviera for, Steven Spielberg arose early amidst the hushed luxury of the Hotel du Cap, a former villa built in the 1800s by a Russian prince and now considered one of the most luxurious hotels in the world.

The 34-year-old filmmaker put on a safari jacket and a NASA baseball cap, and, maintaining the scraggly beard he lately had taken to wearing, drove into Cannes to see how the world, on this final day of the 1982 Cannes Film Festival, would react to his newest movie.

For the journalists who crowded into the Palais des Festivals for the 8:30 screening, it was the final day of a long and mostly lack-luster festival. Movies in general were thought to be in trouble around the world. The talk was of failure and scandal. The eighties had been ushered in by *Heaven's Gate*, a $36-million fiasco that had all but destroyed United Artists, the studio which financed it. And the buzz in Hollywood the coming summer would be of former *Wall Street Journal* reporter David McClintick's book *Indecent Exposure.* The book dealt with the scandal that rocked the film industry in 1977 when it was discovered that David Begelman, the president of Columbia studio had embezzled $10,000 by forging a cheque made out to actor Cliff Robertson. The resulting attempt at a cover-up was still causing reverberations.

Cliff Robertson.

In his book, McClintick would argue that "Hollywood is rife with corruption all right, but the occasional incidents of embezzlement, fraud, cheating, and chiseling — as serious as they are — constitute symptoms of a more pervasive and subtle corruption."

In short, something was very wrong with the way the American movie industry was conducting business and making movies. "The movie business is at the moral level of the South Vietnamese Army," screenwriter Josh Greenfield (*Harry and Tonto*) complained to *Newsweek* magazine in 1978. What's more, movie attendance was down, the costs of making movies were rising (the average movie cost $10 million in 1981), and Burt Reynolds was getting $5 million just for smiling and sitting in a car in *Cannonball Run*. "Now," reported *Time* magazine, "cable TV and cassettes are starting to offer the movies serious competition for the entertainment dollar." Paul Schrader who wrote *Taxi Driver* and directed *American Gigolo,* was not optimistic: "We are supporting a dying business, and the change is scary."

Little of this gloom and doom penetrated the world of Steven Spielberg. Lesser mortals became embroiled in the industry's alley fights and allowed themselves to be corrupted; Spielberg was above the fray, beyond reproach. Envy and avarice, the longest continuing partnership in Hollywood, did not cloud his life. "I'm kind of like the 500-pound gorilla," he said. "If I want to do it, I can do it."

Spielberg as a child used to sneak onto the Universal studios lot, and wander around, enchanted by the movie world he had broken into, dreaming of the day when he somehow could be part of it. He could barely remember a time in his life when he did not want to make films. He devoured the movies produced by the Walt Disney studio. The emphasis on Disney movies was partially due to the fact that his parents censored much of what he watched. He once told an interviewer that they kept a blanket over the television set.

At the age of 12, he wrote and filmed his first amateur production using actors, and by the time he turned 16 he had shot a 140-minute movie titled *Firefight,* about scientists investigating mysterious lights

***Above*: Spielberg on the set of *E.T.* with young Henry Thomas who played Elliott, the director's alter ego. E.T. himself was actually three different mechanical creatures created by designer Carlo Rambaldi: an actor wearing a padded suit; a doll attached to the floor; an electronic robot with 86 points of movement and 40 different facial expressions on four interchangeable heads.**

Above: **The Disney entry into the race to make big, expensive high-tech science fiction adventure movies in the wake of the success of *Star Wars* was *Tron* (1982). The idea was rather novel: human Pac-Man played by Jeff Bridges is miniaturized and sent into the interior of a computerized video game. The special effects were often dazzlingly original. In spite of good reviews, *Tron* was not a hit, perhaps because kids were no longer interested in Walt Disney movies.**

Opposite: **Steven Spielberg on the set of *Indiana Jones and the Temple of Doom* (1984) with Harrison Ford. The second Indy adventure was criticized for its darkness and violence, and what was perceived in some quarters to be its suggestion of racism in a plot that revolved around the dreaded thuggee cult of India. Spielberg later dismissed the movie, and said one of the reasons he made the third adventure, *Indiana Jones and the Last Crusade*, was to bring back the sort of light hearted adventure contained in *Raiders of the Lost Ark*, but absent in *Temple of Doom*.**

in the night sky — a theme he would return to years later when he made *Close Encounters of the Third Kind.*

Studio executives first noticed him when he attended the film department at California State College (his marks were too poor to go anywhere else) and turned out an impressive 24-minute short, *Amblin',* which was shown in 1969 at the Atlanta Film Festival. Sidney Sheinberg, who was then head of Universal's television division, was impressed enough that he signed Spielberg to a seven-year contract. This time, instead of going over the wall to get into Universal, he was coming in through the front gate to shoot television shows. His first assignment was directing actress Joan Crawford in an episode of a series called *Night Gallery*. Less than a year later, in 1971, he got his chance to direct a two-hour TV feature titled *Duel.* In it, Dennis Weaver played a motorist trying to elude a malevolent runaway truck. The movie was shot in just 16 days on a budget of $350,000. It became a big hit in Europe and Japan, and even though it was never shown theatrically in the U.S. it acquired a huge cult following. It's considered by some critics to be the best movie ever made for television.

Close Encounters of the Third Kind.

Duel led to Spielberg's first feature film in 1974, a comedy drama titled *The Sugarland Express.* The movie impressed everyone, but oddly it was not a success with the public, despite the presence of Goldie Hawn. The next year, however, Spielberg directed *Jaws* for Universal. For a time, it was the biggest hit in movie history, grossing $60 million in its first month of release, a figure that, up until then, was unheard of. He had followed it with *Close Encounters of the Third Kind,* and then his only certifiable box office flop, an especially unfunny but expensive (at $27 million) comedy, *1941.* He recovered quickly however, and directed *Raiders of the Lost Ark,* which became the most popular movie released in 1981.

It was Spielberg together with his friend George Lucas, the director of *Star Wars,* who inadvertently created Hollywood's newly discovered obsession with the megahit, the movie that went beyond mere success and became a phenomenon, breaking all existing box office records. As Hollywood entered the eighties, making movies in smaller numbers with bigger budgets that demanded higher profits, anything less than a blockbuster was no longer good enough.

E.T.

When Steven Spielberg took *E.T.* to Columbia Pictures, he was turned down by studio boss Frank Price. Columbia already had an alien picture in development, titled *Starman*, and wasn't interested in another one. Spielberg then took *E.T.* to Universal, which immediately snapped it up. Thus, it was Universal, not Columbia, that ended up with the most successful picture of all time. Columbia meanwhile, doggedly went ahead with *Starman*. It was released in 1985. directed by John Carpenter (*Halloween*) and starring Jeff Bridges as the alien who wants to go home, and Karen Allen as the woman trying to help him get there. *Starman* won Bridges an Oscar nomination for best actor, something E.T. never received, but the public wasn't interested in real-life alien beings, and the movie flopped.

WITH ALL SPIELBERG'S CLOUT AND POWER, he had become increasingly secretive. Therefore, no one knew anything about the new movie he was showing at Cannes. Following the huge success of *Raiders*, he had said vaguely that he wanted to make a film about children, and that it would be called *A Boy's Life*.

But the movie the press was seeing this morning was not *A Boy's Life*. No one knew what to expect, and at this point at the end of the festival, no one really cared. The reporters who slumped into their seats were exhausted after 10 days of movies. They just wanted this movie, and the Cannes Film Festival, to be over.

A couple of moments after 8:30 a.m., the lights went down, the curtain opened, the John Williams music rose ominously and for

a moment the screen was black. Then a title appeared: *E.T. — The Extra-Terrestrial.* After that moment, the movies would never again be quite the same.

The first audience ever to see *E.T.* was enchanted almost immediately. The movie, as written by Melissa Mathison in collaboration with Spielberg, was simple enough: a worm-like extra-terrestrial creature with large, sad eyes capable of seducing multitudes is stranded on earth. He is discovered late one night hiding in the garage by a boy named Elliott (Henry Thomas), who lives with his brother, sister and single mother in a large suburban bungalow that is quintessentially middle American. E.T.'s goal is to go home. It was a desire reiterated constantly not only in Spielberg's work, but in many of the most revered Hollywood fantasies, notably *The Wizard of Oz* ("Oh, Aunt Em," Dorothy gushes, "there's no place like home").

At one point in the film, Elliott and E.T. are bicycling into the country to arrange for the little creature's pick-up. E.T., in order to make time, unexpectedly levitates the bike high into the night sky. When that happened, everyone in the audience gasped, then applauded. If Spielberg had any doubts as to whether he had a hit, they were assuaged with the reaction to that scene. As E.T. finally headed home amidst the overheated swell of the John Williams music, the lights went up, and the dazed, euphoric and teary-eyed journalists staggered out of the Palais into the midday sun, knowing they had witnessed something very special indeed.

Later, Spielberg said that the origins of *E.T.* lay in his desire "to make a movie about young people. And this was the threat realized." The origins, he conceded, also lay in his middle-class childhood, growing up in New Jersey and in Scottsdale, Arizona. "That's how I grew up," he said of the movie. "You saw my house. That house was very much like the house I was raised in. That was my bedroom. And the little girl was an amalgamation of my three terrifying sisters. As for myself, well, I wish I could have been young Henry Thomas who plays Elliott."

At the gala black tie premiere that evening, *E.T.* was even more enthusiastically received than it had been at the press screening. There was a standing ovation, and thunderous applause. Still, it's doubtful, as he flew out of the Nice airport, that Spielberg truly understood the dimensions of the success *E.T.* was about to enjoy. How could he? There had never before been anything quite like its success. Throughout the summer and autumn, *E.T.* would become the largest-grossing movie in the history of the North American box office. Its worldwide grosses eventually would amount to more than $700 million, revenues that, by the end of the eighties, no other film had come even close to surpassing.

Above: More sci-fi _Star Wars_-type adventure. _The Last Starfighter_ (1984) emerged from the video game era, and suggested that the video game had come from outer space. An alien recruiter, played by the late Robert Preston, whisks a young computer whiz into a galaxy far, far away, in order to fight the evil race known as Ko-Dan.

Right: The most curious sci-fi movie of the decade, _Heartbeeps_ (1981), was a robot comedy co-starring Bernadette Peters and the late Andy Kaufman as a couple of robots in love. She is a hostess robot, and he is a valet robot, and they escape from a world ruled by humans. The movie encountered all sorts of problems, and when it was released ran only 79 minutes.

As Spielberg grew older during the eighties, he made repeated attempts to grow beyond the sort of adolescent-oriented adventures that had made him the most successful filmmaker in the history of Hollywood. Spielberg didn't ordinarily read for pleasure, but one of his producers, Kathleen Kennedy, urged him to read Alice Walker's *The Color Purple*, about a young black girl growing up in the South. Spielberg was so taken with the book that he decided to direct it himself in 1984. The resulting movie, *left*, shot for only $15 million, was a major departure for him, and created a great deal of controversy, particularly from some blacks who were incensed that a white, middle-class director would attempt to bring such a personal story of black life to the screen. There was further criticism of the way Spielberg had blunted some of the more controversial elements of the Walker book, but when all was said and done, the movie was tremendously successful, grossing close to $100 million.

Director David Lean was said to have been interested in making J.G. Ballard's novel of a boy's adventures in Shanghai after the invasion of the Japanese, *Empire of the Sun*, into a movie with Spielberg producing. However, it was Spielberg who directed the most masterful and accomplished work of his career, shooting some of the movie on location in China. Ironically, *Empire of the Sun* (1987), was Spielberg's least successful movie since *1941*, another movie with a World War II background.

For years, Spielberg had been wanting to remake the old Spencer Tracy World War II tearjerker, *A Guy Named Joe*, about a fighter pilot who comes back from the dead to help the woman he loves. He finally decided to do it after completing *Indiana Jones and the Last Crusade*. Instead of World War II, Spielberg set *Always* around modern-day forest fire-fighting pilots. Richard Dreyfuss played the old Spencer Tracy role, and Holly Hunter was the woman he loved, even after death. Spielberg had wanted to cast Sean Connery as Dreyfuss's guardian angel, but when the actor was unavailable, he cast Audrey Hepburn instead.

By 1985, Steven Spielberg's independent production company, Amblin Entertainment, was churning out carefully crafted but instantly forgettable adolescent adventures like *The Goonies, above,* about a group of kids who find a buried treasure. It was a combination of a *Hardy Boys* adventure and an amusement park ride.

Drew Barrymore, the granddaughter of the great John Barrymore, was just six years old when she enchanted everyone as Elliott's precocious little sister in *E.T.* Like most members of the movie's cast, however, she did not go on to better things. She appeared in *Firestarter* (1984) and *Cat's Eye* (1985), *above.* But by the beginning of the nineties, at the age of 14, she was best known for her public battle to overcome drug and alcohol abuse.

ALTHOUGH SPIELBERG AND HOLLYWOOD PROBably had little indication of it at the time, *E.T.* would help to usher in a new golden era at the movies. For all the complaints about the emptiness of the American film culture that were heard throughout the decade, and the continuing obsession with what was commercially viable, it could be argued that American movies had found themselves again, and lured back audiences who rediscovered movies as they had not since the heyday of Hollywood in the thirties and forties. Whatever might be said of the aesthetic value of many of the decade's films, they did succeed in attracting huge numbers of people around the world, who, if they liked a movie, would come back to it again and again, then see it yet again when the movie was released on videocassette.

Hollywood appeared to have relearned some old lessons about how to entertain audiences. Formulas were found that worked, and those formulas were used again and again. Lucas and Spielberg had taught Hollywood that if a movie made huge amounts of money once, it could make almost as much, maybe even more, if you produced a sequel employing the same characters. And so there were follow-ups to just about every successful movie. The summers became known as "sequel summers." An archeologist named Indiana Jones, a quartet of unemployed nutcases who called themselves Ghostbusters, a Vietnam veteran named Rambo, a prize fighter known as Rocky, the crew of the starship Enterprise, a secret agent codenamed 007, an Australian outback cowboy named Crocodile Dundee and a long-nailed, gruesome-faced ghoul named Freddy were welcomed again and again by audiences. Stars who played a popular character often found themselves trapped by that character. In 1984, for example, Christopher Reeve announced that, after *Superman III,* he would never again play the Man of Steel. "I felt, well, I think we've done it now," Reeve said. "I've enjoyed it, it's been a great chapter for me, but we're gonna run out of things to do." Two years later, having failed to ignite much interest playing roles that didn't require him to fly around in blue tights, Reeve signed to appear in *Superman IV.*

When Sylvester Stallone finished *Rocky III,* he announced that was it, he was finished with Rocky. After he completed *Rocky IV,* he again made the same announcement. "This is definitely the final time," he assured in 1985. "There is really nothing else to do with him except fight with himself." He laughed at the thought. "He'd go into a mirrored room and beat himself up." By the end of 1989, though, with his appeal declining, Stallone was preparing to fight himself in a mirrored room — *Rocky V* was in production.

Stallone like everyone else, was in the business not of breaking new ground, but of giving the audience what it wanted. The hit-makers in the eighties, particularly Spielberg and Lucas, were very much like the people who came to their movies: white, middle class, weaned on television and films, and anxious to be swept away by the magic unfolding on the large screen in front of them. The movies they wanted to make were also the movies they wanted to see — and millions of other people, it turned out, wanted to see them too.

The times also had something to do with this. Amidst the growing complexities and contradictions of the eighties, audiences once again employed the darkness of a movie theater as a way of escape. "There is this acceleration of change, and we're much more affected by that," noted Paul Newman. "People want to be entertained. They don't want to be bombarded by emotions or questions. I hope it gets better. I don't know whether it will or not."

Ronald Reagan was in the White House telling Americans to feel good about themselves again. The Gipper was a former actor himself, and he had been formed by the simplistic mythology of the movies: good triumphs over evil, might is right, true love lasts forever.

Christopher Reeve considered himself a serious actor before he was chosen to play Superman in 1978, after the names of such better known stars as Nick Nolte and Burt Reynolds had been suggested. Reeve's intensity was perfect for the role, and he played the Man of Steel in three sequels during the eighties.

***Above*: Opera star Luciano Pavarotti was never more acclaimed than he was when he made his movie debut in *Yes, Giorgio* (1982), about a singer who falls for his throat specialist. The public, with its sixth sense about these things, stayed away in droves.**

***Below*: Yes, Virginia, they even made a movie about Santa Claus during the eighties. Called *Santa Claus: The Movie* (1985), it was produced by Ilya Salkind, who previously brought Superman to the screen. In order to add some star power, the producers hired Dudley Moore as an elf who helps Santa save Christmas. He could not help Santa save the movie, however. It bombed.**

If audiences did not want reality from the President of the United States, they certainly did not want it in their movies.

In the seventies, America lost a real war in Vietnam; in the eighties that war could be won at the movies, thanks to that indestructible patriot, John Rambo. The simplicity of the Hollywood view of things, as it always has, played well around the world. In Beirut, Christian and Moslem militiamen stopped shooting and shelling each other long enough to attend *Rambo — First Blood II.* Even as they hated America, they loved the movie. Sly Stallone was their kind of guy. Even Stallone was surprised by Rambo's success. "Oh boy, that was unbelievable," he said one day lounging around the Beverly Wilshire Hotel. "I didn't think the movie was going to be popular at all. I thought that character was just too dark for audiences to respond to. But it did sometimes ten times the business in certain countries that *Rocky III* did. In Europe, it murdered *Rocky.*"

North American film revenues, in the seventies, hadn't budged for years, hovering in the vicinity of $1 billion annually. By the end of the eighties, they had ballooned to over $5 billion. Movie attendance in North America had reached levels not seen in nearly 50 years. Box office records snapped with increasing regularity; everything was on an upward spiral.

Everyone seemed to be going to the movies again. Declining attendance, which scared observers in the seventies, had reversed itself, and almost 500 new films were being released each year. The video cassettes that initially produced dire predictions about the destruction of movie exhibition, actually had the reverse effect. They ended up revolutionizing the business, appealing to an older audience that then turned around and, impatient for the cassette, went out to see the movie when it was in a theater. In turn, this older audience helped reassure producers that there was an audience for more adult-oriented movies. The increased attendance also resulted from the efforts of a determined young Canadian entrepreneur named Garth Drabinsky, who, through his chain of Cineplex Odeon theaters, breathed new life into the moribund exhibition business in North America by refurbishing old theaters, building new ones and generally making going out to the picture show a much more pleasurable experience than it had been for years.

Summer had become an annual binge of movie attendance, netting the industry the year's biggest share of profits. In 1988, for example, audiences plunked down a record $1.7 billion at the box office in order to see summer movies. The next year the figure jumped 20 percent to almost $2.1 billion.

Even so, video revenues began to surpass theatrical profits. Thus, not only was *E.T.* the most popular movie ever released theatrically, it also sold more videos than any other when it was released around Christmas of 1988 — in excess of 15 million copies. According to *Variety*, Spielberg himself, who at one time stated that he would never release *E.T.* into people's living rooms, was said to have realized a profit of $75 million from the video sale alone.

But at the beginning of the eighties, before the release of *E.T.*, there was gloom in Hollywood, and one movie more than any other was responsible for it.

How Hollywood Emerged from the Shadow of Heaven's Gate

KRIS KRISTOFFERSON WENT FOR A RUN ALONG the beach at Malibu. A few days before he was to fly to New York and then Toronto for the premiere of his latest film, the singer and actor jogged seven miles, then took his daughter Casey to school. He had recently won a long battle against those well publicized show-business devils, drugs and alcohol, and as he jogged along the beach at the age of 44, he was a slim, fit 155 pounds and as healthy as he had ever been in his life.

While he was filming in Montana the year before, Kristofferson's marriage to the singer Rita Coolidge had broken up. He jogged 15 miles a day in order to make himself tired enough to sleep. But now his life once more had settled down, and he was looking forward to the premiere of what he was certain was the most important movie of his career. "What a difference a year can make," he exalted one morning over coffee in the kitchen of his friend Vernon White, who lived down the hill from him. "The sun is shining, the birds are singing. It's a Walt Disney world out there."

Kris Kristofferson.

If Kristofferson had any inkling of what was to come, he gave no indication of it on that sun-splashed morning in Malibu. His new movie was called *Heaven's Gate*, and it was directed by Michael Cimino, the *wunderkind* who in 1978 had flared into prominence with *The Deer Hunter*. The epic film about Pennsylvanian blue collar workers sent to Vietnam had won five Academy Awards, including best picture and best director, and had become one of the most talked-about pictures of the decade.

Following the disaster of *Heaven's Gate*, the other great Hollywood scandal of the eighties swirled around the death of actor Vic Morrow, *above*, and the two Vietnamese children he was carrying across a stream while filming an episode of *Twilight Zone: The Movie* (1983) one July night in 1982. Morrow was decapitated when a helicopter, filming overhead came too low and crashed into the actor and the children. The accident raised a hue and cry about safety on movie sets, and about lax enforcement of rules regarding kids working in film (the children should never have been on the set that night). John Landis, who directed the segment, was charged along with four others with manslaughter, but was later found not guilty after a lengthy jury trial. Steven Spielberg was one of the executive producers of *Twilight Zone*, but he was not on the set that night, and was not implicated in any of the subsequent court proceedings.

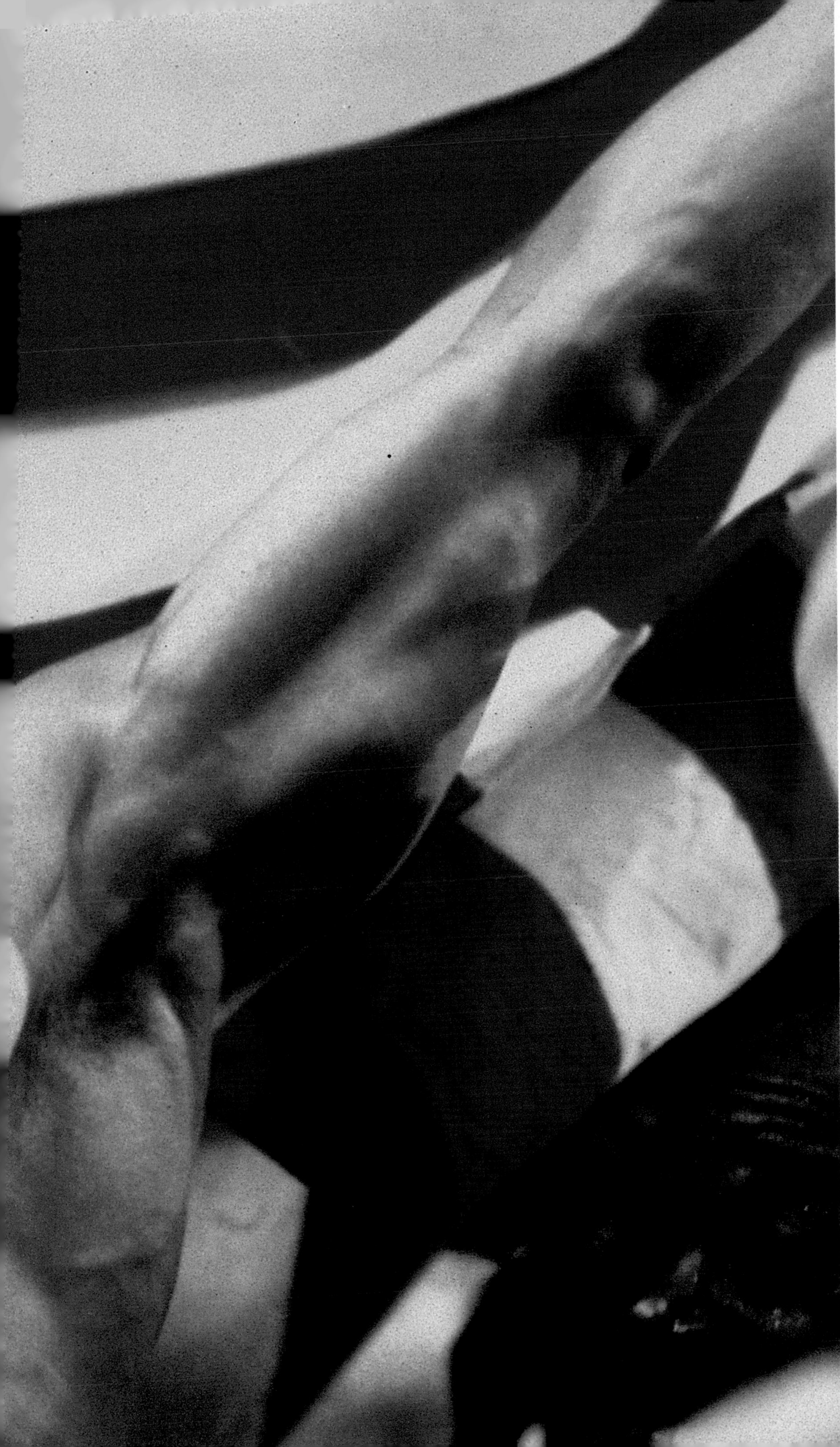

Although Stallone swore he wasn't political and the commies just happened to make great villains, Sly nonetheless managed to take on the Evil Empire with a great deal of glee in 1985. In the summer he was in *Rambo — First Blood II,* winning the war in Vietnam. That fall, he was in the ring for *Rocky IV,* draped in the American flag, taking on Russia's supposedly invincible steroid-stuffed champion boxer (played by Dolph Lundgren, who went on to become a minor action hero himself). Rocky, of course, beat the Russkie and saved American honor. Who even knew the Russians boxed?

Disney, trying anything to regain its lost box office clout in the eighties, even went so far as to go back to Oz in a now all-but-forgotten sequel to the 1939 classic, *The Wizard of Oz*. Dark and gloomy, *Return to Oz* (1985) starred nine-year-old Fairuza Balk from Vancouver, British Columbia, and featured a talking chicken. The movie disappeared almost as soon as it opened, and not even the talking chicken has been heard from since.

Matthew Broderick, the son of the late character actor James Broderick, made a name for himself starring on Broadway in Neil Simon's *Brighton Beach Memoirs,* then went on to make his movie debut in another Simon vehicle, *Max Dugan Returns* (1983). Audiences discovered him in *WarGames* (1983), one of the best and most successful of the computer-whiz-in-trouble movies that proliferated in the early eighties. Broderick is the teenaged genius who accidentally breaks into a Defence Department supercomputer that could set off World War III.

Heaven's Gate was Cimino's first picture since *The Deer Hunter.* The new movie was to be equally epic, a western about the Johnson County war, the classic cattlemen-against-the-homesteaders story, filmed in Montana at a cost reputed to be in the neighborhood of $36 million. In a small, insular community that lived on gossip, the rumors and stories proliferated about *Heaven's Gate*: an arrogant young director way over budget and very much out of control, and a studio with little choice but to swallow hard and pay the mounting production bills. Kristofferson was convinced Hollywood had given Cimino a bad rap. The movie would vindicate everyone involved. Cimino was about to unveil his masterpiece.

If he had no inkling of trouble drinking coffee in Malibu, Kristofferson began to sense something was wrong by the time he flew to New York a week later for the film's premiere on November 18, 1980. Cimino's original 5½ hour version had been pared down to 3 hours and 39 minutes. Even so, United Artists, the studio that financed *Heaven's Gate,* was extremely nervous, and as Kristofferson took his seat next to co-star Isabelle Huppert that night at the Cinema theater on Third Avenue, the atmosphere was tense.

By the time the picture crashed to an end, it was clear United Artists had a major disaster on its hands. Critic Vincent Canby wrote a review in the next day's *New York Times* that sounded the picture's

death knell: "*Heaven's Gate* fails so completely, you might suspect Mr. Cimino sold his soul to the devil to obtain the success of *The Deer Hunter*, and the devil has just come around to collect."

As Kristofferson flew to Toronto the next day, an idea had formed in Mike Cimino's mind: pull *Heaven's Gate* from release, and re-edit the picture. As Kristofferson and Vernon White sat down at the University theater to view the movie once again, the decision had been made to cancel its release until more work had been done.

When a re-edited version of the movie was finally released the following April, it averaged only $500 per theater, which meant that almost no one went to see it. The fiasco ultimately led to the collapse of United Artists, and a restructuring that was still going on at the end of the decade.

There were lots of other expensive flops in the eighties. *Dune*, produced by Dino De Laurentiis, and *The Cotton Club*, directed by Francis Coppola, each of which cost at least $50 million, failed miserably on the *same weekend* in December of 1984. Two more such multimillion-dollar miscalculations were *Howard the Duck*, produced by George Lucas, and *Ishtar*, a misconceived comedy starring Warren Beatty and Dustin Hoffman. (The joke around Hollywood in the summer of 1987 was that *Ishtar* was Arabic for *Howard the Duck*.) Yet nothing, no matter how much of a flop, was able to erase the

Above: Danny DeVito takes it lying down. Michael Douglas couldn't get anyone interested in turning his script about a female romance novelist who gets involved in a real-life South American adventure, into a movie. Then _Raiders of the Lost Ark_ became a hit, and Douglas got the go-ahead to make _Romancing the Stone_.

Right: Henry Thomas, post _E.T._, grew up a little bit, but no one was much interested in seeing him in _Cloak and Dagger_ (1984).

Opposite: A scene from _Heaven's Gate_ (1981). United Artists might have wished so many people lined up at the box office.

Even the robots took on human qualities in the post-*E.T.* era. *Short Circuit* (1986) starred a state-of-the-art robot named No. 5 who escapes from a laboratory with the help of Steve Guttenberg and Ally Sheedy. The film was successful enough that it spawned a sequel in 1988. However, one robot comedy-adventure proved to be enough for audiences.

Opposite: Christopher Lloyd hangs off the clock tower from *Back to the Future* (1985), one of the most popular and adroit adolescent fantasies to emerge from Steven Spielberg's Amblin Entertainment during the eighties. Bob Gale and Robert Zemeckis had written several unsuccessful scripts, including Spielberg's misfired attempt at epic comedy, *1941.* (1979). When the two shopped the property around Hollywood, every major studio in town turned it down. Finally, Spielberg had to take it upon himself to get *Back to the Future* made, and it became the year's biggest hit.

bad taste left in the aftermath of *Heaven's Gate.*

Steven Bach, the former United Artists executive had this to say about *Heaven's Gate* in *Final Cut,* his book about the mistakes that went into making the movie: "Perhaps there is something about the movie business itself, the industry as it is construed today that mitigates against the kind of humanism that might have transformed *Heaven's Gate* from an essay in exploitation to what John Gardner called at various times 'moral' or 'generous' fiction. Perhaps the conditions in which careers are forged and films constructed partake so little of those qualities that we should not expect to find films imbued with them. But occasionally we do, and that is what justifies continuing to make them."

E.T., RELEASED TWO YEARS AFTER *HEAVEN'S GATE,* proved to be one of those films. Its humanity and unadorned appeal to basic human emotions provided Hollywood not only with a role model, but also a problem: in the wake of *E.T.* no one wanted to make a picture that appealed to anyone over the age of 14.

The Spielberg fantasy factory, Amblin Entertainment, named after the award-winning short that got him started, began working at full throttle, contributing to the growing sense that adolescence had been permanently arrested within the movie industry in order to attract huge dollars. Amblin churned out Kids R Us kinds of films: *Gremlins, Batteries Not Included, Young Sherlock Holmes* and *Back to the Future,* among others, and the gargantuan grosses only encouraged Hollywood to abandon intelligence.

Gizmo, nicest of the *Gremlins.*

"What really changed Hollywood in a material way was the first *Star Wars* (1977)," commented director Lawrence Kasdan. "It transformed the balance sheets of an entire publicly held company (Twentieth Century-Fox), so that became the new goal. If you're always swinging for the fences you're only going to get a certain kind of movie. The amazing thing is, even given the attention focused on making blockbusters, they haven't got a clue how to do it."

Nonetheless, everyone wanted to try. For serious filmmakers attempting to make serious films, it was not a good time. "The big fantasy films are a greater risk for the companies," said director Norman Jewison. "But sometimes the companies are more willing to invest

Above: **Everyone questioned not only director Milos Forman's decision to film a movie version of Peter Shaffer's London and Broadway hit, *Amadeus*, based on the life and music of Wolfgang Amadeus Mozart, but also his casting choices. To play the title role, he chose a largely unknown actor named Tom Hulce who previously had appeared in *National Lampoon's Animal House.* Not only was Hulce nominated for an Academy Award (F. Murray Abraham, even more unknown than Hulce won the Oscar for his portrayal of Salieri), but *Amadeus* also won for best picture of 1984. What's more, the film was a huge international success.**

Below: ***Body Heat*** **(1981) made a young soap opera actress named Kathleen Turner a star. If you thought what was in the movie was sexy, you should have read the script.**

in films like that. They feel they will have a better chance at the box office because the audience seems to demand fast-paced films and gets bored very easily."

For Woody Allen, the prolific artist who made the most personal American films, the whole process of moviemaking in Hollywood had become laughable. "The business of long casting sessions, and many lunch meetings with potential stars, it's all nonsense," he argued. "Guys out in Hollywood do this all the time. They get a project okayed and they work two years at all the perquisites. They love flying to New York to discuss something with the costume designer, then flying back to California and meeting three actresses, then having lunch with the rewrite man, and they make the thing into a way of life."

In this sort of atmosphere it was tough even for the acknowledged master of the popcorn movie blockbuster, Lawrence Kasdan. By the age of 34, the South Carolina-born University of Michigan graduate and former advertising copy writer, had penned the screenplay not only for *Raiders of the Lost Ark*, but *Return of the Jedi*, and *The Empire Strikes Back*, three of the most successful blockbusters of all time. Then Kasdan himself directed a deliciously tawdry *film noir*

thriller from his own script entitled *Body Heat.* Kasdan next wanted to move on to something more serious, a movie that dealt with the sixties generation now grown uneasily into the eighties. There was only one problem: no one wanted to make his script, which was titled *The Big Chill.*

"I wrote it for the Ladd Company for whom I had done *Body Heat,*" Kasdan recalled in September of 1983. "That movie had been good for them, and I assumed I would have no problem getting them to finance this. But when they read it, they just didn't think that it could make any money.

"I thought someone else would snap it up, because every studio in town had offered me pictures to direct. I was feeling arrogant and confident. I started going around town and everyone turned it down. The young executives, the people my age, would say, 'I love it, it's funny, it's sad, and I'll be the first one in line, *but* it's not commercial, *but* it doesn't have a hook.' They were the worst of all. A circuitous chain of events led me to Carson Productions (Johnny Carson's independent production house), and they happened to have a relationship with Columbia, and they agreed to make the movie. But it was torture."

No one wanted to let Norman Jewison bring playwright Charles Fuller's successful stage production of *A Soldier's Story* (1984) to the screen. Finally Jewison got Columbia to bankroll the picture on a vastly reduced budget with a largely unknown cast. Howard E. Rollins played the black officer sent to investigate the murder of a black sergeant at a southern barracks during World War II. The movie was an unexpected success.

***Opposite*: The gang's all here. The cast of *The Big Chill* (1983), *from left*, JoBeth Williams, Jeff Goldblum, Tom Berenger, Mary Kay Place, William Hurt, Meg Tilly, Glenn Close and Kevin Kline.**

Although the failure of *Heaven's Gate* was laid directly at the feet of Michael Cimino, it did not end his career. The Italian producer Dino De Laurentiis hired him a few years later to direct *Year of the Dragon* (1985), a thriller saturated with the same confusion of blood and melodrama that had marred *Heaven's Gate.* The movie was set in New York's Chinatown, and there was outrage over its depiction of Orientals. Mickey Rourke, *above*, played the New York cop on the trail of an Oriental drug lord. Fashion model Ariane Koizumi provided the love interest.

Cimino's next film, *The Sicilian* (1987) was a gangster movie based on a novel by Mario Puzo and starring Christopher Lambert — seen here on the set with the director. Once again there was controversy. Cimino's 146-minute version of the movie was drastically cut for its North American release, and novelist Gore Vidal who had worked on the script, sued for a screen credit. Anyone who saw the movie wondered why.

To the amazement of everyone, except perhaps Larry Kasdan, *The Big Chill* was one of the biggest hits of 1983, and the movie, not to mention the title, became synonymous with the growing angst of the Baby Boomer generation. Hollywood executives began to understand there was an adult audience out there that, under the right circumstances, could be drawn to a picture without millions of dollars worth of special effects.

The year 1984 was a record breaker even by Hollywood's newly acquired blockbuster standards. The summer movies alone added an unprecedented $1.5 billion to the industry's coffers. *Indiana Jones and the Temple of Doom*, *Gremlins* and *The Karate Kid* all exceeded the magic $100-million mark. *Ghostbusters* smashed through the $200-million barrier and *Beverly Hills Cop*, with Eddie Murphy, eventually brought in $234 million.

But while the industry luxuriated in the returns from adolescent-oriented fantasy and adventure, it was becoming increasingly clear, in the wake of the success of *The Big Chill*, that serious films could also make money. The same year *Ghostbusters* and *Beverly Hills Cop* cleaned up, *The Killing Fields*, *A Soldier's Story*, *Educating Rita*, *Terms of Endearment* and *Amadeus* not only were taken seriously, but also managed to make a lot of money.

By the mid-eighties the video revolution was at its height. Yet, for the first time in decades, adult audiences were going out to theaters in order to see a movie. Independent films such as *Kiss of the Spider Woman* and *A Room with a View* found an unexpectedly wide audience. On the eve of the release of *Moonstruck*, the comedy that was to become the most successful movie of his career, the veteran Norman Jewison was moved to note that things were changing. "I think there are films out there now dealing with subjects they weren't dealing with five years ago," he said sitting around his Toronto production offices one day. "I think the level and quality of the writing is coming back. And let's face it, I think films are a little more mature. Films are being directed to a little older audience, and a little bit more sophisticated audience. If you continue to make films for 14-year-olds, it does limit your choice of subject matter."

In the summer of 1989, the comic-book pyrotechnics of *Batman* and *Indiana Jones and the Last Crusade* dominated at the box office, but at the same time there was room for the offbeat *Dead Poets Society*, and a romantic comedy for adults called *When Harry Met Sally*. . . And there was something else. The movie brats, who had begun the decade with little more ambition than to enchant with pyrotechnics, were no longer brats at the end of it. They were getting older, and their movies began to reflect that. They had played all their tricks of magic. They now wanted to dig deeper, reach for honest emotion rather than dazzling special effects.

Certainly that was true of the most successful movie brat of them all. By the summer of 1989, *E.T.*'s dad was a real life father (his son's name was Max) and as he finished *Indiana Jones and the Last Crusade*, Spielberg reflected on the movie business he had influenced so heavily throughout the decade. When all was said and done, Spielberg had either directed or produced five of the top ten biggest hits of all time: *E.T.*, *Jaws*, *Raiders of the Lost Ark*, *Indiana Jones and the Temple of Doom*, and *Back to the Future.* (George Lucas who co-produced the Indy adventures with Spielberg, as well as the *Star Wars* saga, could also lay claim to five of the top ten.)

"Everyone's interested in breaking records now, and turning a gentle sonnet into a cottage industry," he said with a sigh. "That's why I won't make a sequel to *E.T.* But the studios are very interested in running the motion picture industry like a business. And if there is a formula, and they can discover it — as Disney has — they will use it until the carbonation and the fizz have gone out of it. Then they'll look for something else."

The Killing Fields **(1984) was based on the true story of *New York Times* reporter Sidney Schanberg (played by Sam Waterston) who goes back to Cambodia to rescue his old friend, Dith Pran, a Cambodian journalist and translator. Ironically, the role of Pran was played by Haing S. Ngor, whose own story of suffering at the hands of the Khmer Rouge was even more interesting. Ngor won an Oscar for best supporting actor, although he was very much the star of the movie.**

ACTION! FANTASY! SEQUEL!

THE LEGACY OF BOND, EASTWOOD AND LUCAS

According to *Orbit Video* magazine, Harrison Ford was the decade's top box office action star. Four of the movies in which he appeared — *The Empire Strikes Back, Return of the Jedi, Raiders of the Lost Ark, Indiana Jones and the Temple of Doom* — made over $1 billion. And that was not counting the huge success around the world of *Indiana Jones and the Last Crusade*. For all his popularity, Ford remained one of the least publicized and most inaccessible of movie stars.

Action movies, fantasy pictures, comedies and sequels dominated the movies in the eighties. The heroes of the action films became the highest paid stars of the decade. The action movie, with its combination of throwaway humor and violence, originated back in the sixties in the James Bond films; and the Bond series was also responsible for the renewed popularity of doing sequels to hit movies. A television actor named Clint Eastwood created the sort of tough-guy action hero later imitated by Sylvester Stallone and Arnold Schwarzenegger. It was the release of Star Wars in 1977 that began Hollywood's love affair with expensive fantasy films, and the box office in the early eighties was dominated by the Star Wars sequels. Lucas then teamed up with his friend Steven Spielberg to produce the Indiana Jones adventures, which traded heavily not only on fantasy but action and humor as well. Now everyone wanted to make the same kind of picture, and the actor who helped originate the modern-day action adventure sequel could only laugh wryly at what was happening . . .

Sean Connery: the original 007 James Bond came back to the role one last time in 1983 in a remake of *Thunderball* titled *Never Say Never Again*. For a time it looked as though there would be two competing Bonds that summer, Connery's aging secret agent and Roger Moore in *Octopussy*. At the last moment, Warner Bros., the distributor of *Never Say Never Again*, blinked and delayed the movie's release until the fall. It did very well, but ironically it was Roger Moore's version of Bond that attracted the larger audience.

IT WAS THE SPRING OF 1987, AND SEAN CONNERY HAD retreated to his home in Marbella, Spain in order to recuperate from something he called "valley fever," a virus he picked up while finishing work on Brian De Palma's film version of *The Untouchables.* Thus in order to talk to him about Malone, the veteran Chicago cop who aided a youthful Elliott Ness against the Al Capone mob, journalists had to interview Connery by satellite from Seville. The electronic press conference was barely underway when Connery was asked about his old nemesis, James Bond. A new actor, Timothy Dalton, was about to play 007 that summer in a Bond picture titled *The Living Daylights.* Did the first Bond have any advice for the fourth Bond in the long-running series? Connery, although he hated these kind of questions, fielded this one courteously — and he was not a man always known to field questions courteously. "Well, Timothy Dalton is an excellent actor," he said, "and I'm sure he doesn't need any advice from me. But I think primarily he should get a good lawyer —" here he was interrupted by laughter "— and be sufficiently well protected for his future. And retain as much humor off and on (the screen) as possible, because I think it's one of the saving graces of the part."

Bond 4: Timothy Dalton.

It was a saving grace, ironically enough, that Dalton was unable to find in bringing his Bond to the screen. But by that time it almost didn't matter. James Bond, British secret agent 007, had become the most popular continuing hero in movie history. He had defied not only a long line of villains out to destroy the world and 007's composure, but time and fashion as well, not to mention a succession of actors who played him always unshaken and unstirred. The Bond pictures popularized the movie series, a form that had fallen out of fashion. In the thirties and forties, movie series had proliferated. But they either started out as low-budget items, or, in the case of the Tarzan films or *The Thin Man* series, they began as so-called A-pictures, then with each succeeding adventure, their budgets were reduced and they were downgraded to B-pictures. But the producers of the Bond pictures hit upon the idea of spending more money, not less, in an attempt to make each succeeding adventure even more exciting than the previous one, thus increasing the box office take. It was the first time in movie history anyone had thought of doing that. Also, no one previously had made action pictures the way the Bond films were made. They were like moving comic books, with little dialogue, lots of humor and nearly non-stop action, everything propelled along at supersonic speed by fast cutting. The action movies of the eighties would come to owe everything to James Bond.

Bond practically created the comic-book movie, yet ironically enough, the man who created him would not have been caught dead reading a comic book, let alone attending the kind of movies the Bond adventures became.

Ian Fleming was a former British intelligence officer turned journalist, who had graduated from Eton and Sandhurst, and worked as the Moscow correspondent for the London *Sunday Times*. He smoked gold-tipped Balkan Soubranie cigarettes, dressed with a casually studied elegance, and thoroughly enjoyed drinking, gambling, golf, snorkeling, bridge playing, fast cars and beautiful women. He often said that he had created Bond at his Jamaican retreat, Goldeneye, "to sooth my nerves before the appalling business of getting married at 44."

Sean Connery, became the era's only bald superstar, and unlike most male movie stars made no attempt to hide his age. Timothy Dalton (*below* with Carey Lowell) had all his hair in place for 007, but very little of the humor that marked the Bonds of Connery and Roger Moore. The sober *License to Kill* (1989), Dalton's second Bond, was the least popular in the series.

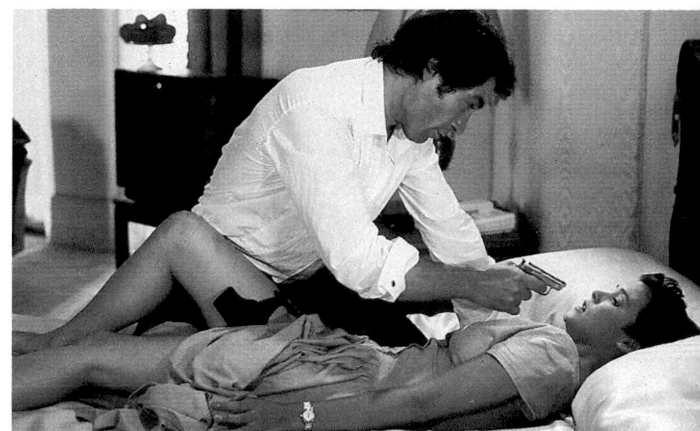

Unlike Connery, Roger Moore came to Bond already a hugely popular actor thanks to *The Saint* television series, not to mention stints in *Maverick* and *Ivanhoe*. His Bond was light and breezy without the dangerous edge Connery brought to the role — although you would never know it in this scene from *Octopussy* (1983).

***Below*: Albert Broccoli.**

In 1961, Harry Saltzman, a veteran Canadian producer working in London, optioned all the books, with the exception of the first, *Casino Royale*. Saltzman then hooked up with a wealthy American producer living in London, Albert R. Broccoli, and together the two of them worked out a six-picture deal with United Artists.

It was decided that the first James Bond adventure would be adapted from the sixth Ian Fleming novel, *Dr. No.* Terence Young, who had worked several times before with Broccoli, was signed to direct. From the beginning, the screenwriter Richard Maibaum began to rework many of the elements in Fleming's books: he toned down the violence, added more women (for all his lady-killer instincts, the Bond of the books is a fairly chaste guy), and, perhaps more importantly, developed a tongue-in-cheek humor almost entirely missing from the books. Connery later would claim to have insisted on the humor himself, but it was producer Broccoli who suggested it, and Maibaum who developed the suggestions. The addition of the humor was what made the Bond pictures unlike previous action films, and it was the humor mixed with violence that would become the most widely imitated characteristic of the series. In part, the humor was added as a kind of defence against anyone making fun of Bond on the screen. "You can't spoof a spoof," Maibaum said later.

Legend has it that as soon as this thirtyish, balding Scot with a tattoo on his arm walked into the office in 1961, Saltzman and Broccoli knew they had their Bond.

It was quite a leap of faith. Sean Connery was the last guy in the world that might be expected to play Bond. Fleming, who initially suggested, of all people, Jimmy Stewart as 007, was said to have been appalled at the choice. Connery was everything Bond and his creator were not. He was from the lower classes, born in a tenement in a tough, working-class district of Edinburgh. His father was a long-haul truck driver. Connery was finished with school and in the navy at age 16, although not for long. "I had spent my entire life waiting to go to war, and it finished in '45, and I went in 1946," he recalled. "I had foolishly signed for 12 years and discovered I was totally unsuited for it, to such an extent that I had ulcers, and I was invalided out after three years when I was 19."

In 1952, he was the Scottish representative at the Mr. Universe contest, and, as a result, was offered a small part in the chorus of a touring company of *South Pacific*. That was his first brush with show business. He was delighted to be earning so much money — the equivalent of $35 a week — for having a good time. He set about improving himself, reading Shakespeare, Proust, Shaw, Turgenev, Dostoevsky, a dictionary never far away.

The Bond films with Connery as star were an immediate success. *Dr. No* was a fairly straightforward spy adventure, but from the beginning it was apparent to the producers that the audiences loved the humor, they adored Connery's sardonic nonchalance as 007, and they were fascinated by the gadgetry. By the time *Goldfinger*, the third Bond film was released (*From Russia with Love*, Bond Two, remains the favorite of Connery and most diehard aficionados), Bond had become a worldwide phenomenon. Fleming, after writing 11 Bond novels, had died of a heart attack at the age of 55. He never knew just how popular his character had become, how long he would endure, nor how far the movies would move away from the novels. *Goldfinger* had established the comic-book elements of the movies. They would be increasingly emphasized as the series got older. Maibaum, as he wrote the next Bond adventure, *Thunderball*, noted, perhaps a little wearily, "all the Bond pictures are brain-busters before they become blockbusters. Each one is expected to top its predecessor."

From the beginning though, Connery was uncomfortable in the role. By the time the actor arrived in the Bahamas to film *Thunderball*, his fourth Bond picture, he was fed up. "They're like comic strips," he said of the series in an interview with the *New York Times*

Bond's Ladies: In the eighties, Carole Bouquet, one of France's most popular actresses, loved Agent 007 in *For Your Eyes Only* (1981). She became better known to North American audiences as a perfume salesperson.

***Left*: Barbara Carrera, from Nicaragua, played a lot of bad girls very well during the eighties. She seduced Sean Connery as Bond in *Never Say Never Again* (1983), and also lured Mike Hammer, another famous fictional detective, into trouble in *I, the Jury* (1982).**

Roger Moore made several unsuccessful attempts to break out of the Bond mode. In *Ffolkes* (1980), known in Britain as *North Sea Hijack,* he was a crusty old naval officer. The public, as it turned out, was not interested in seeing 007 play it crusty. Nearing 60, Moore gave up Bond in 1985. He retreated to his villa in the south of France and didn't work for most of the remainder of the decade. He was supposed to star in a London musical (Andrew Lloyd Webber's *Aspects of Love*) but dropped out at the last moment. Moore reappeared on the screen in 1990 when he co-starred with his old pal Michael Caine in a comedy titled *Bullseye.*

service. "The producers constantly have to come up with bigger and better gimmicks. That's all that sustains the pictures."

Even then he was grumbling about money. "I am fighting for more money and time," he said. "I want to get as much money as I can. And I want to do (the movies) in as little time as possible, so I can fit in other things that mean more to me. These James Bond pictures can take six months of my time, working every day."

Twenty years later, he was still bitter. "I had many problems apart from the greed of the producers," he told the London *Sunday Times Magazine*. "Even they had to divorce. They couldn't stay married because they would be sitting opposite each other at a table thinking, 'That asshole's got my other 30 million.'"

Saltzman and Broccoli did indeed split up, with Broccoli, well into his seventies, continuing to actively produce the pictures. Connery did six, then swore he was finished with the part. Yet he could

not resist Bond one more time in the eighties and made *Never Say Never Again* (echoing Connery's sentiments about saying no to 007), a picture that, in fact, was a remake of *Thunderball.* Once again, the shoot was arduous, went way over schedule, and Connery hated every moment of it, right down to the toupee he had to wear.

Connery not only survived James Bond, but in the middle of the decade he became more popular than ever, thanks to his appearance in *The Untouchables*, for which he won an Academy Award in 1987 as best supporting actor.

"Sean Connery is not like anyone else; he's an original," said Steven Spielberg, who had the idea of having him play Dr. Henry Jones, Indy's father in *Indiana Jones and the Last Crusade.* "He's never been stronger or more sought after, and he's finally recognized as the star he's always been. Hollywood has at last admitted to itself that Sean is one of the great movie stars; he will be remembered throughout recorded movie history."

What's more, closing in on 60, he was named the sexiest man alive by *People* magazine. Connery, who had heard a great deal about his sexuality over the years, characteristically took it in stride. "There are very few sexy men dead," he observed dryly.

Sean Connery never paid much attention to Hollywood throughout most of his movie career. However, when he was cast in *The Untouchables* (1987), he was "discovered" by the American film industry, and won a best supporting Oscar for his performance. *From left*: Andy Garcia, Sean Connery, Kevin Costner, Charles Martin Smith.

ROGER MOORE WAS CHOSEN TO TAKE OVER from Connery in 1973. A former MGM contract player and television star (*Maverick*, *The Saint*), Moore had been rejected during the original Bond search because he was not thought to be "he-man" enough. But now he had aged into the role, and took over as Bond in the Broccoli-produced pictures. Moore brought a lighter, less dangerous, more throwaway air to the pictures. He was not nearly the athlete Connery had been, and the joke was that Moore stood in and did the close-ups for the stunt men.

By 1987, Moore, approaching 60 and having made seven Bond pictures, had grown too old for the part, and the dour and seemingly humorless Timothy Dalton was cast in the role. There was a great deal of talk about returning to the basics of Bond, and Richard Maibaum, who had been away from the series, was brought back to help accomplish that. But by this time the producers had run out of the original Bond novels (not that they had been paying much attention to the Fleming plots). The latest Bond, *License to Kill*, number 16 in the series originally started up by Broccoli and Saltzman, was not based on any of the Fleming books (a new writer, John Gardner had taken up Bond's adventures on the printed page).

In the summer of 1989, Bond seemed slow and dated compared to *Indiana Jones and the Last Crusade* and *Lethal Weapon II*, action

Outland* was described as "*High Noon* in outer space" when it was released in 1981. Sean Connery played the Gary Cooper role of the mining colony marshal standing alone against the bad guys.

Don Johnson became a sensation on television during the eighties starring in a stylish police series titled *Miami Vice*. However, when he tried to make the transition to the big screen as a tough guy cop after neo-nazis in the curiously titled *Dead Bang* (1989), the public wasn't interested. Johnson at the end of the decade was better known as the husband of actress Melanie Griffith.

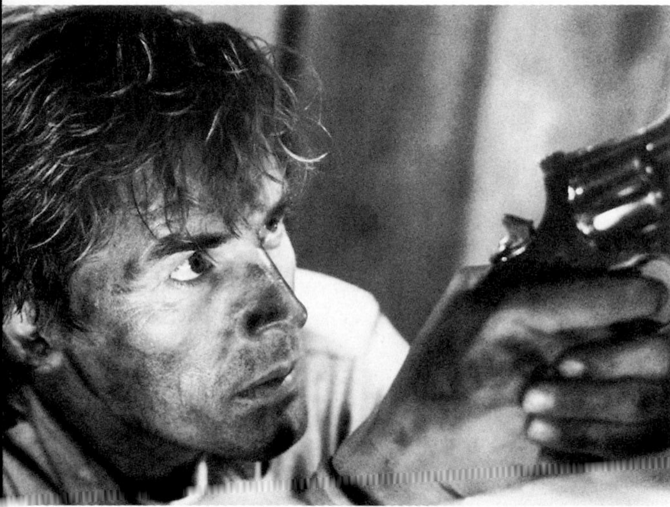

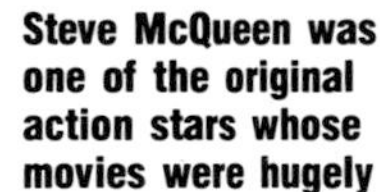

Steve McQueen was one of the original action stars whose movies were hugely successful throughout the sixties and seventies. In 1980, he starred in a shoot-'em-up titled *The Hunter*, before dying that same year of a heart attack following cancer surgery at the early age of 50.

movie sequels that owed their existence to 007, and which now provided the sort of cranked-up thrills that Bond could not. As a result, *License to Kill* failed miserably in North America, and although Broccoli announced still another Bond picture, there was for the first time in almost three decades serious thought being given to the suggestion that the movies' most durable and influential action hero might have reached the end.

Squint Hard, Say Little, Pump Up: How the Action Hero Came to Be

CLINT EASTWOOD WAS IN MONTREAL IN AUGUST 1984 to launch his 39th film, a thriller titled *Tightrope*, in which he played a New Orleans cop investigating the murders of local prostitutes. At the age of 54, he had been a major superstar for two decades. If James Bond more or less invented the action movie, it was Clint Eastwood who had modified it for a North American audience and caused it to become a staple of the business. Everyone squinted, said little, carried a big gun, and tossed off quips as they shot the bad guys. Everyone pumped iron, and looked more at home within the confines of a comic book than in real life. Even television actor Bruce Willis discovered that, if you wanted to be a major male movie star, you had to take off your shirt, pump up, and shoot someone. He did just that in *Die Hard* in 1988. Sure enough, yet another action star had been born.

Tough guy: Bruce Willis in *Die Hard*.

But, as everyone tried to imitate his success, Eastwood in the eighties was trying to move away from it. *Tightrope* was considered something of a departure for him, since it required the main character to come to terms with his own secret desires. It was the morning after its world premiere at the Montreal Film Festival, and the day on which *Tightrope* opened in a thousand theaters across North America. Eastwood stood around his hotel suite in bare feet, going through various newspapers, finding out what critics thought about his new movie. "This isn't much," he said to his longtime friend and co-producer, Fritz Manes, referring to a review in one of the local papers.

"But take a look at this one." He indicated a glowing report in *USA Today*. He disappeared into an adjacent bedroom only to return a few moments later to report that he had talked to a friend of his in New York. The *New York Times* apparently had liked the movie. "But the guy who told me this is a physician," he said with a grin. "So he might not be looking for the same things I'm looking for."

Eastwood was dressed in brushed suede slacks, a green LaCoste pullover, and he was in the final stages of growing the gray-streaked beard he would wear for an upcoming movie called *Pale Rider*, his first western in eight years. He had been making movies for almost three decades, a former drifter from San Francisco who worked as

Clint Eastwood, the actor who created the action star mold from which all others were stamped, made some curious choices in the 1980s. Here he effectively played a tough Marine gunnery sergeant in *Heartbreak Ridge* (1986), whipping a group of recruits into shape so they could attack Grenada, of all places, not exactly one of the finer moments of U.S. military history — but then no one said it was easy making a war movie without a war.

Chuck Norris tried very hard to become a big-time action star in the eighties, just like his hero, Clint Eastwood. He made a number of movies, mostly B-grade action pictures such as *Lone Wolf McQuade* (1983), *above.* A former karate champion who trained stars such as Steve McQueen, Norris said little, squinted hard, and shot a number of bad guys, but the action movie audience never went for him in a big way.

a logger, a lifeguard, and gas station attendant, before landing a contract at Universal Pictures in 1954.

"I'm at the stage now where several generations have fallen in love and fallen out of love sitting in a drive-in or going to some of these movies," he said, a smile creasing his craggy, tanned features. "So you become sort of nostalgic in some people's minds."

In 1963, he was co-starring in a western TV series called *Rawhide* when he accepted an offer for $15,000 to go to Europe to star in a low budget western titled *A Fistful of Dollars* for an Italian director named Sergio Leone, who spoke no English, and had never been to America, let alone western America. The movie, which was based on a Japanese Samurai film, *Yojimbo*, directed by the great Akira Kurosawa, was shot in Spain on a shoestring budget. Leone's bizarre, slightly tongue-in-cheek approach to the iconography of the American western, at once highly realistic and totally preposterous, was an immediate success in Europe. As Eastwood, who played the serape-clad, cheroot-smoking Man with No Name, started work on two more westerns with Leone, *For a Few Dollars More* and *The Good, the Bad and the Ugly*, he was already a star.

Pale Rider **(1985).**

There had never been a movie hero quite like the character Eastwood brought back to America with him from Europe. Eastwood simultaneously played to the mythology of the screen hero, and against it. His anti-heroes did not spend a lot of time worrying about right and wrong. That they invariably did the right thing was almost beside the point. He said little, squinted a lot, and was never fazed by the bad guys.

The Eastwood persona, stumbled upon almost by accident, coming out of the Japanese Kurosawa and filtered through the American west as represented by an Italian director working in Spain, would become the mold from which most action heroes were stamped. The actor who created The Man with No Name was to play him again and again. Eastwood, having found a good thing, was not about to tamper much with the formula.

By July of 1971, when he appeared on the cover of *Life* magazine, Clint Eastwood had become the world's most popular movie star. ("Who can stand 32,580 seconds of Clint Eastwood?" asked the headline over the article. "Just about everyone.")

Consciously or not, he was among the first movie stars to understand that the police picture was becoming the modern-day equivalent of the western. Thus, when he made *Dirty Harry* in 1971, it quickly became the biggest hit of his career.

Dirty Harry would become the prototype for a whole generation of maverick movie-cops. Most anti-heroes in the movies were outsiders working against the establishment. Dirty Harry was an outsider working against the establishment from within. Eastwood went on to replay Harry in four more movies. With the exception of *The Dead Pool*, released in 1988, all of them were hugely popular.

***Bronco Billy* (1980).**

In the eighties, critics had begun to take Clint Eastwood more seriously, both as an actor and as a director. His smaller, more personal films, most notably *Honkytonk Man* and *Bronco Billy*, although not big hits, received critical raves. And there was new appreciation for Eastwood's 1970s westerns, such as *High Plains Drifter* and *The Outlaw Josey Wales*. Eastwood took the appreciation in stride, but he was obviously pleased by the change in attitude.

"I guess earlier in the game I was too successful for my own good on a commercial level," he said. "Or for whatever reason you're just not as fashionable in a certain area for a period of time. But then people liked *High Plains Drifter*. That grabbed a lot of attention. Then *Bronco Billy*, a lot of reviewers seemed to like that film. I guess there are just enough different kinds of films along the way that people started saying, 'Well, there is an element of versatility there.'"

As he approached 60, he talked about a time when he would concentrate on directing, and indeed *Bird*, his film biography of jazz legend Charlie Parker, earned him some of the best reviews of his long career. Still, he was aware of an audience that would not give up its long-held views of him. "I think people are disarmed when they find out I'm not Dirty Harry," he said. "I think they would rather have Dirty Harry." In fact, Eastwood in person was as far away from his cool, taciturn screen image as might be imagined. Of all the superstars, he was perhaps the warmest and most likable, and, seemingly, the most open. "On first meeting," the novelist Norman Mailer wrote of him, "he's one of the nicest people you ever met . . . He's very laid-back. If you don't bother him, he will never bother you. In that sense he is like the characters he plays in his films."

At the end of the eighties he made *Pink Cadillac*, more a lazy statement about how fed up he was with his image than an action

Charles Bronson was another tough laconic action star who could never quite get on the elevator up from the B-movie cellar. A highly respected character actor in the fifties and early sixties (*The Magnificent Seven, The Great Escape*), Bronson, like Eastwood, became a star in European movies. His big break came when he played Eastwood's Man with No Name character in Sergio Leone's western epic, *Once upon a Time in the West* (1968).

Rambo III (1988), *above,* was set in Afghanistan but actually it was shot in Israel. Billy Dee Williams, *below*, co-starred with Stallone in *Nighthawks* (1981) and complained that Sly stole all the close-ups. One of Sly's most unlikely roles was in *Victory* (1981), *insert*, known as *Escape to Victory* in Britain, a World War II drama about a soccer game between allied prisoners of war and their German captors. It was directed by John Huston, and Sly played a Canadian army officer. The prison drama *Lock Up* (1989), *below*, utilized an actual working penitentiary (East Jersey State Prison) and its inmates. That touch of realism didn't help at the box office.

movie, then went off to Africa to make a film version of the Peter Viertel novel, *White Hunter, Black Heart*, in which he played a John Huston-like movie director. By then, he seemed content to leave the action-movie field to the pretenders to his throne, and certainly there were plenty of them around. Like Eastwood, Charles Bronson had been a character actor in Hollywood for years before attaining stardom in Europe. Into the 1980s the granite-faced Bronson, in his mid-sixties and visibly tired of exerting himself, nevertheless, continued to turn out a succession of low-budget action movies. Chuck Norris was a karate-instructor-turned-actor who openly worshiped Eastwood and wanted movie stardom like his. However, the blond, diminutive actor was never quite able to do it. And late in the decade, another martial arts expert, Steven Seagal, appeared on the scene in *Above the Law* and *Hard to Kill*. He was big, muscular, got lost if he had to say more than a line of dialogue, and hinted in interviews that he had once worked for the U.S. Central Intelligence Agency.

But of all the action heroes who followed in Eastwood's wake, no one was more successful at it than a shy, lonely kid from New York, born with a speech impediment, and a chip on his shoulder.

SYLVESTER STALLONE LOOKED LIKE A MOVIE star. In July of 1981, he gleamed in a creamy suit expensively draped over a body which he worked on four hours each day, and lately slimmed down so that the lines were cleaner, without the bulky, unappealing look of the bodybuilder. His hair was black and thick and not a strand of it was out of place. His every move was watched by an off-duty New York detective, one of a number of bodyguards who accompanied Stallone everywhere. He was in Manhattan to promote a World War II action movie called *Victory*, in which he co-starred with Michael Caine. He sat in a corner at a reception after the premiere of the movie, flirting with actress Linda Gray, who played J.R. Ewing's wife on the hit TV soap opera *Dallas*. Stallone's face was animated, his dark eyes glowed, and Gray was obviously charmed. When he stepped onto an elevator a few minutes later, the off-duty detective and the entourage of bodyguards crowding around him, Stallone conceded he didn't even know who he was talking to. "She's on *Dallas* is she? Well, whatdya know." Then he fell silent as the elevator headed down toward the lobby. Everyone looked uncomfortable. His face went slack and his eyes were dead, and in that cramped elevator Sly Stallone seemed very much alone. He had lately reconciled with his wife Sasha, after leaving her and their young son for the actress Susan Anton. He admitted that he had not reacted well to success, that he had made a

Another action tough guy from the eighties, Steven Seagal, like Chuck Norris, was a former karate instructor. Unlike the diminutive Norris, Seagal was big and mean-looking. His first movie, *Above the Law* (1988) was a hit.

Tom Selleck was supposed to play Indiana Jones in *Raiders of the Lost Ark* (1981), but couldn't because of a television commitment. Later, he was cast in a *Raiders* clone titled *High Road to China* (1983). It did not make Selleck a movie star.

Burt Reynolds occasionally tried to be a tough guy during the eighties, as he did in *Stick* (1985), a movie which he also directed. More often than not, though, audiences wanted to see him as the good ol' boy behind the wheel of a car in carefully formulated movies such as *Cannonball Run* (1981). When audiences got tired of the formula of Burt and smiles and cars after the release of *Stroker Ace* in 1983, *below*, his star plummeted with a speed that served to emphasize the fickleness of the movie-going public during the decade.

fool of himself. "I've kind of done things in the past I'm not too proud of," he said. "I was never satisfied, I lost my perspective." But that was not the real trouble. The problem was his movie career. Nobody was going to Sylvester Stallone movies unless he played a punch-drunk boxer named Rocky.

In 1976, Stallone was an overnight sensation. His was the kind of Cinderella story that movies are made of but real life seldom is. He was the poor kid from the Hell's Kitchen section of New York with the droopy eye and the speech impediment (the result, he said, of a doctor misusing a pair of forceps during his birth in a hospital charity ward). He grew up, he said later, in a fantasy world, worshiping bodybuilder and actor Steve Reeves, who starred in several Hercules movies.

Stallone was a struggling actor in Hollywood when he sat down and in three days wrote the script for *Rocky*. Then he held onto the script and wouldn't allow the producers to cast anyone but himself in the starring role. *Rocky* won the Academy Award for best picture in 1976, and the indomitable fighter who wouldn't quit became an American folk hero. No matter what happened to him after that, Stallone conceded, he would always be known as Rocky Balboa to audiences around the world. And yet *Rocky* had become a prison for him. If he made *F.I.S.T.* or *Paradise Alley* or *Nighthawks*, audiences ignored the movies. He was becoming increasingly frustrated and worried. *Victory* did not change his luck. It did no better at the box office than Stallone's other non-Rocky movies.

In Hollywood, if fortunes are going to change at all, they will change very quickly indeed. A year later, in 1982, to the amazement of everyone, Stallone was on top again. He had been signed by a couple of independent producers, Mario Kassar and Andrew Vajna, to play the lead in a movie called *First Blood*. Kassar and Vajna figured that, even if it didn't get its money back in North America, the movie would do well in Europe, where it had been pre-sold on Stallone's name. The script, based on a novel by David Morrell, had been kicking around for years, and all sorts of actors, including Paul Newman, had considered the property and then rejected it. Now, Canadian-born Ted Kotcheff would finally direct *First Blood* on locations in British Columbia. Stallone was playing a Vietnam veteran named John Rambo who arrives in a small town to look up an old buddy, only to find that the buddy is dead, and he himself is on the run from redneck cops. The movie was a hard-edged action-adventure, although it did have vague pretensions to say something in 1982 about the treatment of Vietnam veterans. Stallone did not expect much to come of it. He thought the character of Rambo too dark for a mass audience to embrace. To his surprise, not only did

American audiences like Rambo, but he became even more popular in Europe, where *First Blood* did even better business than it did in North America.

There could only be a sequel. Rambo, who had been killed off in the original novel, was off to Vietnam to win a war long since lost. In 1985 *Rambo — First Blood II* became one of the biggest hits of the decade, and Rambo, like Rocky, was a folk hero to millions. In less than a decade, Stallone had managed to find two characters with such audience appeal that, by the time *Rocky IV* followed *Rambo II* in December of 1985, Stallone was once again the world's most popular movie star. "I don't know sometimes whether to put on boxing gloves or carry a machine gun," he said. His brushes with failure between Rocky movies had taught him a lesson. "I have to stay with what I know best. Rather than bore everyone trying to do something classic, which I probably couldn't pull off anyway, you try to give the audience what it expects. Particularly when you're dealing with millions of dollars and the audience's confidence in you."

But in the process of establishing himself as the decade's most popular and highest-paid star, Stallone also become its most widely disparaged. Critics savaged his work, comedians held him up to ridicule, and, as his second marriage to actress Brigitte Nielsen broke up ostentatiously, amidst much snickering, Stallone once again found himself trapped. In short order he had become tired of all the running and shooting, and so, it appeared, had the audience. *Rambo III*, which, at a cost estimated by *Variety* at $85 million, was perhaps the most expensive movie ever made, did disappointing business when it was released in North America in the early summer of 1988. (Worldwide, it grossed more than $250 million, recovering its cost, and making a tidy profit.) The studios nonetheless wanted more sequels and action pictures — a *Rambo IV* was planned; *Rocky V* was in the works. After the third Rambo, Stallone took time off, painted, played polo, brooded, and rejected action script after action script. When he went back to work again, in 1989, it was to star in a prison picture called *Lock Up*, which no one went to see. That was followed later the

***Tango and Cash* (1989).**

Not all sequels featured heroes shooting people. Chevy Chase made *National Lampoon's Vacation* in 1983, then followed it up with *National Lampoon's European Vacation* (1985). The third sequel, *National Lampoon's Christmas Vacation,* proved to be so unexpectedly popular in 1989 that it revived Chase's flagging career.

Below **and** ***opposite*****: His appearance in** ***Conan the Barbarian*** **in 1982, helped make Arnold Schwarzenegger (the name means "black ploughman") one of the most unlikely superstars of the eighties. No one knew better how to promote Arnold than Arnold himself. In the summer of 1990,** ***Time*** **magazine was calling him the world's most popular action hero, and even though action movies in general didn't do well at the box office that summer, Arnold's latest, a $70-million sci-fi adventure titled** ***Total Recall*** **was a hit. However, Arnold could not escape Conan without first making a sequel. It was called** ***Conan the Destroyer*** **(1984), and it was bad enough to do serious damage to the career of any actor. The same year, though,** ***Terminator*** **was released, and Arnold was never again asked to carry a sword.**

same year by still another action picture, *Tango and Cash,* in which he co-starred with Kurt Russell. Stallone put on a tie and wore glasses in order to play a dapper cop. In the world created by Stallone, this constituted playing against type. But he still had the gun in his hand, and the bad jokes in his dialogue. *Tango and Cash,* however, did somewhat revive his flagging box office fortunes, and he headed for Philadelphia to make *Rocky V.* In the fifth chapter of the story, Stallone had wanted to kill off Rocky. No way, said the studio, MGM/UA. "Everyone," he told *Esquire* magazine sadly, "wants hopping, skipping, jumping, burning."

WHICH WAS JUST FINE WITH SLY'S MAIN rival for muscle-bound action stardom, Arnold Schwarzenegger. For him, stardom was a damned good business opportunity. Forget the angst over being typecast — if people were lining up to see your movies, that's what counted. Consequently, when action-hero stardom came into its own during the eighties, no one cultivated it more carefully or cleverly than Schwarzenegger.

A native of Graz, Austria, Arnold Schwarzenegger had been a skinny kid who, like Stallone, grew up worshiping a muscle-bound movie hero. Reg Park, like Stallone's hero, Steve Reeves, had starred in Hercules movies (*Hercules and the Captive Women*). To be more like Park, Schwarzenegger got into weight training in order to build up his muscles. Despite a funny name and a thick accent, Arnold was determined to become a star — a very rich star; the only kind you could be in America. "I knew I was a winner," he wrote in his best-selling *Arnold: The Education of a Body Builder.* "I knew I was destined for great things." He was about the only one who thought so. As usual, however, Arnold fooled everyone.

By the spring of 1984, Arnold had been Mr. Universe five times; Mr. Olympia seven times; had starred in a popular documentary about bodybuilding titled *Pumping Iron*; and had made his feature film debut, once again as a bodybuilder, opposite Jeff Bridges and Sally Field in a Bob Rafelson movie, *Stay Hungry.* Actually, it wasn't quite his debut — he had been billed as Arnold Strong in a 1970 feature, *Hercules in New York,* and he also appeared briefly in *The Long Goodbye* (1973).

But while the rest of the movie industry still regarded him and the whole business of bodybuilding as a somewhat freakish enterprise, Schwarzenegger was understanding that if he was going to be a star he would have to concentrate on his physical prowess, not his acting talent. "This was always my plan," he said, as he relaxed

For a brief time sword-and-sorcery pictures dominated the action market, thanks to Arnold Schwarzenegger in ***Conan the Barbarian*** **(1982). Even the women got involved. An unknown Scandinavian actress named Brigitte Nielsen played *Red Sonja* (1985), which featured a brief appearance by Schwarzenegger. However, Arnold did much better with audiences when he made his comedy debut in *Twins* (1988), opposite Danny DeVito.**

with a cigar behind a carved wood desk, in the Venice, California headquarters for his Oak Productions. "In 1975, after my first movie, *Stay Hungry*, I always said I wanted to be like Charles Bronson, Clint Eastwood, and do nice action pictures and make $1 million a movie."

The means to this end was provided by Italian producer Dino De Laurentiis, who decided, correctly, that there was only one actor in the world who could play *Conan the Barbarian*, the Hyborian-age warrior created by pulp author Robert E. Howard. The movie, directed by John Milius did all right in North America, but in Europe it was a huge hit. Arnold was on his way, and he knew it. No one had investigated the intricacies of North American stardom more carefully than Arnold, perhaps because no one was a more unlikely star.

***The Terminator* (1984).**

"What happens," he explained, "is, if a movie like *Conan* is successful, they credit you, the actor, with the success. The actor really is only one of five elements that should get credit for something like that. But that's the way they treat things here."

Therefore he would be credited with the unlikely success in 1984 of *Terminator*, a darkly nasty sci-fi action picture written and directed by a young newcomer named James Cameron. Schwarzenegger played a killer cyborg returned from the future to gun down a large portion of the population of greater Los Angeles. "From that movie on," Arnold said later, "I never got another Viking or sword-and-sorcery script again." The Austrian bodybuilder with the thick accent and the funny name had found his niche. *Terminator* launched a series of very expensive high-tech action pictures such as *Commando*, *Predator* and *The Running Man*. Nobody seemed to be having more fun with movie stardom than Arnold. While Stallone worried and brooded, Schwarzenegger became an American citizen — an *all-American* citizen, a staunch cigar-smoking Republican who nevertheless had no qualms about marrying a member of the Kennedy clan, news anchorperson Maria Shriver. He also had no qualms about making fun of his image. In December of 1988 he co-starred with Danny DeVito in a comedy called *Twins*, and for the first time actually kissed a girl. The movie was a huge hit, but Arnold was not one to trifle too much with his audience. He went right back to action pictures in the summer of 1990 — another sci-fi film called *Total Recall.*

"I think the time may come when I will have the same attitude as Robert Duvall or someone, where I want to do a story about people. Or a love story. You have to have that feeling. Right now I don't have that feeling.

"Right now, I feel very comfortable and good about doing action pictures because all my life I loved these pictures."

Star Wars, Indiana Jones and the Creation of the Comic Book Fantasy

HARRISON FORD SAT SLUMPED INTO A CORNER of a sofa in a Los Angeles hotel suite, unable to keep the look of irritation off his face. He was a remote, taciturn man, notorious among the journalists who interviewed him for his monosyllabic answers. He wasn't doing much better today. Ford was in the process of promoting a new movie, a detective thriller titled *Witness,* but reporters kept asking him about Han Solo and about Indiana Jones. The *Star Wars* trilogy plus the two Indiana Jones movies, *Raiders of the Lost Ark* and *Indiana Jones and the Temple of Doom,* constituted the most popular action adventure films of all time. If the escapist antics of James Bond had captured the imaginations of audiences around the world in the sixties and seventies, in the eighties it was the *Star Wars* adventures and Indiana Jones. George Lucas, the creator of *Star Wars* and Indy, had grown up enthralled by fantasy and adventure, addicted to comic books, an avid fan of old movie serials shown on afternoon television — all the elements he would bring to his movies. He also brought back the Saturday afternoon adventure serial hero with a little of James Bond's sardonic humor added. The result was Harrison Ford.

A journalist suggested that perhaps people should stop asking him questions about the action heroes he had portrayed. "Yeah, why don't you?" he snapped. "I get bored with the old aspects of the story that continually get used as hooks."

Off screen, Harrison Ford was a very private man, difficult to get to know, and sensitive about being thought of as nothing more than an action hero. "I don't like it to rest that the last five or six movies have been just me running around with a gun in my hand," he said. He paused. "Well, I can't even remember what the last five movies are. But it still doesn't sound very good to me."

Nonetheless, in *Witness* he once again had a gun in his hand, playing a Philadelphia police officer named John Book who gets

Christopher Lambert was a skinny, unknown American, raised in Switzerland, who had wanted to be a stockbroker, but decided to try acting for a year or so. Director Hugh Hudson decided he would be perfect to star as Tarzan in his lavishly mounted production of *Greystoke: The Legend of Tarzan, Lord of the Apes* (1984). Hudson put the young actor through a grueling exercise program to get him in shape for Tarzan. *Greystoke* did only so-so in North America, but in Europe it helped make Lambert a popular star.

Director Richard Donner took the fantasy adventure back to medieval times for *Ladyhawke* (1985). It starred Matthew Broderick, Michelle Pfeiffer — and a beautifully setting sun.

Dutch-born actor Rutger Hauer, called the 'Paul Newman of Holland,' became internationally known as a bad guy in *Nighthawks* (1981) and (*insert*) in *Blade Runner* (1982). Attempts to turn him into a romantic hero (*Ladyhawke*, 1985) and an action star (*Wanted Dead or Alive,* 1986) were not successful.

Harrison Ford in *Blade Runner* (1982).

involved with a pretty Amish woman (Kelly McGillis) and her son. The boy has witnessed a murder in a railway station washroom, and eventually the killers come after the three of them in the Amish country around Lancaster County in Pennsylvania. *Witness,* directed by the Australian Peter Weir, was a crucial movie for Harrison Ford. He had churned out a series of movies between the *Star Wars* and Indiana Jones films, and they all had been flops. No one went near *Force Ten from Navarone* or *Hanover Street* or *The Frisco Kid.* Even *Blade Runner,* a high-toned sci-fi comic-book action movie, had failed to do the kind of business everyone expected. If Ford could be anything more than an eighties variation on the old Saturday afternoon matinee action heroes, he had yet to demonstrate it. "I don't feel any pressure," he maintained. "I've been around for 25 years now. The people who are going to buy it know all about it, and those that are not, that's their choice."

Ford need not have worried. *Witness* became one of the major hits of 1985, persuading doubters that not only could he carry a movie by himself, but that he was also an actor of depth and subtlety who could do much more than simply wisecrack between action scenes. At the age of 42, his stardom was confirmed. Starting out, it had been a much different story. Ford was told he did not have what it took to be a star. And initially, he had "a horrifying fear" of acting. "I don't think I was ready for stardom 20 years ago," he said. "You might as well say the person who is the chief executive officer in an insurance company across the way had matured in his job. And it's true. Everyone matures with experience. That's one of the facts of life."

Ford was born in Chicago, dropped out of Ripon College in Wisconsin, and moved out to California, where he wandered into acting

Witness **(1985): Alexander Godunov, Harrison Ford, Kelly McGillis, director Peter Weir.**

between a series of odd jobs that included carpentry and working as a management trainee in a department store. A talent scout from Columbia Pictures spotted him, and he was signed to a contract. He appeared on screen for the first time as a bellhop in a James Coburn movie called *Dead Heat on a Merry-Go-Round.* He did small roles in a number of movies and television shows for the next few years. By the time he turned 30, he had two children and was out of the business, working once again as a carpenter. He would later jokingly refer to himself as "carpenter to the stars." He did work for actress Sally Kellerman, musician Sergio Mendes, and producer Fred Roos with whom he became friendly. "Harrison was not conventionally good looking," Roos recalled years later. "He was also tight-lipped, standoffish, and most people thought he had an attitude. He's an incredibly cranky guy. But I thought he was going to be a star, and we got along famously."

Roos persuaded a young director named George Lucas to cast Ford in a movie he was shooting called *American Graffiti.* He was

Director Mel Brooks, who in the seventies successfully made fun of westerns (*Blazing Saddles*, 1974), horror movies (*Young Frankenstein*, 1974) and Alfred Hitchcock movies (*High Anxiety*, 1977) tried to send up the whole *Star Wars* saga in a spoof called *Spaceballs: The Movie* (1987). Unfortunately, it was a one-joke movie that came four years after the release of the *Return of the Jedi*, (1983), long after the *Star Wars* phenomenon had run its course. In making fun of the most successful movies of all time, Brooks ironically made the least successful movie of his career.

In the wake of the success of *Star Wars*, everyone wanted to try their hand at expensive sci-fi fantasy. Tri-Star Pictures did *Lifeforce* (1985), an unintentionally hilarious mess shot in London and directed by Tobe Hooper, best known as the director of *The Texas Chainsaw Massacre* (1974).

given the small role of a hot-rod-driving badass named Bob Falfa. It was also Roos who got Ford his next role, another small part in Francis Coppola's *The Conversation.* And it was Roos who began pestering George Lucas to consider Ford for the director's next film, a science fiction adventure called *Star Wars.*

Originally, Lucas had Christopher Walken, Nick Nolte or William Katt in mind for the part of intrepid space rogue Han Solo. He didn't want to use any of the cast from *American Graffiti*, but he felt at ease with Ford and had him come in and read the male parts for the actresses auditioning to play Princess Leia. Ford soon grew irritated at the way Lucas auditioned other actors while he worked right under the director's nose. "I pretty well badgered George into casting him in *Star Wars*," Fred Roos said. "He wasn't high on George's list. He didn't know him like I did."

When Harrison Ford arrived at the outskirts of London where *Star Wars* was being shot at Elstree Studios, he, like everyone else, was concerned about the script. "You can type this shit, George," Ford reportedly said to Lucas, "but you can't say it." But then, no one in July of 1976 thought *Star Wars* was going to amount to much of anything. Science fiction films, with such odd exceptions as Stanley Kubrick's *2001: A Space Odyssey*, were consigned to the B-movie basement. Lucas wanted to change that. He wanted a fantasy that took place in a galaxy far, far away where spaceships looked realistic and were driven like cars. He wanted a teenager who eventually became Luke Skywalker, a princess named Leia, a rogue named Han Solo, a knight who became Obi-Wan Kenobi, a couple of robots C3PO and R2D2 and a bad guy named Darth Vader who did the bidding of an evil space empire.

The strangest of all the *Star Wars* clones was *Enemy Mine* (1985) in which lizard-skinned alien Louis Gossett, Jr. had the baby of astronaut Dennis Quaid after the two were stranded together on a planet. It was directed by Germany's Wolfgang Petersen.

***Right*: Farrah Fawcett, in one of her attempts to shed her TV image, co-starred with Kirk Douglas in *Saturn Three* (1980).**

In order to develop special effects that would look realistic, Lucas created a company called Industrial Light and Magic in a downtown Los Angeles warehouse, and because the old-time special effects people had all but disappeared, he brought in a group of young, untried mavericks who more or less learned on the job as they worked on *Star Wars.*

Industrial Light and Magic would spawn a whole new special-effects technology unlike anything ever seen before. It was that technology that would become the cornerstone for most of the decade's biggest fantasy hits. Without the highly developed new techniques that began to emerge painstakingly out of the imaginations of Lucas's mavericks, there would have been no *Star Wars*, let alone Indiana Jones adventures or *Ghostbusters* or *Batman*; not to mention *Who Framed Roger Rabbit*, the most sophisticated amalgamation of live action and animation ever put on the screen.

In fact, none of those movies would have been made if it were not for *Star Wars*. It changed the whole attitude toward making movies. Hollywood, which for years had ignored fantasy and adventure, would, after the release of *Star Wars*, be able to think of practically nothing else. *Star Wars* launched the idea of the blockbuster; *E.T.*, in 1982 created the obsession with it. To understand what George Lucas inadvertently created, and its effect on moviemaking, it is necessary to go back a bit to his childhood.

HE GREW UP IN MODESTO IN NORTHERN CALIFORnia, a shy, gangly, awkward kid. Uninterested in sports, he devoured comic books and was fascinated by the family's new black-and-white television set. The origins of both *Star Wars* and *Raiders of the Lost Ark* can probably be traced back to *Adventure Theater* on KRON-TV from San Francisco. The show featured all the old movie serials from the thirties and forties headlining Flash Gordon, Don Winslow, Lash LaRue and the Masked Marvel. Lucas started driving a car when he was 15 years old, and became obsessed with racing. In 1962, at the age of 18, he was almost killed in a car accident. The accident changed his life. "You can't have that kind of experience and not feel that there must be a reason

George Lucas on the set of *Star Wars* (1977). The first *Star Wars* movie was shot at Elstree Studios between March and August of 1976. The crew disliked Lucas because he was so standoffish, and they could not figure out what the movie was about. Lucas so hated the experience that after *Star Wars* was released, he decided he was through with directing. *Below*, Lucas poses with Harrison Ford, Anthony Daniels (C3PO), Carrie Fisher, Kenny Baker (R2D2), Mark Hamill, Peter Mayhew (Chewbacca) and director Richard Marquand on the set of *Return of the Jedi* (1983).

Canadian director James Cameron successfully mixed science fiction fantasy with horror in *Aliens* (1986), but when he attempted to bring the same elements to an underwater adventure, *The Abyss* (1989), *insert*, audiences didn't respond. Nonetheless, Cameron's movie contained brilliantly conceived moments of suspense, and he spared no expense, filming in an unused tank filled with more than seven million gallons of water at the Cherokee Nuclear Power Station in South Carolina to produce some of the most dramatic underwater footage ever seen.

why you are here," he said later to biographer Dale Pollock, who wrote *Skywalking: The Life and Films of George Lucas.* "I realized I should be spending my time trying to figure out what the reason is and trying to fulfill it. The fact is, there is no way I should have survived that accident . . . "

He gave up any idea of pursuing a professional racing career, and ended up at the University of Southern California's film school. His family, particularly his father, wondered what he was doing, since George had never demonstrated any serious interest in film. But Lucas had arrived at USC at exactly the right moment. Hollywood was changing; the members of the establishment old guard, who had protected their jobs for decades, were disappearing, and there was no one to replace them. A few years before, it would have been unthinkable for film schools to turn out people who would make Hollywood movies, but now Hollywood was coming to USC.

Lucas made several prizewinning shorts, including a somberly futuristic piece titled *THX-1138*, and those successes won him a scholarship at Warner Bros. to watch the production of a big-budget movie version of the Broadway musical, *Finian's Rainbow.* It was being directed by another film school graduate (UCLA rather than USC), a *wunderkind* named Francis Ford Coppola, who was five years older than Lucas. Next to the car crash, Francis Coppola was to become the major influence on Lucas's life. He would be mentor, friend, and rival. They were a study in contrasts: Lucas was shy and conservative, Coppola flamboyant and daring. But from the beginning Coppola was impressed with Lucas. "I very quickly became aware of his superior intelligence," was the way he later put it. It was Coppola who, through his newly formed Zoetrope production company, helped Lucas get his first feature launched at Warner Bros., a full-length version of his prizewinning short *THX-1138.* Lucas's family could not believe anyone had given their George a million dollars with which to make a movie, and neither could Warner's executives once they got a look at the finished product. They were appalled at Lucas's grim, unemotional and very uncommercial view of the future, and immediately canceled any further involvement with Zoetrope. Undaunted, Coppola again put his name on the line so that Lucas could make his next feature, *American Graffiti,* a movie based on his adolescent experiences growing up in Modesto. The movie was shot for just $700,000 over 28 nights, and, once again, when the studio (Universal this time) saw the finished product, it didn't want to release the movie. *American Graffiti,* of course, went on to become a huge hit and inspired dozens of imitations. But it did little to help Lucas launch his next project. For some time he had been kicking around the idea of doing the sort of science fiction movie that evoked the serials he used to watch on television's *Adventure Theater.* Universal, yet to release *American Graffiti,* was not interested, and other studios also turned the project down. One of the problems was the treatment Lucas had written. It didn't make a great deal of sense, so when Alan Ladd Jr., who was in charge of production at Twentieth Century-Fox, gave the green light to develop what was to be called *Star Wars,* it was more a leap of faith than the act of a studio executive who understood what he was reading.

THE MOVIE FINALLY OPENED ON WEDNESDAY May 25, 1977. That evening, Lucas and his wife Marcia began to have some inkling of what was happening when they decided to go to Hamburger Hamlet across Hollywood Boulevard from Mann's Chinese Theater. As they came along the street, they were confronted by huge traffic jams, and hordes of people. It suddenly struck them why everyone was here: they were trying to get in to see *Star Wars.*

Time magazine succinctly pinpointed the movie's appeal: "A subliminal history of movies wrapped in a riveting tale of suspense and

Actor John Lithgow looked amazed to find himself playing an astronaut in Peter Hyams' *2010* (1985), which tried to explain everything in a sequel to Stanley Kubrick's classic *2001: A Space Odyssey,* a movie that explained nothing.

***Below*: Tobe Hooper (*The Texas Chainsaw Massacre*, 1974) was credited with directing *Poltergeist* (1982), one of the most popular scare movies produced in the eighties. But producer Steven Spielberg was said to have stepped in and directed much of the footage himself.**

Darth Vader takes on Luke Skywalker in ***The Empire Strikes Back*** **(1980). Actor David Prowse could barely breathe under his cowcatcher mask, and he was not allowed to talk. Noted American actor James Earl Jones later dubbed in Vader's eerie, distinctive rasp of a voice.**

Below**: In order to play** ***RoboCop*** **(1987), the cyborg Detroit police officer, actor Peter Weller originally had to spend as much as 10 hours getting into his costume. Why was he chosen for the role? "Because he was the only actor who would do it," said producer Jon Davison.**

Opposite**: Carrie Fisher and Mark Hamill in** ***Return of the Jedi*** **(1983).**

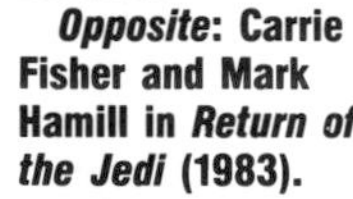

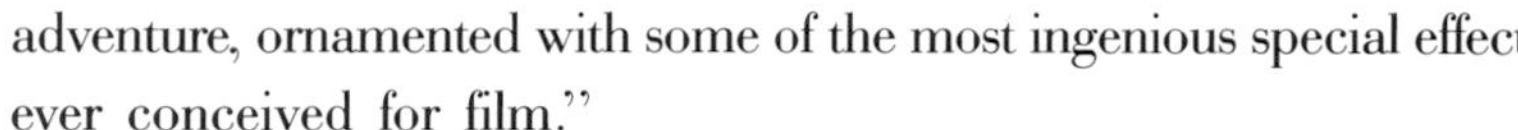

adventure, ornamented with some of the most ingenious special effects ever conceived for film."

By summer's end, *Star Wars* had made over $100 million, and had done it faster than any movie in history. By the end of 1989, the movie, according to *Variety*, had returned $193.5 million in so-called rentals (the proportion of the gross the studio receives after the exhibitors have taken their cut). It was the number-two box office champ of all time, behind *E.T.*

The *Star Wars* phenomenon continued into the eighties. The two sequels, *The Empire Strikes Back* in 1980 grossed $223 million (the next most popular movie of the year, *Nine to Five*, grossed less than half that amount), and *Return of the Jedi* in 1983 grossed $263 million.

Of the three principals, only Harrison Ford would maintain his stardom beyond *Star Wars*. Despite the fact that the three adventures focused most prominently on Mark Hamill's Luke Skywalker, the actor had all but disappeared by the end of the decade. Carrie Fisher, known to millions of children as Princess Leia, to the point where in the early eighties she could hardly walk out of her Upper West Side Manhattan apartment, continued to work regularly, but mostly in co-starring roles. By the end of the decade, she had become a best-selling novelist, whose first book, *Postcards from the Edge*, was being turned into a movie directed by Mike Nichols and starring Meryl Streep, Shirley MacLaine and Dennis Quaid.

Harrison Ford, on the other hand, had lucked out playing the square-jawed hero. Despite his surliness off camera, he was the kind of leading man you could throw into any situation. He was perfect for a project George Lucas and Steven Spielberg concocted shortly after the release of *Star Wars*.

THE WAY THE STORY HAS BEEN TOLD SO MANY times, Lucas and Spielberg were on vacation together in Hawaii. By this time, Lucas, who never did like the process of directing, had decided to give it up and confine himself to producing movies. He wanted to produce something that his friend Spielberg could direct. They started kicking around the idea of doing a variation on the popular James Bond films. Lucas wanted to create a gentleman adventurer along the lines of the heroes of the adventure serials he had watched so avidly as a kid. He already had worked on a couple of outlines, one of them with a San Francisco filmmaker named Philip Kaufman, who later would write and direct the film version of Tom Wolfe's best-selling *The Right Stuff*. Kaufman and Lucas developed a plot, involving a search for the lost ark of the

Sam Shepard was best known as one of America's most acclaimed modern playwrights (*True West, Fool for Love*) before he started to appear in movies during the late seventies (although as far back as 1969, his voice was used in *Easy Rider*). Shepard, the son of an Air Force officer, received the most attention as an actor (and an Oscar nomination) playing the legendary test pilot Chuck Yeager in *The Right Stuff* (1983). Yeager, according to author Tom Wolfe, was the embodiment of "the right stuff" that evolved into the Mercury Seven Astronauts. Philip Kaufman who adapted the book, and directed, saw the film as a modern epic of how the U.S. entered the space race. In Reagan-era America, this unabashed saga on manly American heroism should have been sure-fire at the box office, but curiously enough, despite the best efforts of the distributor, Warner Bros., the public could not be lured in to see the movie. Shepard, with his lean looks and laconic manner continued to do small parts in big movies throughout the eighties. He remained the most enigmatic of stars, however, refusing to talk to the press or in any way play the movie star game.

Australian actor Paul Hogan was a rigger on the Sydney Harbor Bridge who dropped out of school at the age of 15. He began on Australian television as an irreverent commentator on the news of the day. As the star of the ***Paul Hogan Show*** he became Australia's most popular entertainer. When ***Crocodile Dundee*** was released in 1986, it outgrossed ***E.T.*** in Australia, and went on to become the most successful foreign film ever shown in North America.

covenant, that drew heavily on a book called *Spear of Destiny*, about Adolf Hitler's obsession with religious artifacts. Spielberg and Lucas decided to make three movies starring the archeologist Indiana Smith. In June of 1979, the two met with a young, unknown screenwriter named Lawrence Kasdan and began to flesh out the plot details of what would become *Raiders of the Lost Ark*. Spielberg thought the name Smith too common, and so the hero's name was changed to Indiana Jones. Spielberg also wanted Indiana to be more of a low-life alcoholic type, while Lucas envisioned a playboy in black tie. The compromise was a more rugged, romantic hero, not unlike the Han Solo character Harrison Ford had played in *Star Wars*, only less amoral than Solo, possessed of a few more scruples. What Lucas did not want, though, was Harrison Ford himself. He was determined to use a different cast in the Indiana Jones movie from the one he used in the *Star Wars* adventures. So a young television actor named Tom Selleck was the first choice to play the lead in *Raiders*. At the last moment, however, Selleck couldn't get out of a commitment to do a TV series called *Magnum, P.I.*, and had to be replaced. Who to replace him with? Why not the actor who Indiana Jones had been fashioned after in the first place? Harrison Ford.

BY THE END OF THE EIGHTIES, THE KIND OF action adventure fantasies and their sequels inspired by Bond and given new life by the likes of George Lucas and Steven Spielberg were as close as Hollywood could get to a sure thing. Even so, audiences and filmmakers alike appeared to be getting tired of all the repeats. Spielberg and Lucas announced that, with the release of the third adventure, that was it for Indy. Harrison Ford suggested he was too old for this sort of thing, becoming the first action star to publicly admit, for the moment at least, age might be catching up to him. "Read my lips," he told journalists with his usual charm. "Bye-bye Indiana." Besides, he was on to other things. He had already demonstrated his knack for romantic comedy, co-starring effectively — and without a gun — with Melanie Griffith in Mike Nichols' charming *Working Girl*. In the summer of 1990, he was starring in a courtroom drama, *Presumed Innocent*, based on the best-selling novel by Scott Turow.

Clint Eastwood's Dirty Harry seemed more tired than dirty when he made his fifth appearance in *The Dead Pool*, released in the late summer of 1988. The former Australian bridge rigger and TV performer Paul Hogan, who had starred in *Crocodile Dundee*, the sleeper hit of the decade, and also the most successful foreign film ever released in North America, made one dull sequel that nonetheless made more money than the original, then pronounced himself through with Dundee. ("All this money is a bit wasted on us," said Hogan's partner, John Cornell, who directed *Croc II*). Whether Hogan actually was through with the character would undoubtedly depend on how his non-Dundee ventures performed at the box office.

Often as not, economics, not good intentions, were what finally brought a movie series to an end. *Superman*, based on the DC Comics hero, was turned into a hit movie in 1978, starring Christopher Reeve in the title role, and directed by Richard Donner. But after three lackluster sequels in the eighties, the public wanted no more of the Man of Steel. *Star Trek*, the old television show, was successfully revived as a series of movies that continually beamed up huge profits for Paramount. But by the time the crew of the starship Enterprise set out on its fifth voyage in the summer of 1989 for *Star Trek V: The Final Frontier*, only diehard Trekkie fans were interested. The movie flopped and the future of the movie series was in doubt.

When it was released in the summer of 1984, *Ghostbusters*, directed by Ivan Reitman and starring Bill Murray, Dan Aykroyd and Sigourney Weaver, had grossed over $220 million. Frank Price, the former head of production at Columbia, the studio that developed the project,

There had been talk for years of turning the old *Star Trek* television series into a movie, but it didn't happen until after *Star Wars* became a hit. There were four *Star Trek* sequels throughout the eighties, featuring the old TV cast, including, *from left*: DeForest Kelley, William Shatner and Leonard Nimoy.

***Right*: Producer Jerry Weintraub was home watching television when he saw a news item about a boy who had taken karate lessons in order to protect himself. From there, Weintraub evolved the idea of *The Karate Kid* (1984), and hired Ralph Macchio to play one of the most unlikely action heroes of the eighties.**

The original *Police Academy* was conceived and directed by Hugh Wilson, who created the popular TV situation comedy, *WKRP in Cincinnati*. He wanted to break into movies and thought the easiest way to do it was via the sort of youth-oriented comedy that was then all the rage. When *Police Academy* was released in the summer of 1984, it was such a hit that it spawned five more sequels. They came as close to the kind of B-movie comedy series that proliferated during the forties as the eighties would allow.

Below: Cop and dog movies were briefly popular. Tom Hanks starred in *Turner and Hooch* (1989). Jim Belushi, *below*, younger brother of John, costarred with a German Shepherd in *K-9* (1989).

called the possibility of a sequel "a huge check sitting in the drawer waiting to be cashed." Well, not quite. When the much-talked-about sequel appeared, in the summer of 1989, it did less than half the business of the original. What's more, it had cost so much to get Reitman and the *Ghostbusters* cast back that Columbia's profit on the picture was thought to be as low as $5 million. It was an amazing turnaround, but perhaps understandable. The audience's attention was elsewhere. That summer there was a new superhero getting all the attention.

B*ATMAN* HAD BEEN AROUND SINCE 1939, CREATED by an 18-year-old Detective Comics staff cartoonist named Bob Kane. Until the arrival of *Superman* a couple of years before, comic books mainly reprinted cartoons that already had appeared in the newspapers. But with the success of a character created specifically for comic books, DC Comics was looking for other superheroes. "And I came up with *Batman*," Kane remembered, 50 years later. "The first influence was Leonardo da Vinci's flying machine created 500 years ago with a man on a sled with bat wings and a caption under it that read, 'Your bird shall have no other wings but that of a bat.'

"The second influence was Douglas Fairbanks, Sr. in *The Mark of Zorro*. The third influence was a movie called *The Bat Whispers*, where Chester Morris played Boston Blackie, who wore a bat costume. The only difference was that he played a villain, and I adapted the costume into that of a hero."

The first *Batman* adventure appeared in Detective Comics in May of 1939. Like the Man of Steel, the Caped Crusader was an ordinary guy by day — in this case millionaire Bruce Wayne, rather than mild-mannered reporter Clark Kent — and a caped crime-fighter by night. Unlike Superman, Batman had no super powers, and his Gotham, unlike the Metropolis of Superman, was a much darker and more troubled city. But otherwise, it was comic strip heroics as usual, featuring a well muscled hero, his sidekick, Robin, and an array of grotesque villains intent on destroying Gotham. If Batman — in those days he was known as *The Batman* — was different, it was because he was a grim vigilante who, as often as not, was on the run from the police, who were jealous of his crime-fighting prowess.

Batman became hugely popular in the forties, was on radio and featured in two Saturday afternoon serials. In the sixties, *Batman* became a campy ABC television series that was clever and funny, but whose outrageousness all but destroyed the straight-faced comic strip.

In 1979, following the huge success of the first *Superman* movie, the idea of bringing *Batman* back to the big screen was brought to the production team of Jon Peters and Peter Guber. Guber-Peters would later become one of the most flamboyant and controversial production teams in Hollywood, and would eventually get themselves hired as the bosses of Columbia Pictures, but in 1979, they were just a couple of producers who were having trouble getting an expensive movie made. Peters in particular was excited at the prospect. "When I was a kid," he remembered, "my heroes were Elvis Presley and Batman. I used to put on a Batman costume and pretend I was the Caped Crusader."

The producers had no interest in redoing the campiness of the television series. The movie *Batman* would emphasize the mythic aspects of the original comic book stories. Ivan Reitman, Steven Spielberg and Joe Dante were among the directors connected at one time or another to the project, and there was even talk of getting Bill Murray to play the Caped Crusader in a comedy version. But Peters would say later that it wasn't until a 30-year-old director named

It wasn't easy for actor Michael Keaton, seen here with co-star Kim Basinger, to play the title role in *Batman* (1989). He had to be bolted into his costume, and the bat-mask allowed no peripheral vision. To make matters worse, nobody had bothered to build a zipper into the bat-suit. The Caped Crusader, in full costume, could not go to the bathroom. No wonder he didn't look happy.

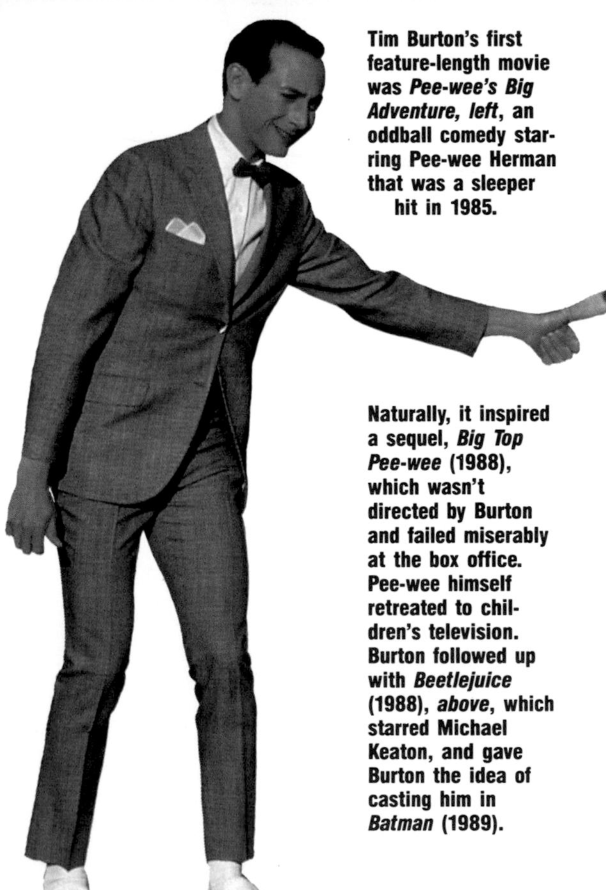

Tim Burton's first feature-length movie was *Pee-wee's Big Adventure, left*, an oddball comedy starring Pee-wee Herman that was a sleeper hit in 1985.

Naturally, it inspired a sequel, *Big Top Pee-wee* (1988), which wasn't directed by Burton and failed miserably at the box office. Pee-wee himself retreated to children's television. Burton followed up with *Beetlejuice* (1988), *above*, which starred Michael Keaton, and gave Burton the idea of casting him in *Batman* (1989).

Tim Burton came onto the scene that the vision of *Batman* began to come together. Burton was a former Walt Disney animator who made his movie debut with *Pee-wee's Big Adventure*, a strange and delightfully whimsical comedy that had been an unexpected hit. He then followed it up with another piece of inventive and funny weirdness, *Beetlejuice*, and again it was a hit. Warner Bros. production president Mark Canton brought Burton together with Guber and Peters. "I always saw myself as a passionate yet detached fan," Burton said, "in the sense that I grew up more with the Batman TV series than the comic books. But I loved the character." Still, he had reservations. "The comic book image of Batman did not make sense to me in a movie. I just kept asking myself this one question: if this guy is so handsome, so powerful, so rich, I mean, why is he putting on a bat-suit. I can't find any psychological foundation for that."

Burton was influenced by a darker revitalized Batman who appeared in a comic book called *The Dark Knight Returns*. This was more like the character Kane had created — "a weird menace to all crime." Burton liked that. His Batman, the one created by screenwriter Sam Hamm, would be the dark knight returned to a Gotham of almost operatic darkness and depravity (a Gotham, as it turned out, that may also have been inspired by the huge success of the musical version of *The Phantom of the Opera*).

Burton also liked the idea of a 37-year-old actor named Michael Keaton playing Batman. Keaton had made an impressive movie debut in a Ron Howard comedy called *Night Shift*, and he had just had something of a comeback part in Burton's *Beetlejuice.* But, as Mark Canton pointed out, "you can think of 400 guys before you think of him."

Keaton also did not see himself as Batman. He was a slim, sharp-featured unprepossessing-looking man with thinning hair. Nonetheless, he was somewhat curious. "I read it and I knew it was a good script," he said, "but I didn't think I was going to do it. I thought, 'Too bad, because this is really good.' Meeting Tim was the turning point. When Tim said, 'You look like the kind of guy who would put on a bat-suit, and go out and do some damage,' then I knew I could work from that." Nonetheless, fans of the comic book *Batman* were horrified when the announcement was made that Keaton would portray the Caped Crusader. It was a furor that died down only when the movie was released.

For all the discussion about returning *Batman* to his origins, the Caped Crusader eventually was defeated by his worst enemy, the Joker. Kane originally had created his most popular villain in collaboration with Bob Finger who wrote most of the Batman adventures. They based the Joker on the German actor Conrad Veidt, who appeared in a movie taken from a Victor Hugo novel called *The Man Who Laughs.* Peters and Guber wanted Jack Nicholson, who they had worked with on *The Witches of Eastwick.* Initially, he, too, balked at the idea. Eventually, Nicholson was flown to London, persuaded to do the part, and signed for $6 million. It was inspired casting, but the more shooting went on at Pinewood Studios, the more the script was rewritten to include the Joker. By the time the movie was released, the star of *Batman* was not the masked hero, but the cackling bad guy with the permanent smile. Thanks in large part to Jack Nicholson and the magnificently gothic sets created by Anton Furst, *Batman* became the movie phenomenon of 1989. It was the year's most popular film, grossing $251 million. That kind of money, of course, could mean only one thing — a sequel. Jon Peters concurred. "We're planning two or three," he told columnist Army Archerd. "The sets are in mothballs, and the Batmobile is in my garage."

The Joker: Jack Nicholson.

Former child star Kurt Russell tried repeatedly to become a major star throughout the eighties, but never quite made it. *Above,* he starred in *Big Trouble in Little China* (1986), a fantasy-action adventure inspired by the Indiana Jones movies that the public ignored.

Swedish actor Max Von Sydow became internationally known for his appearances in Ingmar Bergman's movies. He did not hesitate, however, to do some well-paid slumming. *Above,* he appeared as Ming the Merciless in *Flash Gordon* (1980), one of the least successful comic strip adventure fantasies of the decade.

Horror movies featuring slasher killers, inspired by the low-budget success in 1978 of John Carpenter's *Halloween*, proliferated among independent filmmakers during the eighties. One of the most successful was *A Nightmare on Elm Street* (1984), conceived and directed by low-budget horror specialist Wes Craven about a child-killer named Freddy Krueger (Robert Englund) who is burned to death by vigilantes, but returns to haunt the dreams of children. The movie, one of the most original horror films of the decade, inspired four sequels.

Inserts: Chris Sarandon was one of a number of actors to play Dracula during the eighties. He appeared in *Fright Night* (1985). Meanwhile, the *Halloween* pictures which started the whole slasher/horror cycle, continued throughout the decade. *Halloween 5* was released in 1989.

Horror authors weren't content just to sell their novels to the movies. Novelist Stephen King tried his hand at directing with ***Maximum Overdrive*** (1986), and the result was more laughable than scary. British horror writer Clive Barker was much more successful, however, with ***Hellraiser*** (1987), ***left***. It was popular enough to inspire a sequel. The ***Friday the 13th*** movies became the most successful horror series in the eighties. There were seven of them, beginning in 1980, all featuring a hockey-masked killer named Jason, loose at a summer camp and killing teenagers, particularly teenaged females who liked sleeping with teenaged males. In horror movies in the eighties, sex was punishable by death.

THE POWER OF A NAME
THE MALE MOVIE STARS

Kevin Costner personified the sort of romantic leading man North American movie audiences have always admired; he was cool, easy-going, and he had a lazy smile that was hard to resist. Before Costner came along, baseball movies were considered box office poison. Such was the power of his name that he was able to make two of them, back to back, *Bull Durham* (1988) and *Field of Dreams* (1989).

If audiences craved action, comedy and adventure in the eighties, they also craved names. The male movie star became the most powerful part of the filmmaking process. Unlike the old days when the studios created the stars and told them what to do, now the movie stars called the shots. A box office name attached to a project could mean the difference between a movie getting made and not getting made. Salaries grew to astronomical proportions, but in return for the money, the stars had to produce hits. This made them increasingly nervous, and less willing to commit to projects unless they were certain they were going to be successful. A whole new breed of male movie stars became popular during the decade, and generally they were either comics or romantic leading men. Of the leading men, none was more popular than a young New York actor who, in 1981, had just received his first important break . . .

Charlie Sheen was the son of actor Martin Sheen and the brother of Emilio Estevez. He was first noticed in a bit part in *Ferris Bueller's Day Off* (1986), but it was after Oliver Stone cast him as the young recruit in *Platoon* (1986) that he became a name. Stone used him again in *Wall Street* (1987), but otherwise Sheen's career was erratic, and movies such as *No Man's Land* (1987), *above*, passed all but unnoticed.

Matt Dillon was discovered while he was walking along a street. He made his movie debut in 1979 as a troubled teenager in *Over the Edge*. He played a lot of those throughout the decade in movies such as *Tex* (1982), *The Outsiders* (1983), *Rumble Fish* (1983) and *The Flamingo Kid* (1984). But as he got older toward the end of the decade, he became harder to cast. He made something of a comeback in 1989 in the low-budget *Drugstore Cowboy*.

TOM CRUISE WAS 18 YEARS OLD. HE WAS JUST ONE of a gaggle of young actors gathered in New York City in 1981 to promote an army drama called *Taps*, co-starring Timothy Hutton and George C. Scott. This was Hutton's first movie since his Academy Award-winning performance in *Ordinary People*, and the reed-thin, nervous young man, the son of the late comic actor Jim Hutton, was thought to be very hot. All eyes were on him. But even so, Cruise was hard to ignore. In *Taps*, his role as a psychotic cadet was the film's showiest part. He arrived at the interviews wearing a black fedora pulled down at a jaunty angle. He was brash, he had a great knife-edge grin, and you could not help but notice the sheer pleasure he and the other young actors exuded in just being here, part of the process of releasing a major Hollywood picture. Still, you could not have suspected what was going to happen to him. There were all sorts of hot young male stars emerging over the next few years, the so-called "Brat Pack" that included Rob Lowe, Judd Nelson and Emilio Estevez. There was Matt Dillon and Sean Penn and Mickey Rourke. But none of them would achieve anything close to Tom Cruise's popularity. Cruise's sudden rise to fame was indicative of just how much the male movie stars dominated the industry in the eighties. Movie star power at times was awesome. A hot box office name — a Cruise or an Eddie Murphy say — could at least ensure that a movie would "open," that is, attract an audience the first weekend. After that, it was usually up to the potency of the picture, and the word of mouth it generated. Because the industry relied so heavily on stars, they often exercised more control than the people who actually made movies; the tail very much wagged the dog.

Timothy Hutton in *Taps* (1981).

In the heyday of the studio system, stars had been held in a kind of luxurious servitude. Clark Gable might have been king at the box office, but he was also under contract to MGM. Therefore, if the studio wanted him to hunt and fish in order to enhance his masculine image, then Clark Gable learned to hunt and fish. If the studio did not want him consorting with actress Carole Lombard, then he slunk around with her secretly until the studio gave its blessing and allowed the couple to marry.

The studios told stars where to go and what to do and what pictures they would make. In a sense, that worked well for them. Anthony Quinn remembered the feeling of security the studios provided, as he paced around his apartment strewn with paintings and sculptures at the Carlyle Hotel in New York. "All of us who grew up in those days — William Holden, Burt Lancaster, Kirk Douglas, Gregory Peck — we had people literally worrying about us 24 hours a day. We were out playing tennis or golf, but we knew people were trying to find projects for us, worrying about our future. Now *nobody* is."

In the eighties, movie stars created themselves. Tom Cruise did not look particularly interesting. He was good-looking in a bland, unthreatening sort of way, and his voice tended to squeak at all

Cocktail **was often cited as a good example of the power of Tom Cruise's name in the eighties. A silly melodrama about a hotshot New York bartender looking to marry a rich woman (he settles for a poor girl, who, naturally, turns out to be rich), the movie grossed $175 million in the summer of 1988. The only reason Cruise even made the movie in the first place was because his next project, *Rain Man*, was delayed. However, there may have been more to *Cocktail*'s curious audience appeal than most critics imagined. When Cruise tried to pull off the same sort of carefully manufactured commercial success in the summer of 1990, this time with a race car movie titled *Days of Thunder*, his public did not respond with nearly the same enthusiasm.**

Mickey Rourke's shambling, disheveled rebel without a cause persona was not particularly popular in North America during the eighties, but it did well in Europe, particularly in France, where Rourke was a huge star, and films such as *Homeboy,* which could not even get a release in North America, did terrific business. A former boxer, Rourke first attracted notice in the supporting role of the arsonist in Lawrence Kasdan's *Body Heat* (1981). The next year he was cast in Barry Levinson's *Diner,* and the year after that he appeared in Francis Coppola's *Rumble Fish*. It was *9 1/2 Weeks* (1986) that established his European stardom. He portrayed an enigmatic commodities broker who gets involved in a kinky sexual relationship with Soho art gallery assistant Kim Basinger. Rourke made some curious choices during the decade, none of them particularly commercial. He went from playing a drunk in a film adaptation of Charles Bukowski's *Barfly* (1987), to portraying St. Francis of Assisi (*Francesco*) to once again playing another enigmatic sexual stud, this time in *Wild Orchid*, a rather ludicrous failed attempt in 1990 to reproduce the success of *9 1/2 Weeks*.

Matthew Modine was another of the young actors who proliferated during the eighties and who never quite became superstars. Modine appeared in movies such as *Vision Quest* (1985), *above,* with actress Linda Fiorentino, *Birdy* (1985), Stanley Kubrick's *Full Metal Jacket* (1987) and *Married to the Mob* (1988).

James Woods, *left,* and Brian Dennehy, seen here in *Best Seller* (1987), played respectively a lot of bad guys and cops during the eighties. Woods longed to be cast as the nice guy leading man, but he was at his best playing creepy types living on the edge. Dennehy, a Vietnam veteran, seemed content to play heavy-set, no-nonsense police officers.

the wrong moments. The old studio system probably wouldn't have been interested in him. But there was no studio to get between Cruise and his audience, and the audience, for whatever reason, had decided it liked him better than just about anyone else.

TOM CRUISE HAD BEEN BORN THOMAS CRUISE Mapother IV in Syracuse, New York. He was the only boy in a family of three girls. His electrical engineer father constantly moved the family around. "I've kind of had a diverse life," he said. "Growing up, I never lived in the same place more than a year and a half. I went to eight different grade schools, three different high schools." He was always the new kid in class, and always felt as though he was being watched. To make matters worse, he suffered from dyslexia, a reading disability. "So I always felt kind of on the outside; I never felt that anyone understood me. I didn't feel I could talk to anyone."

The family was living in Ottawa, Ontario when Cruise's parents divorced. He was 11 years old at the time, and his mother and

The Outsiders (1983): *From left,* Emilio Estevez, Rob Lowe, C. Thomas Howell, Matt Dillon, Ralph Macchio, Patrick Swayze, Tom Cruise.

sisters moved him back to Lovall, Kentucky, where the family had its roots. His mother remarried, and the family moved to New Jersey. Cruise had never even considered becoming an actor until his senior year when someone talked him into going out for a play. "All of a sudden, after all those years of feeling like nothing, I had something to say. I found that I could express myself through acting. It felt right. I think the dyslexia had a lot to do with it. It's like God gives you a good mind and then he kind of holds your hand back and says, 'Uh, you're gonna have to work for it, pal.'"

He landed the first professional part he ever auditioned for, a supporting role in a teenage romance directed by Franco Zeffirelli titled *Endless Love.* He worked on the film for one day. After that he suffered for his art for a time, working in New York as a busboy, subsisting on hot dogs and rice. Then he went to meet the casting director for *Taps,* "and somehow I just knew I was going to do this film." Initially he was given a small part, "but then during the rehearsals and military training, I was upgraded to the co-starring role."

After *Taps,* Cruise was offered starring roles in all sorts of teen exploitation pictures. He had already taken one of them, *Losin' It,* before deciding this was not the way to go if he was to be taken seriously as an actor. He was convinced that many actors were prostituting themselves. "You have to set your values," he said. "You have to decide what you want for your career."

He went off and played a small role in *The Outsiders* in order to have the experience of working with director Francis Coppola. Even then he intuitively understood that Hollywood had to pay more attention to young actors.

"I was doing *The Outsiders* when I was offered *Risky Business,*" Cruise recalled. "I was going to go on and do *Rumble Fish,* but then this script by Paul Brickman came along. And I thought, 'Oh, my God, finally, this is an intelligent, stylish piece of material.'"

Tom Cruise in *Risky Business* (1983).

Risky Business made Tom Cruise a star in 1983. The wit and insight of Brickman's screenplay aside, what audiences responded to most was the sight of Cruise dancing around his living room in a pair of briefs miming Bob Seger singing "Old Time Rock 'n' Roll." "The scene itself was a line in the script: 'Joel dances through the house,'" Cruise recalled. "And Paul Brickman had always had the opening frame of it, and we went through the house, and talked about it, and decided I would wear my underwear and the shirt. He wanted me barefoot, but then he showed me the opening frame

Gene Wilder was the quietest and most unlikely of stars during the eighties. The former Jerry Silberman, Wilder first attracted attention in a small part in *Bonnie and Clyde* in 1967. The next year he was nominated for an Academy Award for his role in *The Producers*, and thereafter made a series of comedies throughout the seventies. He was most successful when paired with Richard Pryor, first in *Silver Streak* in 1976, and then in the eighties in *Stir Crazy* (1980) and *See No Evil, Hear No Evil* (1989). However, Wilder's biggest comedy success during the decade came when he starred all by himself as a man obsessed with a model in *The Woman in Red* (1984). He met his wife Gilda Radner when the two co-starred in *Hanky Panky* (1982). They co-starred again in *Haunted Honeymoon* (1986), *below*. Three years later, Radner died tragically of cancer.

Patrick Swayze was a dancer who had appeared in supporting roles in movies and television before he was cast as a rebellious young dancer at a summer resort in a low-budget ($6-million) movie titled *Dirty Dancing*, in which he co-starred with Jennifer Grey, *above*. It became one of the sleeper hits in the summer of 1987, and Swayze, almost overnight, was a star. Rather than pursuing the romantic image the movie established for him, Swayze followed up in 1989 with two action pictures (*Road House* and *Next of Kin*) that went nowhere at the box office. In the summer of 1990, he was back playing the romantic lead in *Ghost*.

John Travolta had been one of the hottest young stars of the seventies, thanks to *Grease* and *Saturday Night Fever*. In the eighties, he did not fare so well in vehicles such as *Staying Alive* (1983), a sequel to *Saturday Night Fever* directed by Sylvester Stallone that, as you can see from the *above* photo, was a little out of touch with the gritty urban fairy tale origins of the original movie.

***Opposite*: Tom Cruise with Kelly McGillis in *Top Gun* (1986).**

and said, 'Somehow I want you to jump out in this frame, and that's how we're going to start it.'" Cruise thought that if he could wear socks, and added a little dirt to the polished hardwood floor, he would get a perfect slide into the shot. "Then I came up with the idea of using the candlestick as a microphone. Paul said, 'I want you to use the whole living room. Just do whatever would cause your parents to have a heart attack if they were sitting in the living room.' It was really Paul and I just playing."

The audience reaction to the scene taught Cruise valuable lessons about how to make use of himself in the movies. He could play it serious, but he also knew when to put the heart-throb on screen and use it to his advantage.

After *Risky Business* was released, the pressures grew dramatically. "They offer you these huge sums of money, and your agent and everyone is just kind of like drooling at the mouth. And I get the script and say, 'My God, are you crazy? Get out of here.' I keep the focus on my craft, I'm not in it for the money."

To the surprise of jaded Hollywood observers, the earnest talk in the wake of *Risky Business* was more than pompous hot air, released in order to fill out the quotes for promotional interviews. It was the declaration of the way in which he proceeded to pursue a career. If he did a frankly commercial action picture such as *Top Gun* (cue the heart-throb with the shark's grin), then he used the added clout which the astronomical success of that movie gave him to launch the much riskier *The Color of Money*, in which he cheerfully played second fiddle to the veteran Paul Newman. *Cocktail* once again required the calculation of the heart-throb with that damnable grin — in a movie that, like certain scenes in *Risky Business*, and particularly *Top Gun*, adroitly treated Cruise not so much as an actor, but the star of his own feature-length rock video.

But that was his concession to his image. *Cocktail* was quickly followed by *Rain Man* (1988), a substantial film. Dustin Hoffman may have won the Oscar as the autistic savant brother, but it was Tom Cruise whose name provided the box office bait that enabled the picture to become one of the biggest dramatic hits of the decade.

Cruise then took on what he considered the most challenging role of his short career, portraying paraplegic Vietnam veteran Ron Kovic in Oliver Stone's *Born on the Fourth of July*. "Tom has the classical facial structure of an athlete, a baseball player," Stone said. "He's a kid off a Wheaties box. I wanted to yank the kid off the box and mess with the image — take him to the dark side."

Thanks to Cruise's determination not only to explore that dark side but also to take the audience there with him, what passes in Hollywood for audacity was rewarded with an Oscar nomination

SEABEES

Tom Berenger looked a lot like the young Paul Newman, and was actually cast as the young Butch Cassidy in a so-called prequel called *Butch and Sundance: The Early Years* in 1979. In the eighties he established his own persona in movies such as *The Big Chill* (1983) and *Someone to Watch over Me* (1988), *above*.

John Goodman became everyone's favorite second banana during the eighties. He was Roseanne Barr's husband on her hit television series, and in the movies he played best pal to everyone from Al Pacino (*Sea of Love*, 1989), to Richard Dreyfuss (*Always*, 1989) and Bette Midler (*Stella*, 1990). By the time he appeared in *Arachnophobia* in the summer of 1990, he only had to walk on the screen and audiences started applauding.

in 1989 Oliver Stone said later that *Born on the Fourth of July* could not have been made had Cruise not agreed to be the star. That was not unusual in the eighties.

A star, even a fairly minor one, could mean the difference between a movie being made or not being made. Dustin Hoffman, along with Warren Beatty and Robert Redford, developed reputations for keeping multimillion-dollar projects in a state of limbo for years, simply by refusing to commit themselves. Hoffman stoutly defended the practice, as he sought to explain how he approached the business of making a commitment to a movie. "I find that stars — and I use the word star to mean that person who can work at will — can do one of two things. You just take virtually everything that comes along — and there are stars that do that. Just to keep working. And they think, 'Oh, one out of five will be good.' Or they'll say, 'I don't care if the film is good, but if the part is a good part, I'll take it.' I think Michael Caine is quoted as saying that. Then you'll get people — and I'm one of them — who say, 'I not only want the part to work, I want the film to work as well. Well, that's a toughie, 'cause if there are 165 films released in a year, how many of them are good? So the chance of doing good work is very difficult. So I've been careful, because I get upset when I'm in a movie that is not working — it bothers me, to put it mildly."

ONE OF THE MOST NOTORIOUS EXAMPLES OF movie star power out of control occurred when Robert Redford, an acknowledged superstar, became involved with Richard Zanuck and David Brown.

Zanuck and Brown were two of Hollywood's most successful producers. Their credits included *Jaws* and *The Sting*, "and about 13 others, some of which we don't mention," David Brown said. They had acquired the rights to a courtroom novel titled *The Verdict*, by a Boston attorney named Barry Reed. If *The Verdict* wasn't the greatest book ever written, it did contain that essential element that any movie star will kill for — a strong main character. Frank Galvin was an alcoholic lawyer, the underdog hero taking on the Catholic Archdiocese and the medical establishment in order to redeem himself. Galvin had Academy Award nomination written all over him.

No sooner had Zanuck and Brown acquired the rights than Dustin Hoffman phoned expressing interest, and so did Roy Scheider, who was furious when he discovered he didn't have the part. Frank Sinatra wanted to do it, and to their utter amazement, Cary Grant phoned to make inquiries.

"Never before in our careers have we had the kind of property

that attracted that kind of attention," Zanuck said.

But everyone else appears to have been relegated to the sidelines once Robert Redford made his appearance. Redford was the golden boy of the movies. He made noises about not liking to act, while at the same time carefully cultivating and maintaining a boyishly romantic screen persona that was a throwback to the leading-man stardom of the thirties. Redford loved to play beautifully flawed heroes. But Frank Galvin wasn't beautifully flawed. He was a drunk.

"When he realized he'd have to let the warts show, let it all hang out, then he backed off," Zanuck said. "Every time a scene was written in which he looked boozy and ill-kempt, unshaven, he resisted. He wanted to be a family man. Frank Galvin, in his estimation, had kids and was a nice, clean-cut guy — a kind of boy scout ver-

Paul Newman, in a scene from *The Verdict* (1982). Unlike most other stars, Newman didn't have to start out playing supporting parts. He was the star the first time he appeared on the screen in *The Silver Chalice* in 1954, and for many years, with his blue eyes and quick, almost arrogant smile, he personified American male movie stardom. Interestingly, Newman owed his early success to the late James Dean. When *The Silver Chalice* failed miserably and Newman was compared very unfavorably to the young Brando, he might have quickly returned to obscurity. However, Dean was killed in a car crash just before he was to start work on *Somebody up There Likes Me*. Newman replaced Dean, the movie became a hit, and his stardom was assured.

Robert Redford established himself on Broadway in 1963 in the Neil Simon hit, *Barefoot in the Park*, but remained essentially another pretty boy in the movies, until Steve McQueen turned down a chance to co-star with Paul Newman in *Butch Cassidy and the Sundance Kid* (1969). Redford took over the role as Sundance and became one of the most potent box office stars of the seventies. He turned 50 years old in 1987, and yet he somehow remained the quintessential golden boy of American movies. In interviews he disdained that sort of image, even as he cultivated it in the films he made. He was never more golden than when he appeared in *The Natural* (1984), as a mysterious, aging baseball player named Roy Hobbs. The movie contained many of the elements Redford drew on — it was set in the early part of the century, an era to which Redford returned repeatedly (*Inside Daisy Clover, The Great Gatsby, The Great Waldo Pepper, Out of Africa*); the romantic hero was larger-than-life but flawed; and the ending was bittersweet but essentially happy. In 1990, he was once again making a film for his favorite director, Sydney Pollack. *Havana* was set in Cuba on the eve of the Castro revolution, and featured Redford as a gambler, yet another flawed larger-than-life romantic hero.

One of the screen's great comedians, Peter Sellers died in 1980. His last movie appeared that same year, an inconsequential comedy called ***The Fiendish Plot of Dr. Fu Manchu***. However, rather ghoulishly, director Blake Edwards strung together some unused segments from Sellers' classic ***Pink Panther*** movies and released them as ***The Trail of the Pink Panther*** (1982). The public, to its credit, ignored the indignity.

Marlon Brando, perhaps the greatest actor of the post-World War II era, appeared briefly in ***The Formula*** (1980), playing a nasty oil magnate in an otherwise totally forgettable thriller starring George C. Scott. It was widely thought throughout the decade that Brando had retired from movies, but, in 1989, he reappeared for a 10-minute role in an apartheid drama titled ***A Dry White Season***. In the summer of 1990, he played a Don Corleone-type gangster in a comedy titled ***The Freshman.***

sion of the character. This is not what we conceived at all."

At that point, James Bridges, of *The China Syndrome* and *Urban Cowboy*, had signed to direct, replacing Arthur Hiller who had become fed up with the delays. The playwright David Mamet had written his version of the script, and Bridges had done three or four rewrites, trying to get something Redford was happy with. Exasperated, Bridges departed as well, and Jay Presson Allen, who wrote the script for *Prince of the City*, took a crack at *The Verdict.*

In all, Zanuck and Brown reckon that 10 different versions of the script were written, and still Redford hesitated. Finally, the two producers did something almost unheard of in modern day Hollywood — they fired the superstar. "We were sick of it, quite frankly," Zanuck said. They went to Paul Newman, who at the time was just finishing *Absence of Malice*. He immediately agreed to play Frank Galvin, warts and all. By now Sidney Lumet was the director, and when he took a look at all the scripts that had been written, he decided to use the one written by David Mamet — the very first one. The movie was successful, and Newman was nominated for an Academy Award in 1982.

Richard Zanuck and David Brown.

At one point during production of *The Verdict*, Newman turned to Zanuck and Brown and asked them when they were going to come up with another project for himself and Redford. "We already have," Zanuck said, only half joking. "It's called *The Verdict.*"

THE NUMBER-ONE BOX OFFICE STAR IN THE world in 1980 was a 43-year-old good old boy named Burt Reynolds. Robert Redford, the number-two box office star was also in his forties. Clint Eastwood, number three in popularity was closing in on 50. In short, there were very few actors on the screen with whom the youth audience could identify. That was about to change. Even as Burt Reynolds thanked the world for making him king of the movies — "To my mind I've just been given the best award of all, the vote of the people" — his popularity was slipping away. By the end of the decade, the most powerful star in the movies would be back doing a television series. His decline occurred so quickly that it was hard to believe. What could be given overnight could be taken away just as quickly.

The days when a star could survive three or four decades were over, although a clutch of veteran male actors did endure: Paul Newman, into his sixties, remained the longest-reigning superstar, at least until 1989 when he suffered two flops in a row, *Fat Man and Little Boy* and *Blaze*. Clint Eastwood, closing in on 60, also faltered. If anything, the popularity of Jack Nicholson actually increased, thanks to his decision to play the Joker in *Batman*. A whole generation of kids discovered that razor-sharp grin and those leaping, cheese-wedge eyebrows hanging over the glittery, darkly dangerous eyes.

Nicholson had remained a savvy, street smart player of the Hollywood star game since first gaining notice in 1969 as the alcoholic lawyer who hit the road with Dennis Hopper and Peter Fonda in *Easy Rider*. He kicked around Hollywood for years, playing in low-budget horror flicks and biker movies, doing some writing and direct-

Jack Nicholson with Danny DeVito and Shirley MacLaine in a scene from *Terms of Endearment* (1983). Nicholson's career was revived in the eighties when he accepted the part of a washed-up astronaut who lives next door to Shirley MacLaine. Apparently he had his work cut out for him on the set, mediating disputes between MacLaine and Debra Winger, who played her daughter. The work on and off camera paid off. Nicholson won his second Oscar, this time as best supporting actor.

ing, increasingly frustrated at his inability to make it. Nobody wanted to be a star more than Jack Nicholson, but he played ambition close to the vest. On the screen, he was always the outsider, thumbing his nose at authority. In truth, Mr. Outsider knew how to play a very inside game when it came to surviving in Hollywood.

In the seventies, he appeared in some of the most ambitious and original American movies of the era: *Five Easy Pieces, The Last Detail, Carnal Knowledge* and *One Flew over the Cuckoo's Nest,* for which he received his first Academy Award. In the eighties, older and more fleshy, his hair thinning, he took the good roles where he could find them, most notably in *Terms of Endearment* in 1983. When Burt Reynolds decided not to play the part of the washed-up astronaut, Nicholson took it over, and won a second Oscar, this time for best supporting actor.

After two decades at the top, he had long since ceased to be impressed with his own popularity, although he did concede one day, sitting around his suite at the Carlyle Hotel that he wasn't much different than anyone else when he arrived in Hollywood. "I wanted to go out there and see the stars," he said. "Sure, I was starstruck. Am I starstruck now?" He issued a lazy, elusive smile. "Yeah, that would be a fair thing to say. Not accurate necessarily, but fair."

Danny Glover and Mel Gibson.

It was as hard to think of Jack Nicholson starstruck as it was to think of him without thinking of a movie star. Jack was the real goods, there was no dispute about that. But otherwise the business of stardom was as often as not a function of perception and timing. For example, Danny Glover was on the screen in *Lethal Weapon* (and the follow-up sequel) as much as Mel Gibson. Yet it was Gibson who emerged from the movie labeled a superstar, not Danny Glover.

The same was true of a fortyish television star named Tom Selleck. He was big and handsome, and *Magnum, P.I.* had been a huge hit on CBS television. But the movies he had starred in performed indifferently. Then, in 1987, he appeared with Ted Danson and Steve Guttenberg in a comedy titled *Three Men and a Baby.* It was a huge hit, and the perception now was that Selleck, rather than either Danson or Guttenberg, was a movie star with box office clout. There was little hard evidence to back up this thinking. Selleck's

***Above*: Unknown Lou Diamond Phillips was chosen to play the role of pop singer Ritchie Valens in *La Bamba*, a surprise hit in the summer of 1987.**

***Below*: Howie Mandel was a bright young stand-up comic from Canada who should have done much better in movies during the eighties than he did. He appeared in *A Fine Mess* (1986) and *Walk Like a Man* (1987), but became much better known for his co-starring role in television's medical drama, *St. Elsewhere.* He was also the voice of little Gizmo in *Gremlins* (1984).**

***Opposite*: Jack Nicholson brought a new kind of craziness to the screen when he starred in Stanley Kubrick's movie adaptation of Stephen King's best-selling *The Shining* (1980). Nicholson's character was a writer trapped for a winter in a snow-bound hotel with his family, and driven to a madness widely imitated by stand-up comics throughout the decade.**

Ryan O'Neal became popular first in television's *Peyton Place*, and then as a leading man in the seventies, most notably in *Love Story* in 1970, for which he was nominated for an Academy Award.

In the eighties, however, he worked infrequently in comedies such as *So Fine* (1981), *below, Irreconcilable Differences* (1984) and *Second Chance* (1989), and was better known as the father of actress Tatum O'Neal, and the man who lived with actress Farrah Fawcett.

next two films, *Her Alibi* and *Innocent Man* both died at the box office. Nonetheless, Tom Selleck was now considered to be a movie star.

Robert De Niro was acknowledged as one of the best actors of his generation, maybe the finest screen actor since Brando. He won an Academy Award for his performance in Martin Scorsese's *Raging Bull* in 1980, but the movie itself was not a hit. De Niro's name on the marquee was not thought to be any guarantee of box office success, even when he made a calculated commercial action movie such as *Midnight Run* (1988). The same was true of the highly respected William Hurt. He starred in *Body Heat* and gave one of the decade's most poignant performances in *Kiss of the Spider Woman*, for which he won an Academy Award, but he was not considered someone whose name alone could attract the paying customers. Richard Dreyfuss, perhaps second only to Nicholson when it came to being likable on the screen, cleaned up his personal life, and experienced a comeback in the eighties with the hits *Down and out in Beverly Hills*, *Tin Men* and *Stakeout*, but he was not considered to be an actor who could carry a movie on his own. And age seemed to work against Matthew Broderick as much as anything. As an adolescent he had hits with *WarGames* and *Ferris Bueller's Day Off*. But the older he got, the less inclined an audience was to see him in movies such as *Biloxi Blues*, *Family Business* and *Glory*.

Matthew Broderick.

The two hardest-working leading men during the decade, Gene Hackman and Michael Caine, appeared to skip from film to film unconcerned about vicissitudes of the box office or the encroachments of age (both men were in their late fifties). Between 1987 and 1989, Hackman made nine feature films. Caine made six, as well as two television movies.

Hackman, particularly after his performance as an FBI agent in *Mississippi Burning* (1988), became perhaps the most respected American movie actor since Spencer Tracy. On a movie set, he could be difficult and irritable, but on screen his performances were seamlessly natural.

"I dunno, I guess I've been doing this for so long, I don't know what else to do," Hackman said to journalist Nancy Mills late in 1989, relaxing in his trailer between scenes he was shooting for a thriller, *Narrow Margin.* "It's hard for me to live in a proper home any more, I've been on so many movie sets . . . You kinda get tired of it after awhile, but after you're off a couple of months, you kinda want to get back in it. It's a very strange life. It's like being in the circus, I suppose."

Caine explained his attitude toward work this way: "I do make a lot of movies. I suppose that's because I have a very high standard of living. I don't get paid $5 million like all those other actors. If

Gene Hackman, with Willem Dafoe in *Mississippi Burning* (1988), was one of the hardest-working and most respected leading men of the eighties. From a working-class background, Hackman dropped out of school at the age of 15, enlisted in the Marine Corps, then drifted from job to job until, in his thirties, he decided to realize a lifelong dream and become an actor. He played a lot of cops in the eighties, and was nominated for an Academy Award for his performance in *Mississippi Burning*.

Denzel Washington came out of the TV series, *St. Elsewhere*, to co-star as South African activist Stephen Biko in Sir Richard Attenborough's *Cry Freedom* (1987). Kevin Kline, who played the white journalist who befriended him, was noted for his work on stage before coming to movies in *Sophie's Choice* (1982) and *The Big Chill* (1983).

Jeff Bridges was a terrific actor, and much in demand by the decade's most important directors, but somehow major stardom eluded him throughout the eighties. He took his shirt off for *Against All Odds* (1984), co-starring Rachel Ward, but his only hit of the decade came when he played a killer opposite Glenn Close in *Jagged Edge* (1985).

***Opposite*: Dustin Hoffman in drag for *Tootsie* (1982).**

you're Dustin Hoffman and you get $5 million for *Tootsie*, and then you get $15 million, what with your share of the percentage, you're not in a hurry to make another film. I'm not going to mention what I make, but it's a lot less than that. But I have the same standard of living as Dustin, so I have to do something."

He took his stardom very much in stride. "No one enjoys being a star more than Michael," said his friend, actor Bob Hoskins. Caine, like Hackman, delighted in working hard to make the acting look easy. Critic Pauline Kael called him a great actor after she saw him in *Educating Rita*, and three years later he won an Academy Award for his performance in Woody Allen's *Hannah and Her Sisters.* Unfortunately, Caine could not be at the Oscar ceremony. He was marooned in the Caribbean, with a shark that didn't work, trying desperately to finish his part in *Jaws: The Revenge.* Ironic that, as he was honored for some of the finest work of his career, he was making one of the worst movies he had ever been involved in.

"People say to me, 'You've had several flop pictures — do you ever worry you'll never work again?' I say no. The writers and directors may not work again. But I'll always be there, because I'm a skilled professional actor."

The Romantic Hunks: Eighties Kind of Guys

THERE WAS ANOTHER KIND OF ACTOR THAT became popular during the eighties, a throwback to the old-fashioned style of leading man who could appeal to women and be admired by men. It was a delicate balance to strike, particularly when the young romantic leads tended to become known, much to their horror, as "hunks." Richard Gere was one of the hunks after he made *An Officer and a Gentleman* (1982). Dennis Quaid was another, although he was never very successful in finding a movie anyone wanted to see, and so was Michael Douglas, a former television actor who, until the eighties, was best known as Kirk Douglas's son and the man who produced the Academy Award-winning *One Flew over the Cuckoo's Nest.* He starred with Kathleen Turner in two action comedies, *Romancing the Stone* (1984) and *Jewel of the Nile* (1985) that were hugely successful. However, it was his role as the philandering husband who has a fling with Glenn Close in *Fatal Attraction* that finally established his sex appeal. He added a ruthless edge to that appeal in *Wall Street* (1987), in which he played a corporate raider; and in *The War of the Roses* (1989), battling Kathleen Turner for the ownership of the archetypal yuppie dream house.

Dennis Quaid dyed his hair blond to play Jerry Lee Lewis in ***Great Balls of Fire*** **(1989). The movie was supposed to be a big hit, but the character of the young Jerry Lee was so unlikable, audiences stayed away. Quaid wanted to do his own singing, but Lewis wouldn't hear of it.** ***Below*****: Dudley Moore made a lot of comedies during the eighties, but his only success came playing a tipsy millionaire in** ***Arthur*** **(1981), co-starring with Liza Minnelli. A sequel,** ***Arthur 2: On the Rocks*** **(1988) flopped.**

But none of these so-called hunks came close to the popularity enjoyed by the two young actors who, more than the others, defined male romanticism on the screen during the eighties.

KEVIN COSTNER HAD BEEN KICKING AROUND Hollywood for six years, and he had never even *spoken* a line of dialogue in a movie, and therefore had yet to qualify for membership in the Screen Actors Guild. He had confidence in himself, though, and he remembered later that he was driving along a freeway after auditioning for a new movie called *The Big Chill* when he decided once and for all that he was going to be a movie star.

Costner had grown up in Southern California, and his dream was to become not an actor, but a baseball player. He briefly went into marketing after graduating from Cal State (Fullerton), and was newly married when he decided that acting was going to be his life. "I felt the true joy of discovering what I wanted to do," he said later. "It may have been a huge weight on everyone else, but it was a huge weight off me."

Kevin Costner in *No Way Out* (1987).

Soon his decision seemed about to pay off. His *Big Chill* audition was well received, and he was cast as Alex, the suicide victim who causes the cast to gather for a weekend of rumination and introspection. "My scene was at the end of the movie. It was a flashback, about 10 or 15 minutes in duration, but it wasn't integrated into the rest of the movie."

Costner filmed his scene and settled back to wait. Then he got a phone call from Lawrence Kasdan, the director of *The Big Chill.* Kasdan had some bad news. It was apparent after a couple of previews that the long flashback scene at the end, the scene which featured Alex, wasn't working for audiences. Kasdan had decided to cut it. Costner's movie debut was left on the cutting room floor.

"In truth, it was more of a blow to my parents and my friends," he said. "I knew the day I got the role that I was in, that I had made it. I was exactly where I needed to be, and that this was the start for me." He paused, then smiled wryly. "Although I must say, the fact that it was a $100-million hit bugged me a little bit."

Kasdan promised Costner he would have a part in the director's next movie. Costner never doubted for a moment that Kasdan

would keep his word. "I'm kind of gullible in a sense. I don't think I'm foolish about it, but I have a hard time not believing those things, because when I say those things, I believe them too."

Kasdan's next movie turned out to be a western called *Silverado*, and the director cast Costner as a charismatic young gunfighter full of confidence and derring-do. *Silverado* didn't do well, but everyone in the movie business noticed Costner. *The Big Chill* incident had already become the stuff of movie legend, and there was a perception in Hollywood that Costner was a star in waiting. "In *Silverado*, Kevin jumped off the screen," said Eric Pleskow, who was the chief executive officer of Orion Pictures. Pleskow offered Costner his choice of pictures on Orion's schedule, and, to everyone's surprise, the actor picked a political thriller titled *No Way Out* that

They didn't exactly look like *The Magnificent Seven* or *The Wild Bunch*, nonetheless, *from left*, Kevin Costner, Scott Glenn, Kevin Kline, and Danny Glover had a go at reviving the western in a movie titled *Silverado* in 1985. That same summer, Clint Eastwood starred in his own western, *Pale Rider*. *Silverado*, despite director/screenwriter Lawrence Kasdan's attempts to give the action a contemporary *Raiders of the Lost Ark* pace, did not do well at the box office. *Pale Rider* did all right, but its small success was attributed to the potency of Eastwood's name. As a result, the western once again returned to its state of limbo.

Mikhail Baryshnikov defected from the Soviet Union in order to dance in America. He made an impressive movie debut in 1977 playing a ballet dancer in ***The Turning Point***. In the eighties, he appeared in ***White Nights*** (1985), playing a defected Russian ballet dancer whose plane crash-lands in the Soviet Union. The movie, directed by Taylor Hackford and co-starring Gregory Hines, was a success, and Baryshnikov showed the sort of screen charisma that makes actors stars; but, rather than pursue a movie career, he became artistic director of the American Ballet Theatre in New York.

Kevin Bacon, with actress Lori Singer, also danced his way briefly to success. He starred in a music and dance movie titled ***Footloose*** (1984), about a young city slicker who discovers the kids in the small town to which he has just moved aren't allowed to dance. Although Bacon did not perform the film's more ambitiously athletic dance moves, he was, nonetheless, immensely likable in the part and should have become a bigger star during the decade.

Opposite: Mel Gibson in ***Mad Max Beyond Thunderdome*** (1985).

just about everyone else had passed on. To everyone's further surprise, *No Way Out* was a sleeper hit. The same summer, Costner starred in *The Untouchables*, a big-budget gangster movie directed by Brian De Palma, which became one of the most popular movies of 1987. "He has a quality I think is quite refreshing in that he has an openness," suggested Sean Connery, Costner's co-star in *The Untouchables.* "Quite a few of the younger American actors, I don't know what it is, they're more angry about things than they need to be. But he has more balance, and he has a certain kind of naivete that he uses extremely well."

Bull Durham, a baseball romance in which Costner played a washed-up minor league player trying not to be in love with Susan Sarandon, was released the following summer, and was still another surprise hit. He followed that with *Field of Dreams*, a Capra-esque drama in which he played a Midwestern farmer who builds a baseball diamond in a corn field — the most unlikely hit of all his movies. In just three years, Costner, in his mid-thirties, had transformed himself into the screen's most likable romantic hero, in the tradition of a Gary Cooper or a Jimmy Stewart. He wore stardom easily. "Kevin Costner is one of those people who's so wonderful you hope to God he never changes," said Lawrence Gordon, who produced *Field of Dreams.*

IF MOVIE STARDOM WAS SOMETHING KEVIN COSTNER could have a good time with, it scared the hell out of Mel Gibson. "The strongest person in the industry is the *star*," he said. "When you find that out, it's kind of weird."

Gibson was 28 when he made this observation. He had come to a place he claimed he never started out for, and, once there, found it alien and confusing. He was a movie star who had starred in an Australian action picture, *The Road Warrior* (1981), and an Australian love story, *The Year of Living Dangerously* (1982). But neither one of those pictures was the kind of financial success that decreed the degree of stardom Gibson supposedly was enjoying.

He was sitting in an unadorned suite in a second-rate hotel in downtown Toronto where he was on location finishing a drama titled *Mrs. Soffel.* He held a cigarette in one hand, and a Heineken beer in the other. His hair was cut very short, making him look even younger than he was, and he was dressed in worn jeans and a loose fuchsia-colored shirt. The blue eyes that set so many women to swooning darted about nervously when he spoke, and the boyish smile flashed on and off like a malfunctioning neon sign. It was one of the first times he had been interviewed and he was not reacting

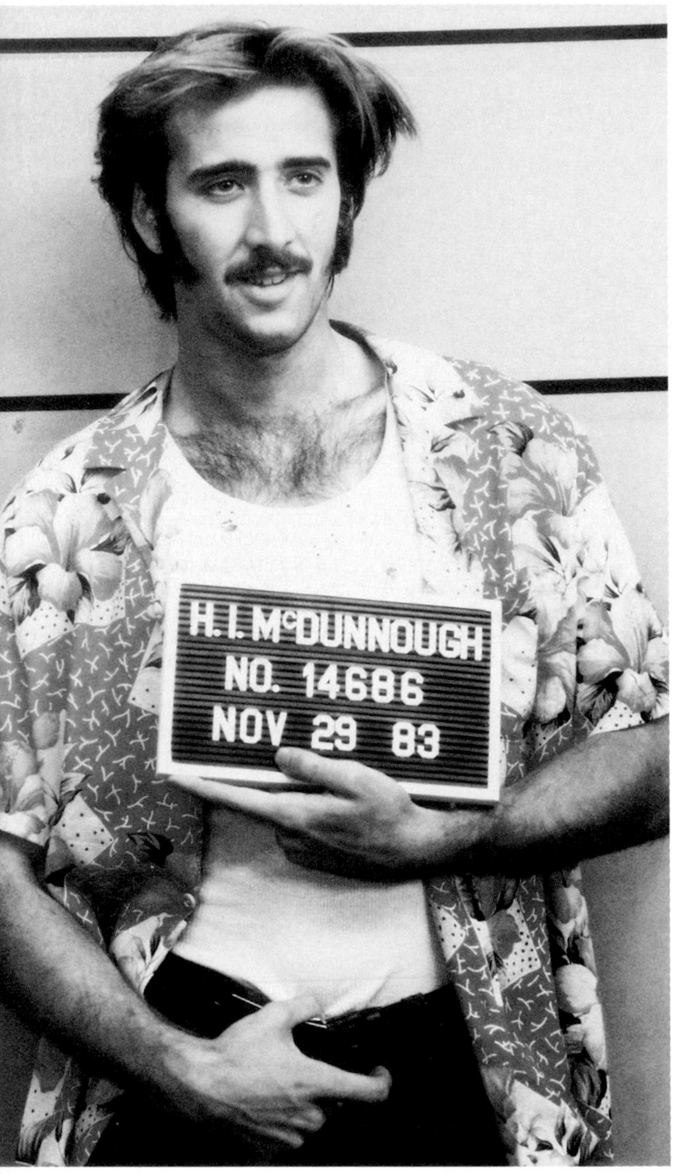

Nicolas Cage, in a scene from ***Raising Arizona*** (1987). Originally, he was Nicolas Coppola from Long Beach, California. It was his uncle, Francis Coppola, who helped Cage get into movies, by casting him in a small part in ***Rumble Fish*** (1983), the first of three of Coppola's films he appeared in. He was often criticized for his edgy, off-kilter performance in ***Peggy Sue Got Married*** (1986), in which he had the unlikely role of Kathleen Turner's husband. But in ***Raising Arizona*** and ***Moonstruck*** (1987), his quirkiness was put to good use. By the end of the decade, still in his twenties, he had managed to put together an impressive body of work, and in 1990 he had his best role yet, playing Sailor Ripley, "an outlaw in love," in David Lynch's controversial ***Wild at Heart.***

well to the process.

"The studio executives who backed *The Year of Living Dangerously* wanted me to be hot," he said, the self-professed working-class actor attempting to explain something as slippery and unfathomable as this stuff about sex appeal. "It was like a push of some kind. You know, they were shovin' me here and there into these photo sessions, making sure my picture was in *People* and *Rolling Stone.* So everyone started to say, 'Who is this guy?'"

Gibson considered himself Australian, but actually he was born in Peekskill, New York, where his father was a railroad brakeman. His grandmother was Australian though, a former opera singer, Gibson said, so when Gibson's father was injured in an accident, he decided to move his family of 11 Down Under. Mel was 12 years old at the time. "It was," he said, "a complete culture shock. Total and complete."

The Year of Living Dangerously **(1982).**

Gibson grew up going to the movies, but he intended to become a journalist, not an actor. It was his sister who put his name in for an audition at the National Institute of Dramatic Art in Australia. "They take a handful of people out of thousands," he recalled. "I went in and they grabbed me. So I decided, 'What the hell, I might as well have fun.' I was only 19."

From the beginning, his looks made him leading-man material. "An acting teacher used to say to me, 'You want to be a character actor.' But what they did to me at drama school was to shove me into all these straight parts. Eventually, I was forced to find a way around it. Straight parts are the hardest parts to play. The potential for being boring is limitless."

Gibson had not even finished his three years at the school when an unknown, untried director named George Miller chose him to play the lead role in a futuristic action picture titled *Mad Max* (released in North America in 1980). The budget was only $300,000. "I thought it was a piece of shit," Gibson said. "And it sort of is, in a way. But, there was something that came through . . . Basically, we were working in that B-road film, schlock trash genre."

But no more. Now, as he sat in the barren Toronto hotel suite, drinking down yet another Heineken, lighting another cigarette, Mel Gibson, who, in his short career, had never played anything but the leading man, was a movie star. And movie stars were expected to have hits.

"That comes by all the time," he conceded, "but I ultimately make the decision on what I should do. You have to make your own decisions." He shrugged. "Anyway, so what if they're not hits? The primary reason for doing a film is so people will see it. You want it to be a hit. It doesn't always work that way, even if it's good. But you've got to take the risk."

Even as he spoke, Gibson was pretty much finished with risks. He left the hotel that afternoon and was arrested for impaired driving. His subsequent conviction appeared to shake him out of the hard-drinking, hard-working, hard-living lifestyle he had been pursuing. He finished *Mad Max Beyond Thunderdome*, then retreated to his ranch in Australia, stopped drinking, and pulled himself together.

When he reappeared in Hollywood, a town he previously professed to dislike intensely, he co-starred in that staple of commercial American cinema, the buddy-cop action movie. This one was called *Lethal Weapon* (1987), and in it Gibson portrayed a suicidal maverick cop named Martin Riggs partnered with the more conservative and mature Danny Glover to create a lot of gunfire and tie up traffic on Los Angeles freeways. By the time he came to do the inevitable sequel to *Lethal Weapon*, he appeared to have relaxed and, like Costner, learned to enjoy his stardom. "I figure if you have to work for a living, you might as well make fun of it. What I do certainly isn't a cure for cancer."

Sidney Poitier was the first black American actor to become a major star. In the eighties, he appeared to prefer directing to acting. However, he did step in front of the camera a couple of times, in *Shoot to Kill* (1988), *above*, and in *Little Nikita* (1988). In both instances, curiously enough, he played FBI agents.

***Below*: John Malkovich came out of Chicago theater to win an Oscar nomination for his performance in *Places in the Heart* (1984). Throughout the decade he was never easy to typecast. He was an unlikely choice to play the heartlessly womanizing Valmont in *Dangerous Liaisons* (1988), nonetheless, he was flawless in the role, and gave the best performance of his screen career to date.**

The Court Jesters: Comedy Is Easy; Serious Is Hard

IN DECEMBER 1982, A YOUNG LONG ISLAND COMIC named Eddie Murphy was about to appear in his first motion picture. He was convinced that, as soon as the movie opened, his career would be finished. During filming, the director Walter Hill had to work hard with him in order to get a sustained performance, and even then the results were less than satisfactory. Each time Murphy finished a take, he would phone his manager, Bob Wachs, and complain that he was a fool for ever agreeing to do this. They hadn't even wanted him in the first place. Originally, the producers hoped to sign Burt Reynolds and Richard Pryor. When the two stars decided to pass, they fell back on Nick Nolte, a rugged blond actor badly in need of a hit, and 21-year-old Eddie, who was part of the new cast of NBC television's *Saturday Night Live*, but was otherwise untried. Nolte was

being paid $2 million. Eddie Murphy was receiving a paltry $200,000.

Now it was Christmas time in New York, and there were a lot of big pictures about to open. The perception was that Eddie's movie, an action cop picture titled *48 HRS*, was not particularly important. Nobody seemed to think much of the fast, violent, and vulgar movie. Nolte played a down-at-the-heels San Francisco cop who gets a young hood named Reggie Hammond released for 48 hours in order to assist him in tracking down a vicious cop-killer. Nolte's career, having shown great promise when he appeared in the television mini-series, *Rich Man, Poor Man*, had floundered after a couple of well-intentioned flops, *Who'll Stop the Rain* and an adaptation of the John Steinbeck novel *Cannery Row*.

Nick Nolte in *Cannery Row* (1982).

Eddie had driven in from his working-class home in Hempstead, Long Island in 1979 and began performing at a club called The Comic Strip, co-owned by a man named Bob Wachs. Wachs later claimed he recognized Murphy's talent immediately. "This kid has instincts you cannot believe," he said. "I mean I couldn't believe it. His material was a little rough, but he had this smile, and this voice."

Murphy remembered things somewhat differently. "He threw me out of the club the first time. But then he finally saw my act and put me up for *Saturday Night Live*."

Murphy was in the midst of his third season as part of the cast that had replaced Chevy Chase, Dan Aykroyd, John Belushi and the rest of the original Not-Ready-For-Prime-Time-Players. The replacements were not considered to be nearly as good as the originals, and certainly Murphy was unimpressed with his colleagues. When he landed a spot on the show, "I did not go crazy. I was only a featured player. Did you see the cast? *That's* why I didn't go crazy."

As Eddie entered the East Side theater where *48 HRS* was having its premiere, he was all but unnoticed by the crowd. A few people called his name, 'Hey, Eddie — Eddie!' But otherwise he could have been any kid going to the movies. He couldn't shake the feeling that the evening was headed for disaster.

When the movie started, he could hardly believe what he saw

Burt Lancaster and Kirk Douglas co-starred together several times over the years (*Gunfight at the OK Corral, Seven Days in May*), but no one had written an original screenplay specifically for them until James Orr and Jim Cruickshank came along with *Tough Guys* (1986), a comedy about two ex-cons trying to make it in the modern world. Lancaster was 73 at the time, Douglas, 70.

Harry Dean Stanton was almost legendary in Hollywood as a character actor, specializing in eccentric, slightly weird characters lost on the American landscape. He appeared in *One from the Heart* (1982), *Paris, Texas* (1984) and *One Magic Christmas* (1985), and although he desperately wanted to be a star, he could never quite rise above his character status.

***Opposite*: Originally Sylvester Stallone was supposed to star in *Beverly Hills Cop* (1984). When he and the producers could not agree as to what kind of picture it would be, Stallone left. Eddie Murphy was hired, more humor was added, and *Beverly Hills Cop* became the biggest hit of Murphy's career.**

Emilio Estevez was one of the so-called "Brat Pack" of young actors who flourished during the eighties. Like several of his contemporaries, Estevez got his start in Francis Coppola's ***The Outsiders*** (1983). He tended to do best in ensemble movies such as ***The Breakfast Club*** (1985) and ***Young Guns*** (1988), or co-starring with other stronger actors, such as Richard Dreyfuss in ***Stakeout*** (1987). Not content with just acting, Estevez tried directing as well, and made ***Wisdom*** (1987).

Sean Penn may have been the most talented of the young actors who came into the movies during the eighties, but he had trouble attracting audiences to his movies. His most successful film was ***Colors*** (1988), in which he played a hot-headed Los Angeles police officer. Otherwise, he was best known for being married to Madonna, and taking swings at various photographers who tried to photograph the couple.

up there on the screen. "It was wild," he reported later. "It blew my mind." It also blew everyone else's mind. By the time Murphy, as Reggie Hammond, walked into an all-white western bar and started ordering everyone around, the audience was delirious. After the movie, Murphy went to leave the theater and was mobbed. It was all he could do to get out the door. Later, at a reception in the Rainbow Room on the 64th floor of Rockefeller Center, Paramount executives who, only a few hours before, were convinced that *48 HRS* would get lost in the crush of Christmas movies, now realized they had a hit on their hands, and elbowed each other out of the way in order to get their photographs taken with Eddie Murphy. In two hours, he had gone from being a cast member on *Saturday Night Live* to a movie star. It was one of the fastest transformations in movie history.

The next morning, Murphy showed up for an interview wearing a leather jacket and cap. The carefully trimmed mustache made him look older than his 21 years. He was subdued, and when he spoke you had to strain to hear what he was saying. There was no sign of the wildly irreverent Reggie Hammond. Murphy struck you as a sober and responsible young man who knew full well what was happening to him, and wanted to take advantage of it. He had already decided to get away from *Saturday Night Live* as fast as possible. "I have ideas for things you can't do on television," he said. "I don't know what's with NBC. They wanted to structure a big, exclusive TV deal, then they suddenly backed off it. Now, when I don't want to do TV, they offer me a big special. I'm saying, 'Guys, I just want *out.*'"

That morning, as he lounged back confidently on a sofa, Eddie Murphy had seen the future. "It's wild," he said. "If you have a hit movie you can ride on that for five years. You're hot." He flashed that trademarked grin for the only time during the conversation. "All of a sudden, I'm hot."

He had no idea just how hot. Murphy was to become the biggest star of the eighties. He was no great shakes as an actor — he was the first to admit that. But he was funny, and in the eighties, if you could make people laugh, you could be king at the box office. Nobody made people laugh harder than Eddie Murphy. *Trading Places, Beverly Hills Cop, The Golden Child, Beverly Hills Cop II, Coming to America,* everything he appeared in, no matter how trite, was a hit. He was the one star whose mere presence on the marquee could guarantee success. No other male star could make that claim. Everyone else had their hits and misses, not Eddie. His only brush with failure came when he made a featured appearance in a Dudley Moore comedy called *Best Defense.* Even a concert film titled *Eddie*

Murphy Raw, featuring Eddie doing stand-up comedy, grossed over $50 million. At the end of the decade when Eddie decided to write and direct, as well as star in a limp 1920s comedy called *Harlem Nights*, it grossed $17 million on its opening weekend, despite the worst reviews of Eddie's short movie career.

Everyone enjoyed Eddie's irreverence, his unflappable ability to talk himself out of any situation. He was the black ghetto kid against the establishment, and even white audiences loved his insouciance. But the movies themselves, for the most part, did not do Eddie justice. They were slickly manufactured vehicles for his stardom, a throwback to the days when people went to see their favorite stars, and if the movie they were in was good, that was just fine, but hardly necessary to an evening's entertainment. Eddie's fans appeared willing to forgive him anything, as long as he was up there on the screen.

By the time he turned 28, his friends referred to him as Money. *Rolling Stone* magazine called him, accurately enough, "Paramount's billion-dollar box office sovereign, the nation's foremost comic commodity." He liked to dress in black, admired Elvis, and he exuded

Eddie Murphy played the pauper who becomes a prince in *Trading Places* (1988), with Dan Aykroyd, *right*. In *Coming to America* (1987), he is the prince who comes to America seeking a wife and becomes a pauper. Like just about everything Eddie did during the eighties, both movies were huge successes. They were both directed by John Landis.

***Above*: Wilford Brimley, *far right*, seen with Don Ameche and Hume Cronyn in a scene from *Cocoon: The Return* (1988). Brimley usually played gruff yet lovable old codgers but, interestingly, he was never as old as he often played. Brimley was only in his fifties when he first portrayed one of the oldsters made young again in *Cocoon* (1985).**

***Opposite*: Steve Martin, Chevy Chase and Martin Short co-starred in *Three Amigos* (1986), a comic takeoff on *The Magnificent Seven*, in which three out-of-work singing western movie stars are hired to save a Mexican town from a gang of desperados.**

Veterans Art Carney and David Niven co-starred in the little-seen *Better Late Than Never* (1983). That same year, Niven was dead at the age of 74.

the aura of power, surrounded constantly by an entourage consisting of men with names like Rough House, Fruity and Ray-Ray. He lived like a young king in palatial homes in Los Angeles and in Engelwood Cliffs in New Jersey. He was the most glaring and successful example of the potency and power of movie stardom in the eighties, particularly when it was used to make the world laugh.

THE GUYS WHO COULD GET A LAUGH TENDED TO come either from stand-up comedy or television. One group of comic performers worked quietly, far away from the influence of Los Angeles or New York in, of all places, Edmonton, Alberta, producing a series eventually aired on NBC following *Saturday Night Live* called the *Second City Television Network (SCTV)*.

SCTV was a fictional cut-rate cable TV station, and each week the cast merrily satirized the medium that fed them. *SCTV* lacked the viciousness of *Saturday Night Live*, but more than compensated with its inventiveness. The show eventually would contribute the talents of John Candy (*Splash; Planes, Trains and Automobiles; Uncle Buck*), Rick Moranis (*Ghostbusters; Honey, I Shrunk the Kids*) and Martin Short (*Three Amigos, Innerspace*) to the movies. The most memorable character Candy played on *SCTV*, the sycophantic sleazeball, Johnny LaRue, tended to typecast him for the movies. His breakthrough in film came playing Tom Hanks' playboy brother Freddy, in the 1984 comedy *Splash*. "Actually, that was the first time anyone had come to me with something that required a performance," Candy said. "There was a little bit of a graph there, I could do something with the role. Usually, I'm supposed to be stuffing my face with food or destroying this or destroying that. Big, broad comedy — Y-e-aaaaah! Drop the drawers!"

John Candy.

However, it was NBC-TV's long-running late-night revue show, *Saturday Night Live*, that was the era's farm team for comedy stars, beginning with Chevy Chase, and continuing with Dan Aykroyd, the late John Belushi, and of course, Bill Murray.

"The first guy (who made it) was me," Chevy Chase said. "The first thing I did was *Foul Play*. Why? Because I lived *Animal House*, I didn't need it. But also because people felt I had a look that was

Comedy was king during the eighties, and if a male star could get a laugh, he could usually get a hit. *Top*: Steve Martin and John Candy had one of the biggest hits of their respective careers when director John Hughes teamed them up for *Planes, Trains and Automobiles* (1987).

Above: Rick Moranis graduated from *Second City Television* into nerdy second banana roles in movies such as *Ghostbusters* (1984) and *Club Paradise* (1986). Finally, he got a chance to star in *Honey, I Shrunk the Kids.* Again he was rather nerdy, but sweetly so, as a dad who accidentally does exactly what the title says he does. The movie was an unexpected hit in the summer of 1989.

Opposite: Tom Selleck was thought to be a likable television star (*Magnum, P.I.)* who was not succeeding in movies when Touchstone Pictures signed him to co-star with Steve Guttenberg and Ted Danson in *Three Men and a Baby.* The comedy, a remake of a French film, was one of the biggest hits of 1987, and probably saved Selleck's screen career, at least for a time.

Andrew McCarthy was another member of the so-called "Brat Pack" who never quite became a major star during the eighties. Nonetheless, he did have an unexpected success co-starring opposite Kim Cattrall in a comedy titled *Mannequin* (1987), about a department store clerk who falls in love with a mannequin who comes to life. For some reason it was a big hit and inspired a sequel in 1990.

a leading-man type. I had everything going for me. It was luck. I was embarrassed all the way through *Foul Play*."

"But there was nothing like *Saturday Night Live*," Dan Aykroyd observed. "There was that electric rush of being out there. We'll never get anything like it again."

"It was a dangerous place," Chase agreed, "like a port city. The anxiety level was way up."

***Ghostbusters* (1984): Bill Murray, Dan Aykroyd and Harold Ramis.**

Aykroyd, who co-wrote *Ghostbusters* with Harold Ramis, said the script came out of everything he learned on *Saturday Night Live.* "It was like the convergence of all our years of training and work. I just knew we had a successful venture of some kind on our hands because of the people involved.

"I always write 'em big," he continued, laughing. "I'm not a businessman when I sit down. I don't care what it costs. I just want images, pictures, entertainment — that's what I'm interested in."

Aykroyd, who was born in Ottawa, Ontario, and who grew up wanting to be a policeman, originally had written the script for *Ghostbusters* with his friend John Belushi in mind. But then, in 1982, Belushi died of a drug overdose at the Château Marmont Hotel in Los Angeles. So Aykroyd showed the screenplay to Ivan Reitman, who was also Canadian-born, and who had co-produced *National Lampoon's Animal House*, the picture that for a long time was the most successful comedy movie ever produced. Reitman liked the idea of *Ghostbusters* but thought the draft unfilmable. Harold Ramis, who co-wrote *Animal House*, was brought in to work on the screenplay with Aykroyd. "Dan's script really was magnificent, the scale of it," Ramis said. "You don't have to censor yourself when you're writing, so Dan had written every kind of delightful ghost you can think of. There were manifestations on just about every page of the script. That was part of the problem, and also the story was not quite there. We created a whole back story of how the *Ghostbusters* came to be ghostbusters, the whole rationale for the plot, the character that Sigourney Weaver played, a lot of things."

"To me, the story was about three guys who go into business for themselves," summed up Ivan Reitman. "It's a comedy about these guys in a strange business, ghost-hunting, and what it's like to do it."

The stars of *Ghostbusters* could not get over the picture's success when it opened at the beginning of June 1984. The Friday night it opened, everyone drove over to Westwood to look at the crowds lined up around the block to see the movie. For weeks they telephoned each other every day, trading news of the astronomical box office revenues. The movie would go on to gross $220 million. No one could quite believe it. Everyone was delighted — except Bill Murray.

On a Friday night in the autumn of 1984 in historic Quebec City, the crowd gathered inside an anonymous mall movie theater to see a sneak preview of Murray's latest movie, a drama titled *The Razor's Edge*. It was a remake of the old 1946 Tyrone Power movie based on a hopelessly outdated Somerset Maugham novel about the ways in which the First World War and Paris can make a wealthy and self-satisfied young man come uneasily of age.

The audience seating itself knew nothing of *The Razor's Edge* or of its antecedents. It knew only that Bill Murray was second only to Eddie Murphy when it came to being funny at the movies. You could set off a nuclear explosion next to him and he would blink a couple of times, look nonchalant, and make a joke about it. In the movies at least, nothing fazed him. No one did the self-mocking charm the way Bill Murray did it. Everyone loved Bill Murray.

Abruptly, a figure loped down the aisle of the crowded theater and moved to a microphone in front of the audience. It took a moment for the crowd to recognize the tall, balding man with the pock-marked face. There was a stir, and then the most amazing wave of warmth swept out of the audience and embraced him.

Bill Murray stood at the front of the theater and said, "Uh, I just want to introduce the film a little bit. I don't want to misrepresent the movie. It's not a *yahoo* kinda movie. It's a movie we spent a lot of time on. There are some funny things in it, but it's not a comedy.

For 30 years Jack Lemmon switched with ease from comedy to drama, usually portraying the put-upon Everyman. In the eighties, however, he concentrated on drama. He starred in *Tribute* (1980), *above*, a dramatic comedy about a man dying of cancer. In *Missing* (1982), he won an Academy Award nomination playing an American businessman searching for his son-in-law in revolution-torn Chile.

Walter Matthau and Jack Lemmon were close personal friends who often co-starred together, although in the eighties their only joint appearance was in Billy Wilder's *Buddy, Buddy* (1981). With his grizzled basset hound features, Matthau remained one of the screen's most entertaining comic character actors. He worked often during the early part of the eighties, but toward the end of the decade, his screen appearances became less frequent, although he did star in one big-budget flop, Roman Polanski's *Pirates* (1986).

Rodney Dangerfield claimed he got no respect. No one ever asked him to be in a movie until Harold Ramis cast him as an obnoxious but funny country club millionaire in *Caddyshack* (1980). He was an instant hit with an audience generations younger than he, and that audience flocked to see him in two subsequent comedies, *Easy Money* (1984) and *Back to School* (1986).

Below: No one took George Hamilton very seriously as an actor, until he started being funny. He appeared in the comedy *Love at First Bite* in 1979, playing Count Dracula, and to his delight, it was a big hit. However, when he tried a follow-up comedy in the same vein, *Zorro, the Gay Blade* (1981), it flopped, and Hamilton did not work in movies for the rest of the decade. Over the vehement objections of Paramount, Francis Coppola cast him in a role in *Godfather III* early in 1990.

So I want you to relax, and not shift around too much — and don't spill any drinks on each other."

The audience laughed and applauded, and failed to read the subtext of Murray's announcement. Bill Murray was not present in Quebec City merely to introduce a movie. He was there to be taken seriously. Eddie Murphy was content to be funny. Arnold Schwarzenegger happily churned out action movies. But Murray, at the age of 33, was looking for something more. Most people spend their lives wishing they had a sense of humor, hoping they can make people laugh. That ability came so naturally to Bill Murray that he didn't want it.

"I enjoy making people laugh, don't get me wrong," he said later. "It's a great kick. There's nothing like standing in a movie theater and watching people laugh at something you did. Very difficult to top that. But as far as life goes, they still bury you one at a time, you know? And when you're there in the last hours by yourself, you gotta look at the big picture. There's a lot of life that isn't laughs, and that's what you've gotta make something of."

Bill Murray in *Caddyshack* (1980).

Columbia desperately wanted the star of *Meatballs, Caddyshack* and *Stripes* to be part of *Ghostbusters*. The quid pro quo became simple: Murray would do *Ghostbusters*, and in return Columbia Pictures would make *The Razor's Edge*.

Now *Ghostbusters* was the biggest hit in the history of Columbia Pictures, and its success had changed Murray's life forever.

For all Murray's popularity, *The Razor's Edge* didn't stand a chance. It failed both critically and commercially, as everyone suspected it would. Murray reacted by taking nearly four years off, living in Paris for a time like Larry Darrell, the world-weary hero of *Razor's Edge*. When he came back to the screen, it was in two comedies, *Scrooged*, and the sequel to *Ghostbusters*, the movie that committed him to an audience that only wanted him to be funny. For the moment, he had given up the idea of being taken seriously. On the set of *Ghostbusters II*, he continually played the funny guy, breaking up the crew and cast, particularly his co-star, Sigourney Weaver. On her last day of shooting, director Reitman pronounced himself satisfied with her close-up and Weaver stood up to take a bow. As the applause died down, Murray appeared to study her closely, then shook his head. "Is it just me," he asked, "or can *everyone* see through

Sigourney's dress?"

The crew cracked up, and so did Sigourney Weaver. Everyone *still* loved Bill Murray.

"I'm at peace making comedies," he said one morning taking a break from shooting *Ghostbusters II*. "I realize they have a much bigger function than I thought."

BEING TAKEN SERIOUSLY WHEN EVERYONE wanted you to make them laugh was not easy. Michael J. Fox was not able to do it at all, and, for a time, the reluctance of either Steve Martin or Robin Williams to meet audience expectations caused them career problems. Tom Hanks, on the other hand, didn't spend a great deal of time worrying what people thought of him, and ended up gaining everyone's respect.

Hanks had starred in a short-lived TV sitcom titled *Bosom Buddies*, which required him to pretend he was a woman and run around in a dress. Tom Hanks could make you laugh, but he was also handsome enough to kiss the leading lady, and there

Bill Murray, alone and lonely in the remake of *The Razor's Edge* (1984), his one attempt at being serious during the eighties. He was born in Chicago, the son of a lumber company salesman who died when Murray was only 17. Uninterested in school, he began taking classes at Second City in 1969, mainly because his older brother Brian Doyle-Murray was there. By the early seventies, he was touring in the *National Lampoon Radio Show,* and when producer Lorne Michaels passed him over for the original *Saturday Night Live* cast, he landed a job on another late-night TV show, *Saturday Night Live with Howard Cosell.* He replaced Chevy Chase during *Saturday Night Live*'s second season. He wasn't particularly interested in making movies, initially turning down his first film, *Meatballs* (1979), because he wanted to play baseball. Although he thought *Ghostbusters* (1984) would be a huge hit ("Bigger than *Tootsie* and smaller than *Star Wars*" was the way he put it), he also turned it down, until Columbia agreed to allow him to star in *The Razor's Edge.*

***Above*: The return of the Rat Pack. When Burt Reynolds starred in *Cannonball Run II* (1984), he reunited the group that in the sixties had dubbed itself the "Rat Pack." The pack consisted of, *from left,* Dean Martin, Shirley MacLaine, the late Sammy Davis, Jr. and the chairman of the board himself, Frank Sinatra. Sinatra's only other big-screen appearance during the eighties was in a thriller, *The First Deadly Sin* (1980).**

***Below*: Robert Duvall was one of the screen's most admired actors during the eighties. He won an Oscar for his role as a country singer in Horton Foote's *Tender Mercies* (1982). But much to his chagrin, the award failed to make him a bankable star.**

***Opposite*: Tom Hanks with Daryl Hannah in *Splash* (1984).**

were not a lot of comic performers who brought those qualities to the screen.

When *Bosom Buddies* was canceled, Hanks, in 1983, landed the lead in two comedy movies. One of them, *Bachelor Party,* was designed as a summer exploitation comedy. "There's a real particular audience that will go for it," Hanks said at the time. "The audience that's out of school."

The other movie was *Splash,* a comedy about a guy who falls in love with a mermaid. It was a project that had been in and out of fashion with eight different managements at various studios. It finally landed at Walt Disney Studios, where it became the first offering of a new production company called Touchstone Pictures. Disney had set it up in order to do more mature, and therefore more commercial movies. Knowing that a rival studio was developing its own mermaid picture, Disney wanted *Splash* made as quickly as possible. Brian Grazer, the producer who originated the project, and director Ron Howard were off the hook for having to hire a big-name star (although all sorts of big names were rumored to have turned it down).

Tom Hanks in *Big* (1988).

Hanks was surprised at how easy it was to get the lead. "It sounds a little too simple, but essentially I walked in to meetings a bunch of times over a period of a few weeks, and that's how it happened. It wasn't, 'Okay, Tom, you gotta beat up these three other guys. We're gonna throw you into this big arena — it's a battle Royal, and the last person who stays inside gets the part.' It wasn't anything like that. I got the phone call from Ron Howard himself saying I had the job."

Splash, made for just $9 million, ended up grossing nearly $70 million. It not only established Touchstone as a viable production company, but it also made Tom Hanks a star. He would become one of the hardest-working comic stars of the eighties, a smooth, facile performer who appeared to drift with effortless affability through such vehicles as *Volunteers, Dragnet, The Money Pit* and *The 'Burbs.* Hanks remained surprisingly underrated as an actor, perhaps because, as he conceded, he was usually charged with portraying "a very average guy in a non-average situation. I have to maintain an interesting persona without being goofy or nutty or wacky or stupid

By the time the eighties rolled around, Peter Ustinov had been appearing in movies for 40 years, and had won two Academy Awards for best supporting actor (*Spartacus*, 1960 and *Topkapi*, 1964). During the eighties, he wrote books and plays, appeared on television and on the stage, and occasionally found time to do a film. He seemed to prefer detectives. He played Charlie Chan in *Charlie Chan and the Curse of the Dragon Queen* (1981), and more notably, Agatha Christie's Hercule Poirot in *Evil under the Sun* (1982), a role he inherited in 1978 when Albert Finney, who originally played Poirot in *Murder on the Orient Express*, refused to do him again. When Poirot ran out of steam at the movies, Ustinov, undaunted, played him on television.

or dumb — which is really my forte." It was not until he played a 12-year-old caught in an adult's body, in the 1988 comedy *Big*, that his unassuming comic genius was finally acknowledged. At the end of the eighties, he was taken seriously enough that when director Brian De Palma came to adapt Tom Wolfe's bestseller *The Bonfire of the Vanities* for the movies, he cast Tom Hanks in the lead.

HANKS' MAJOR COMPETITION WHEN IT CAME TO being affably funny was provided by a young Canadian named Michael J. Fox. He became the decade's biggest little comedy star, although he never really thought of himself as a comedian, and like Bill Murray, longed to do more serious work. Even he made jokes about his size: "You know what the difference between a short actor and a short star is? The short actor stands on an apple box, and the short star has them dig ditches for everyone else."

The son of a Canadian army officer, Fox grew up in Vancouver, one of five children. He loved hockey, learned how to play the guitar and was noted for his hyperactivity. He did a few acting jobs for the Canadian Broadcasting Corporation, and then, at the age of 18, headed south to try his luck in Los Angeles. "I was ready to come home at one point," he recalled. "But I owed a lot of money to the IRS, and I was afraid if I went to Canada I would never be able to come back to the States again. So I was really in an urgent situation, which I think was good for me, because it made me really care about auditions, research them, and go in and try and kick butt."

***Back to the Future* (1985).**

One of the auditions he went on was for a new situation comedy called *Family Ties*. The creator of the show, Gary David Goldberg, was not impressed. "I was probably the first actor who read, so it was easy for him to pass by me, because they were probably going to read 40 or 50 people. So I just kept on the casting lady, kept calling her, because I knew she liked me. And then, toward the end, Gary let me come back again, and this time he liked me."

Fox, playing the conservative yuppie Alex Keaton, became the unexpected star of *Family Ties*. "Even if Michael was on stage for just a few minutes, it was electric," recalled Gary Goldberg. "We'd

When Michael J. Fox was funny, as he was in ***The Secret of My Success*** **(1987), a comedy about an upwardly mobile country boy who comes to the big city, then audiences flocked to see him. When Michael J. Fox was serious, as he was in Brian De Palma's Vietnam drama,** ***Casualties of War*** **(1989),** ***insert,*** **audiences stayed away.**

look around and say, 'Why is the audience leaning forward?' Michael had the ability to let the audience in, to get people to breathe with him."

Over the seven-year run of the series, Fox won three Emmys but, more importantly, he came to the attention of Steven Spielberg. Spielberg was producing a movie titled *Back to the Future*, based on a script by Bob Gale and Robert Zemeckis that had been turned down by every studio in town before Spielberg's Amblin Entertainment decided to take the gamble, with Zemeckis directing. They had cast a young actor named Eric Stoltz to play the role of Marty McFly, the teenager who goes back to the 1950s in a DeLorean car. Five weeks into shooting, they were unhappy with Stoltz's work. An actor with a lighter touch was needed. Fox came into the role at a moment's notice. During the day, he shot *Family Ties,* and at night, he was on the set of *Back to the Future.* When the movie was released, in the summer of 1985, it became the year's biggest hit (grossing $208 million). Abruptly, Fox was starring in the most popular movie, and the top-rated TV series.

But Michael J. Fox soon learned that laughter had its limits. If

Gregory Hines was one of the few black actors able to land leading roles in American movies during the decade. Even so, Hines, seen here with Billy Crystal, was not regarded as a box office star, despite his success with Crystal in *Running Scared* (1986) and in *White Nights* (1985) with Mikhail Baryshnikov.

Below: Richard Pryor, in a scene from *Stir Crazy* (1980). Pryor began the decade as the most popular black actor at the movies. By the end of the eighties, his popularity had been eclipsed by Eddie Murphy, who, ironically, grew up wanting to be just like Richard Pryor. When Murphy directed *Harlem Nights* in 1989, he cast his idol in a co-starring role.

he made a comedy such as *The Secret of My Success*, it was a hit. But if he tried to do something more serious — *The Light of Day*, in which he played a guitar player in a Cleveland rock band; *Bright Lights, Big City*, where he was a cocaine-dependent magazine fact-checker, or *Casualties of War*, which featured him as a soldier in Vietnam — then his fans were not interested.

"Audiences can be very unforgiving," said Paul Schrader, who directed Fox in *Light of Day*. "People don't like to see their icons change roles."

"Drama is hard," Fox had decided by the end of the decade, while filming not one, but two sequels to *Back to the Future*. "I've done comedy all my life. I was a small kid, so, you know, make them laugh and they won't beat you up."

MOST OF THE DECADE'S COMIC STARS TOOK for granted their ability to make people laugh. They were, for the most part, the kids at the back of the class who never grew up, and they did not take laughter much more seriously than that. The genius of Robin Williams and Steve Martin lay in their refusal to take lightly their ability to evoke laughter or to do much of anything that was either safe or predictable. Perhaps because of this, it was a long time before anyone knew quite what to do with them.

Both Steve Martin and Robin Williams had started out as stand-up comics. Williams was a comedian with a talent for improvisation that was breathtaking to witness. He would appear unexpectedly at a club like the Comedy Store on Sunset Strip in Los Angeles and hit his audience with something like the Born Again Trout. "Yeah," he said, "it's like every time you catch a trout and throw it back again, that's a Born Again Trout." Williams then described the trout returning to his trout pals who naturally wanted to know what God was like. "It's insane," the trout would report, "he wears a penalty jacket and drinks beer. It's insane, I tell ya. He's just . . . *out there*."

Television first discovered Williams. He played Mork, the alien being from the planet Ork, in the sitcom *Mork and Mindy*. In 1979, at the age of 26, he went from struggling comedian to television phenomenon in less than five months. "Nanu, nanu," became part of the pop lexicon of the day. Instead of going into the sort of mindless teen comedy movies that might have appealed to his TV audience, Williams struck out for more risky territory. He made his movie debut in 1980, playing the title character in director Robert Altman's movie musical of *Popeye*, one of the decade's most bizarre movies. He followed *Popeye* with the movie version of John Irving's blackly comic best-selling novel, *The World According to Garp*. Then he fooled everyone's expectations once again with his portrayal of a saxophone-playing Russian defector in Paul Mazursky's *Moscow on the Hudson*. For *Popeye*, Williams gained 20 pounds and wore all sorts of uncomfortable rubber and latex. For *Moscow on the Hudson*, he learned to speak fairly fluent Russian and took exhaustive saxophone lessons.

"I think I chose the roles I have because they are not easy," Williams said in 1984. He thought about this, and laughed. "Probably I'll end up next year doing something like — 'Look, it's Mork! He's back! He's crazier than ever!'" His face crumpled into feigned pain. "Oh, man, I said I wouldn't do that. I had to pay for the ranch, man. I needed the money!"

His face resettled again, and he became a studio executive talking to a failed Robin Williams in a voice lacquered with phony warmth: "Robin you're so *daring*. We'll get back to you. That was a very daring move — a little stupid. But we love ya. If you go back to TV, call us."

Despite the continuing acknowledgment of his comic talents, he was going from bad to worse at the movies, making clinkers such

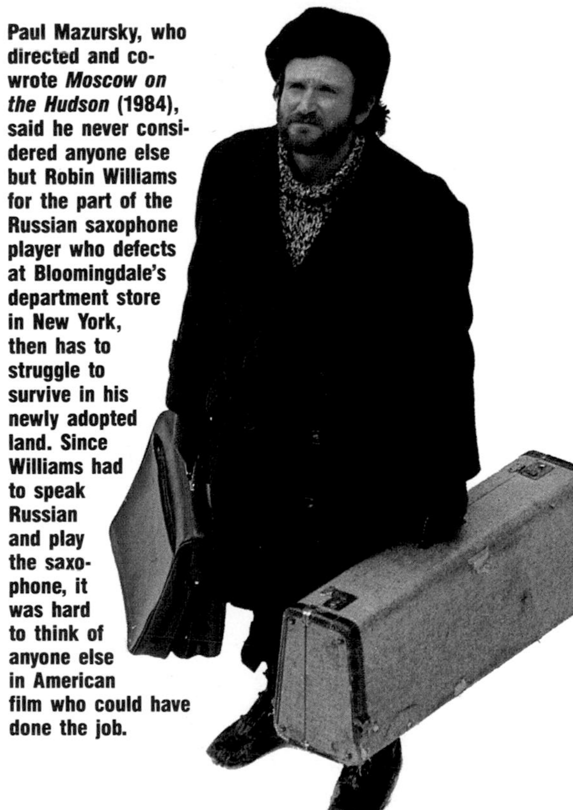

Paul Mazursky, who directed and cowrote *Moscow on the Hudson* (1984), said he never considered anyone else but Robin Williams for the part of the Russian saxophone player who defects at Bloomingdale's department store in New York, then has to struggle to survive in his newly adopted land. Since Williams had to speak Russian and play the saxophone, it was hard to think of anyone else in American film who could have done the job.

Not surprisingly, given his talent for it, Robin Williams improvised much of his on-air dialogue for *Good Morning, Vietnam* (1987). However, *Dead Poets Society* (1989), a film Williams agreed to do at the last minute, was much more tightly scripted. Although he was billed above the title, Williams' role of John Keating, the English teacher who inspires the students at a private boys' school, was actually quite small, and Williams completed it in just a couple of weeks.

as *Club Paradise* and *The Best of Times.* Finally, in 1987, Touchstone Pictures came along with a script based on the experiences of a real-life disc jockey named Adrian Cronauer, who had broadcast on Armed Forces Radio during the war in Vietnam. The resulting movie, *Good Morning, Vietnam,* had a lot more to do with Williams' talent for improvisation than it did with the real Cronauer's experiences during the war — Cronauer admitted that if he'd said the things on air Williams says in the movie, he would have been finished. Williams finally had found the perfect showcase for his talents, and *Good Morning, Vietnam* earned $123 million. His movie stardom was finally established after nearly a decade of failed attempts.

But then Williams appeared to be up to his old tricks once more, doing the last thing in the world his audience expected of him. This time he was an idealistic teacher at a private boys' school in the 1950s, urging his young charges to "*carpe diem,*" (seize the day) and read poetry. To the amazement of everyone, *Dead Poets Society* earned $95 million at the box office when it was released in the summer of 1989.

Even so, Williams was under no illusions about the future. "You make enough strange films," said the comedian who made more strange films than any other star during the decade, "and even if they are accepted, they can still cut you off, pull the plug, and say, 'It's wonderful, and we're going to run that wonderful effort on a double bill with *Heaven's Gate.*'"

STEVE MARTIN ALSO STARTED OUT AS AN UNlikely phenomenon. He was the wild and crazy guy in the white suit, with the arrow through his head — the silver-haired straight man who somehow lost it in front of an audience.

Martin had grown up in Southern California and, as a kid, once worked at Disneyland. In real life he was absolutely nothing like the persona he presented on stage, and was genuinely amazed to think anyone would mistake him for a wild and crazy guy. "Are you kidding? Can you imagine acting like that 24 hours a day? You couldn't do it."

"He looks like he could be the prime minister of Belgium," said director Carl Reiner. "He's a deceptive man. You look at him, you never know what he is thinking. But what I love about him, he's an easy laugher. If he likes a joke, he laughs out loud, and it's so against type, because he's really so quiet. Also he's a very decent guy. We know him so well, and when my wife and I see him on a television appearance, we're always so surprised by his behavior, because's he's not that way."

Steve Martin in *Roxanne* (1987).

Even as Martin played in sold-out arenas to the size of crowd that ordinarily turned out for a rock concert, he was thinking beyond stand-up comedy. He wanted to make movies, and when he starred in his first comedy, *The Jerk*, in 1979, it was a huge hit. The reviews, however, were terrible, and Martin was devastated. "I didn't want to be known as a *schlockmeister*. That's one thing I wanted to work at, so there wasn't the perception I made teen films."

Therefore, he decided to follow *The Jerk* with a musical drama titled *Pennies from Heaven* (1981). Author Dennis Potter had adapted his successful British television series to an American film directed by Herbert Ross, with Martin playing the cynical song sheet salesman who fantasizes himself into the hit songs he peddles. While

In the seventies, Al Pacino was often compared to Robert De Niro and mistaken for Dustin Hoffman. He was one of the most popular and admired actors in film, and was nominated five times for an Academy Award. In the eighties, however, he worked much less successfully. His attempt at a comedy, *Author! Author!* (1982), was a failure, and although he had a hit with *Scarface* (1983), the movie was controversial for its violence and language. His next film, *Revolution* (1985), was an out-and-out disaster, and Pacino retreated until the end of the decade when he made something of a comeback in a popular crime thriller titled *Sea of Love* (1989), *below*.

At the beginning of the decade, John Belushi gave promise of being one of the biggest comedy stars of the eighties. He had graduated from television's *Saturday Night Live* into two hit movies, *National Lampoon's Animal House* in 1978 and *The Blues Brothers* (1980). In 1981, he starred in *Continental Divide* and in *Neighbors*. Then in 1982, he was found dead of a cocaine overdose at the Château Marmont Hotel in Los Angeles, and instead of being remembered as a comic star, his name became synonymous with the drug excesses of a generation.

Below: *Stand by Me* (1986) was not only the best adaptation of a Stephen King story filmed during the eighties, it also helped introduce, *from left,* Jerry O'Connell, Corey Feldman, River Phoenix and Wil Wheaton.

the movie suggested the depth of Martin's talent, it was totally uncommercial. Martin's audience wouldn't go near it.

"There's a thing that happens to a career," observed Carl Reiner, who had directed *The Jerk*. "When *Pennies from Heaven* followed *The Jerk*, it was a downer. It was not what the audience expected of Steve."

What's more, when Martin did attempt to recover the comic turf he had deserted, he found the ground hard to retake. Well-intentioned comedies such as *Dead Men Don't Wear Plaid, The Man with Two Brains* and *The Lonely Guy* all failed at the box office. Martin was frankly alarmed, a career worked on for a lifetime was in danger of being lost.

"I didn't know what to do," he said later. "But I did know this is a business where you have to make hits. They're spending $13 million to make these movies, and you had better deliver. If you want to be an artist, go write a book."

Then he got a telephone call from his friend Carl Reiner. "Carl

phoned me and said, 'I've got a script here.' I said, 'What is it?' He said, 'A girl gets in a guy's body.' I said, 'It sounds silly.' He said, 'Just read the script.'"

All of Me was the story of a wealthy, mean-spirited spinster who becomes trapped in the body of an upwardly mobile young attorney. Reiner wanted Martin as the attorney. Lily Tomlin was to be the spinster. Martin liked the script, but nonetheless, he was gun shy. "I was in and out of it several times. You know: to do it, not to do it. But every time I would waver, I would read the script again."

All of Me, released in 1984, resuscitated Steve Martin's movie career, and established him as a major comic star. He seemed able to do anything from the romantic fire chief with the funny nose in *Roxanne*, to the mean-spirited con man in *Dirty Rotten Scoundrels*, to the hard-pressed but loving dad who would do anything for his kids in *Parenthood*. Even so, there was the suspicion that the surface of Steve Martin's talents had only been scratched. The best of him was yet to come.

Opposite: Steve Martin in a scene from _Dead Men Don't Wear Plaid_ (1982).

Below: Dean Stockwell has enjoyed three acting lives. He began as a child star in movies such as _Gentleman's Agreement_ and _The Boy with Green Hair._ Then as a young leading man, he appeared in _Compulsion, Sons and Lovers_ and _Long Day's Journey into Night_. In the sixties he fell out of fashion, but in the eighties his career revived once again thanks to German director Wim Wenders, who cast him in _Paris, Texas_ (1984). Thereafter, he gave a succession of strong character performances, most notably in _Blue Velvet_ (1986) as Gar, the bordello operator who lip syncs Roy Orbison singing "In Dreams," and as the mob chief, in _Married to the Mob_ (1988).

Paul Newman

When Paul Newman, a well-known supporter of liberal causes, tried to bring his politics to the screen, a mistake usually resulted. ***Fat Man and Little Boy***, released in 1989, was one such mistake. Certainly it was one of the most ill-timed movies of the eighties, an intricately mounted, expensively produced story of the creation of the atomic bomb, directed by Roland Joffe of ***The Killing Fields*** and ***The Mission***, a man who preferred to have his pictures accompanied by a message. This time, though, the message — the bomb is bad — fell on deaf ears. It had already been done as a television miniseries, and besides, ***glasnost*** was in flower, and the fear of a nuclear war had never been less prevalent than at any time since the end of World War II. Paul Newman, ***opposite***, played Leslie R. Groves, the general assigned to oversee the Manhattan Project, the $2-billion assignment to create the bomb in remote Los Alamos, New Mexico. The large cast also included John Cusack, Bonnie Bedelia and Laura Dern. Incidentally, the Fat Man and Little Boy of the title were the names of the bombs. To be accurate, the movie should have been called ***Little Boy and Fat Man***, since Little Boy was dropped on Hiroshima August 6, 1945, three days before Fat Man was dropped on Nagasaki.

WORKING GIRLS

TAKING WOMEN SERIOUSLY IN THE EIGHTIES

Good women's roles were difficult to come by during the eighties. Movies in which women dominated were almost unheard of. One of the few exceptions was ***Steel Magnolias*** (1989), directed by Herbert Ross and based on a stage play by Robert Harling concerning the trials and tribulations of a group of women who frequent a hair salon in a small Georgia town. ***From top left:*** Dolly Parton, Sally Field, Daryl Hannah. ***Bottom:*** Shirley MacLaine, Olympia Dukakis, Julia Roberts.

While the men of Hollywood hit their stride in the eighties, the women tended to be left behind. Despite feminism's many advances, women had a difficult time during the decade. Actresses who in earlier times had dominated films were often treated as second-class citizens. The problem was a simple one: women had little box office clout. Audiences preferred men in action adventure pictures and in comedies; women were relegated to playing the hero's girlfriend. Paradoxically, women who started audiences laughing were the decade's biggest stars. But they were the exception rather than the rule. The sex symbol, a staple of movies throughout their history, largely disappeared. There were beautiful, even sexy, women in movies, but, lacking any real box office clout, an actress had to be taken seriously, and this meant working hard, spending years searching out strong leading roles, and winning awards. There was one actress better at this than anyone, and during the Christmas of 1982, she was sitting in a Manhattan theater becoming increasingly upset . . .

Geneviève Bujold was a Quebec-born actress who appeared to be on the verge of stardom in 1978 with the release of *Coma*. She seemed to lose interest in the eighties, however, making infrequent screen appearances in such films as *Monsignor* (1982), *Tightrope* (1984), and in several Alan Rudolph movies: *Choose Me* (1984), *Trouble in Mind* (1985), *The Moderns* (1988).

Anjelica Huston was better known as John Huston's daughter and Jack Nicholson's girlfriend before she won an Academy Award for her performance in *Prizzi's Honor* (1985), starring Nicholson, and directed by her father. Subsequently she shone in a variety of supporting performances in *Enemies, a Love Story* (1989) and, *above,* in Woody Allen's *Crimes and Misdemeanors* (1989).

IT HAPPENED MIDWAY THROUGH THE WORLD premiere of *Sophie's Choice.* The audience seated inside the Cinema One theater on New York's Upper East Side began to stir. Meryl Streep noticed the movement immediately. This was a black tie charity benefit for Amnesty International, and anyone who was anyone was at the theater to see director Alan J. Pakula's version of William Styron's highly regarded novel about a Polish survivor of the Nazi death camps.

The role of Sophie was the most important of Streep's career. She had fought long and hard to be sitting here, and, as the audience continued to squirm, Streep was furious. In a city where the temperatures this December night in 1982 were soaring 20 degrees above normal, someone had neglected to turn on the air conditioning inside the theater, and now the audience was sweltering uncomfortably. Streep could hardly believe it.

Meryl Streep in *Sophie's Choice* (1982).

Even later, after everyone had left the overheated theater, many of the audience red-eyed and weepy in the aftermath of the film's tragic conclusion, Streep could not shake her anger. At a glittering reception inside the atrium of the newly completed Trump Tower, where elevators seemed to lift off like the mother ship from *Close Encounters of the Third Kind,* she dutifully posed for photographers with co-stars Kevin Kline and Peter MacNicol, hiding her fury behind a carefully applied smile.

William Styron, author of *Sophie's Choice,* hovered in the background, red-faced, a drink clutched in his hand, taking congratulations from a whole pride of literary lions gathered for the occasion: Norman Mailer, Kurt Vonnegut, Irwin Shaw and Arthur Miller. The actress Lauren Bacall was also present, and so was actor Richard Widmark, Mike Wallace from *60 Minutes,* the singer Carly Simon, feminist Gloria Steinem, and *Washington Post* editor Ben Bradlee. It was a helluva party, a dazzling acknowledgment of the movie, and of Meryl Streep's stardom. *Sophie's Choice* not only won her the award for best actress of 1982, it also established her as the premiere actress of her generation. Throughout the decade it would become *de rigueur* for young actresses to aspire to the sorts of roles that Meryl Streep played. With her seriousness of purpose, her stated desire to top herself each time out, Streep laid out the ground rules that everyone else wanted to play by. Let the men do frivolous roles in action movies and comedies.

But all that would come later. The first thing the next morning, stardom was not on her mind. Malfunctioning air conditioning was. "There's just no excuse for it," she said, seating herself on a brushed suede sofa in a beige suite at the Westbury Hotel. "The heat acted as an external distraction."

She sighed heavily and crossed long legs beneath the leather skirt she had purchased a few days before. She wore a green-striped raw silk blouse with the skirt, and her hair was feathery blonde, cut short for the character in her next movie, *Silkwood*. She was to spend so much time over the next few years camouflaging herself, coloring her hair and changing her accent, that one would tend to forget the fine-boned beauty that was on display that morning.

Most actors lead lives of failure, awaiting those rare moments when

Novelist William Styron, who wrote *Sophie's Choice* (1982), said he always imagined Ursula Andress in the part. But it was Meryl Streep who was eventually cast by director Alan J. Pakula. Streep suggested Broadway actor Kevin Kline, *below,* for the part of Nathan, Sophie's charismatic, volatile lover. It was the actor's first film. Kline had an awesome reputation as a stage actor, particularly in *The Pirates of Penzance.* He was once described by *New York Times* critic Frank Rich as "the pride of the American theater — a homegrown actor who might yet be our Olivier." By the end of the decade, he had become one of the most versatile actors around, winning an Academy Award for his comic performance in *A Fish Called Wanda* (1988), then going off to play Hamlet at the New York Shakespeare Festival.

Silkwood **(1983) was the first but not the last time Meryl Streep would play a real-life woman. In this case it was Karen Silkwood, a young nuclear worker at the Kerr-McGee nuclear plant in Oklahoma, who died in a mysterious car accident after she campaigned against unsafe working conditions at the plant. The movie, directed by Mike Nichols, also gave a boost to Kurt Russell's career, and resulted in an Oscar nomination for Cher, who had not previously been taken seriously as an actress.**

the moon and the stars are in their proper places, the gods are smiling and there is finally, often unexpectedly, success. Streep, however, had known almost nothing but success. Even her childhood fell neatly into place. In New Jersey she was a cheerleader. She was on the swim team. She was the homecoming queen. Growing up, she remembered seeing a lot of Walt Disney movies and watching Lucille Ball on television. "I didn't think about becoming an actress, really. I don't think I consciously decided to become an actress. I was living like a hippie in Vermont and working at a small theater, but then that wasn't good enough. I applied to Yale and got in. And when

I was there they were *very* serious about acting. Every year after that I just got more and more dedicated to it."

Even in the early days, she was never self-conscious about being on a stage and saying words that weren't hers. "I think men are more nervous about acting than women. Maybe it's the nature of men and women. Women are used to being vehicles for emotion. Men like to think they move mountains and aren't vehicles for anything. Certainly I never felt silly about it. The more I acted, the more I came to believe it was a pretty great thing I was doing."

In three years at Yale she played 40 different roles. Joseph Papp saw her and cast her in *Trelawny of the Wells* at New York's Shakespeare Festival. That was followed by a couple of television roles, notably as the Catholic wife of a German Jew in the TV movie *Holocaust*, and then supporting roles in movies: *Julia*, *The Seduction of Joe Tynan*, *The Deer Hunter*, *Manhattan* and *Kramer vs. Kramer*, for which she won an Academy Award in 1979 for best supporting actress. The next year she had her first starring role, playing the haunted Sarah Woodruff in *The French Lieutenant's Woman*. It was the first of many parts that would require her hair color and her accent to be changed.

But that was the sort of thing expected of serious actresses throughout the decade. They had to make movies that had something to say, to act as a role model for others. The sex symbol, the staple of movies since the beginning, the role that, through the years, had provided stardom for everyone from Theda Bara to Marilyn Monroe, all but disappeared.

Originally, movies were much more about women than they were about men. At a time when women in real life were second-class citizens, they dominated films. The first actor ever to receive billing in a movie was a woman, Florence Lawrence, who, in 1910, became known as "The Imp Girl." The first real star was also a woman, Mary Pickford, who, by 1916, was not only the highest-paid woman in the movie world, but was on a par with Charlie Chaplin, who at that time was the highest paid man ("It took longer to make one of Mary's contracts than it did to make one of Mary's pictures," grumbled Samuel Goldwyn).

Lillian and Dorothy Gish were also much more popular than most of their male contemporaries. In her nineties, Lillian Gish appeared at the Cannes Film Festival in order to promote *The Whales of August*, a film she appeared in with Bette Davis. At a press conference, she pointed out that the problems of women and stardom really had not changed over the years. "In my business the men get younger, and the women get older," she observed. "I started out playing the child of Lionel Barrymore. And then I played someone that he liked

Amy Irving, *above*, through much of the eighties was best known as the wife of director Steven Spielberg. However, she shone in a low-budget comedy drama titled *Crossing Delancey* (1988).

***Below:* Tina Turner was best known as a pop singer when she was featured opposite Mel Gibson in *Mad Max Beyond Thunderdome* (1985). She played Aunty Entity, the nasty queen of Bartertown. Despite the fact that Turner brought a great deal of flair and humor to the role, it was the only time she appeared on screen in the eighties.**

Get Serious: Diane Keaton made so many serious films throughout the eighties, that it was easy to forget she became a star and won an Oscar getting laughs in Woody Allen movies. In *Crimes of the Heart* (1986), adapted from Beth Henley's play, Keaton, along with Jessica Lange (*middle*), was one of the sisters who rallied around after Sissy Spacek (*right*) shot her husband. As was usually the case with movies featuring strong women's roles in the eighties, the actresses had to work for practically nothing in order to get it made.

Sissy Spacek as Loretta Lynn in *Coal Miner's Daughter* (1980).

Madonna wasn't yet a pop star when she made an impressive movie debut as the missing woman in *Desperately Seeking Susan* (1985). Thereafter, however, her hit records didn't help her movie career, either in *Shanghai Surprise* (1986) or *above* in *Who's That Girl* (1987). In the summer of 1990, she finally seemed on the verge of the movie stardom she so eagerly sought, thanks to a co-starring role opposite Warren Beatty in *Dick Tracy*.

— you know, romance. And then I played his wife. And I *know* if he had lived I would have played his lover, because that's the way movies go. The men get younger and the women get older."

Even so, the most popular movie of all time, *Gone with the Wind*, is not about Rhett Butler. It's the story of Scarlett O'Hara. *The Wizard of Oz* is all about a little girl trying to get home, not a boy. During the thirties and forties, the screen was crowded with strong women: Greta Garbo, Mae West, Bette Davis, Joan Crawford, Marlene Dietrich, Vivien Leigh, Katharine Hepburn, Rosalind Russell, Ginger Rogers, Jean Arthur — the list goes on and on. The movies in which they appeared were more often than not shaped for them, and they invariably got top billing. The men were relegated to the background. Who today can even remember any of Greta Garbo's leading men? ("What when drunk one sees in other women," the critic Kenneth Tynan wrote, "one sees in Garbo sober.") And, with the exception of W.C. Fields and (briefly) Cary Grant, no one remembers any of the men Mae West appeared with. The same is true of Marilyn Monroe and Shirley Temple (who, in 1939, was the highest-paid star in Hollywood). In the fifties, audiences flocked to the movies to see Audrey Hepburn or Grace Kelly or Ava Gardner as avidly as they went to see a Rock Hudson or a William Holden. In the early sixties, the most popular stars in the world each year usually were women.

Doris Day fought for the top spot for several years with Elizabeth Taylor, before Julie Andrews came along and eclipsed them both.

But, as the seventies faded into the eighties, the men began to dominate as never before. If Eddie Murphy liked a script, Paramount fell over itself to get it made. If Sally Field or Jane Fonda or Barbra Streisand or Sissy Spacek wanted to get something done, it took years of effort and usually meant a salary cut. "And that's exactly how we did it," Sissy Spacek said, describing how she and co-stars Diane Keaton and Jessica Lange finally made the movie version of Beth Henley's Pulitzer Prize-winning play, *Crimes of the Heart* in 1986. "They said, 'How about this: we make the movie, and we don't pay you very much.' And we said, 'Okay.'" She shook her head and laughed ruefully. "I tell you, it's brutal out there. 'Cause I made two movies nobody wanted to make (the other was *'Night, Mother,* also based on a play). So you had to give an ounce of blood. Now mind you, if we'd added a couple of car chases..."

Diane Keaton in *Mrs. Soffel* (1984).

Part of the problem with women in movies was at the box office. The major studios knew going in that *Crimes of the Heart* was never going to be as successful as an Eddie Murphy comedy, thus it would not provide the actresses involved with the sort of clout that got movies made in the Hollywood of the eighties. The most celebrated actresses of the decade ignored the dictates of commercialism. Unlike the men, they were in search of quality, and instead of trying to establish easily identifiable images, they were usually trying to escape them. Diane Keaton become famous in the seventies co-starring in Woody Allen comedies, most notably, *Annie Hall,* for which she won an Oscar in 1977. But in the eighties, she concentrated on dramas such as *Shoot the Moon, The Little Drummer Girl* and *Mrs. Soffel.* When she was finally persuaded to do another comedy, *Baby Boom* in 1987, market research indicated that the audience no longer thought of Diane Keaton as a comedienne. This surprised her. "I always liked to do comedy," she maintained. "It's just that I didn't come across any good ones, and once you've been in those Woody Allen comedies, it's sort of like, forget it."

Women tended increasingly to become accessories, and the overcoming of this kind of stereotyping became the all-consuming ambition of the most important actresses in the eighties. Talent had to

Dolly Parton was a well-known country singer, but no one thought of her as a movie star before she made her movie debut in 1980, opposite Jane Fonda (*left*) and Lily Tomlin (*right*) in the hit comedy *Nine to Five.* The three actresses became friends and talked constantly about working together again, but nothing ever materialized.

When writer-director James L. Brooks cast Holly Hunter in *Broadcast News* (1987), her only previous exposure was in *Raising Arizona.* In short order Hunter, who played a highly-strung network news producer, found herself nominated for an Oscar and featured (with co-stars William Hurt and Albert Brooks) on the cover of *Newsweek* magazine. That initial blaze of success did not sustain, however. Her only other major film, *Always* (1989), was less than a glowing success.

***Above*: Jennifer Beals starred in *Flashdance* (1983), a phenomenon in the early eighties. Her stardom should have been assured, but thereafter she appeared on screen infrequently. She co-starred with the pop singer Sting in a curious version of the Frankenstein story titled *The Bride* (1985).**

***Left*: Jodie Foster, in costume for *Carny* (1980), started out as a child star working for Disney. By the time she was 12 years old she had gained notoriety with her appearance in Martin Scorsese's *Taxi Driver* (1976), playing a child prostitute. It was that movie that caused John Hinckley to become so infatuated with her that it led to his attempted assassination of President Ronald Reagan. She was in danger of being remembered only as a footnote in history before she appeared in *The Accused* (1988), and won an Academy Award for her role as the victim of a gang rape.**

***Opposite*: Daryl Hannah usually played the fantasy object of various leading men. In *Clan of the Cave Bear* (1985), though, she played a Cro-Magnon woman named Ayla.**

be acclaimed; you needed to win awards — nobody, for example, took Jodie Foster seriously until she played the victim of a gang rape in *The Accused* (1988) and won an Oscar. If you didn't already have respect, you had to earn it, and the ways in which actresses accomplished that were sometimes quite extraordinary. Cher did it by employing a combination of obsessive drive, clever self-promotion, chutzpa, and — oh, yes, talent. Initially, of course, the former Cherilyn Sarkisian from El Centro, California, was taken any way but seriously. Throughout most of the seventies, she was a joke, exiled to Vegas, earning, she said, $325,000 a week, and wishing she was an actress. She was, after all, Cher of Sonny and Cher, bad rock songs from the sixties, ersatz glamor, a hit television show, a reputation for dressing outlandishly. Not exactly Meryl Streep territory.

Cher in *Mask* (1985).

It was only after she moved to New York and convinced the director Robert Altman to give her a part in his off-Broadway production of *Come Back to the Five and Dime, Jimmy Dean, Jimmy Dean* that her fortunes began to change. (We should all suffer like Cher: while earning $500 a week off-Broadway, she lived with her family in an $8,000-a-week suite at the Mayflower Hotel.)

Altman then cast her in the movie version of the play, and the director Mike Nichols came backstage in New York and offered her the role of Meryl Streep's lesbian roommate in *Silkwood.* But even then, Hollywood would not give her much more than the benefit of the doubt. She should have won an Academy Award for her role as the tough biker mom in *Mask* (1985), but she wasn't even nominated. The director Norman Jewison had to talk her into playing the widowed Italian bookkeeper in his comedy *Moonstruck* in 1987. It won her the Oscar she coveted, but, more importantly, it provided her with box office clout, and respectability. Typically, perhaps, Cher on Oscar night remembered to thank her hairdresser and neglected to thank Norman Jewison. But even that moment of tastelessness did not alter the perception that Cher finally was traveling first class in an industry that often treated women very much as second-class acts. It was a difficult time, even for strong, independent stars such as Jane Fonda and Barbra Streisand, who forced the industry to take them seriously long before Meryl Streep came along.

Kate Capshaw was a former schoolteacher who reminded casting directors of Julie Christie. She was best known as the night club singer who screamed constantly in *Indiana Jones and the Temple of Doom* (1984). But she played a lot of girlfriends in movies such as *Windy City* (1984), *Power* (1985) and *SpaceCamp* (1986). In 1989 she played against her sweet image as a sexy American bar girl in *Black Rain*.

Lea Thompson, a former professional ballet dancer, was another one of the sweet young actresses who worked a lot during the eighties but could not quite break out of the girlfriend roles into genuine stardom. She was best known as Marty McFly's girlfriend in *Back to the Future* (1985). But she also appeared in such films as *Howard the Duck* (1986) and *Some Kind of Wonderful* (1987).

***Opposite:* By the time she directed and starred in *Yentl* (1983), Barbra Streisand's insistence on being photographed only from the left side had become the stuff of Hollywood legend.**

STREISAND, THE FORMER SWITCHBOARD operator from Brooklyn with the incredible voice ("I was known as the kid with the voice") who grew up dreaming of being a star, had already conquered Broadway (*I Can Get It for You Wholesale, Funny Girl*), recordings, and television (in a series of elaborate CBS specials) when she made her movie debut as the actress Fanny Brice in the 1968 musical *Funny Girl*. As with just about everything else in her career it was a huge success. Streisand won an Oscar (although she had to share it with Katharine Hepburn) and remained a major force on the screen throughout the seventies. But, after starring in a chaos-ridden remake of *A Star Is Born* (1976), and a romantic comedy with Ryan O'Neal in 1979 called *The Main Event*, she was gone from the screen (except for a limp, little-seen 1981 comedy, *All Night Long*) until she made a heavily promoted comeback in a 1983 musical titled *Yentl*. The movie was

Barbra Streisand in *Nuts* (1987).

based on an Isaac Bashevis Singer story (the author later loudly denounced what Streisand had done to his work), and not only was she starring as a Jewish girl impersonating a boy so she could study the Torah, but she was producing and directing the movie as well. *Yentl* had come to the screen with great difficulty. No one, it seemed, wanted Streisand as a director. She was a woman, which in Hollywood was already a strike against her, and she had a reputation for being hard to work with (her fights with co-star Kris Kristofferson and director Frank Pierson on the set of *A Star Is Born*, are legendary). Streisand felt the resentment. "There's a hostility with the fact that I did so many jobs, I can feel it," she said, holding court

In the seventies, Barbara Hershey insisted on being known as Barbara Seagull. In the eighties she had matured into one of the most beautiful and accomplished actresses in the movies. She appeared briefly in *The Natural* (1984), *(below)*. Her many other movies included *The Stunt Man* (1980), *Hannah and Her Sisters* (1985), *Beaches* (1988) and *The Last Temptation of Christ* (1988).

one afternoon in a Manhattan hotel suite.

Yentl was a success; it was mostly critically praised, and it should have been a turning point in Barbra Streisand's career as she entered her forties. Yet it did nothing for her. She made one more movie, *Nuts*, in 1987, then she disappeared from movies for the rest of the decade. *Yentl*, the movie she labored so long to make in order to prove she was as good as the boys, was all but forgotten.

JANE FONDA PROVED TO BE MUCH MORE resilient. As Streisand labored to make *Yentl* work, Fonda had been a successful producer for years and, at the beginning of the decade, had become the most powerful woman in Hollywood. It was the last thing anyone would have expected of her when she began acting in the late fifties. "There were two things immediately against her," remembered the director Sidney Lumet who directed her father, Henry Fonda, in *Twelve Angry Men*, and nearly three decades later directed Jane in *The Morning After*. "First of all, she was the most beautiful thing I'd ever seen come down the pike, so right away you assume, all that beauty, clearly she can't act. And secondly, because her father was such a brilliant actor, the assumption is that the kid won't be any good. So I didn't see any of her potential."

Jane Fonda in *The Morning After* (1986).

But she fooled everyone and had become, in her mid-forties, the most popular actress in North America. Lumet put it down to her inexhaustible energy and commitment. "She lives her life that way, and she conducts her career that way. Whatever talent was there, she was going to use all of it."

Meryl Streep would take over from Fonda as role model in the mid-eighties. But at the beginning of the decade, Fonda was the most admired — and occasionally reviled — actress in the business. Launched into her fourth decade, she remained one of the world's great beauties. Crisp, reserved, articulate, superbly groomed, she could still show a refreshing vulnerability, that caught visitors by surprise. She had worked hard over the years to be taken seriously, to get beyond being known merely as Henry Fonda's daughter or as the sexy piece of fluff who had starred in *Barbarella* in the sixties for her husband, French director Roger Vadim.

Controversy lingered over her occasionally virulent anti-war activism during the years of the Vietnam conflict in the late sixties and early seventies, when she was known by her detractors as Hanoi Jane. The controversy continued to flare up periodically. When she was shooting *Stanley and Iris* in 1989 in Waterbury, Connecticut, Vietnam veterans protesting her presence forced production to switch locations to Toronto. For the most part, though, she tried to downplay the effect her political views had on her career. "I feel people separate me as an actress from my political being," she said. "They like the fact that I stick up for what I believe in, that I'm feisty. People say, 'We don't always agree with you, Jane, but go to it.' I get that a lot."

Jane Fonda, Katharine Hepburn, Henry Fonda in *On Golden Pond* (1981).

She was intelligent, strong-willed and independent enough in the seventies to start producing her own pictures — *Coming Home, Nine to Five, The China Syndrome* — at a time when women didn't do that sort of thing. She established a precedent that would be emulated by most other serious actresses in the eighties, who discovered, as Fonda had, that it was the only way to get projects they cared about onto a movie screen.

What's more, she had amassed a fortune with her Jane Fonda Workout books and videos. For many North American women, she had become the guru of physical fitness.

At the height of her career both as a producer and an actress, she finally had succeeded in bringing her father together with herself and Katharine Hepburn in the film version of the stage hit *On Golden Pond*. To everyone's amazement, the movie was a huge success, and it won for the elder Fonda, in his final performance, the Academy Award that had been denied him over the course of his long career.

But *On Golden Pond* would be Jane Fonda's last hit of the decade. She became better known for her workout empire than she did for

For a time after the huge success of *The Blue Lagoon* in 1980, it looked as though Brooke Shields was on her way to becoming the decade's most successful teenaged star. But her next movie, *Endless Love* (1981), flopped, and thereafter everyone seemed to lose interest. She wasn't in the sequel to *The Blue Lagoon* that began production in 1990.

***Below*: Diane Lane was a child star in the seventies who grew up in the eighties to play sexy vamp roles in movies such as *The Cotton Club* (1984).**

Right: **Meg Tilly first received notice in *The Big Chill* (1983). Thereafter she co-starred in movies such as *Impulse* (1984), *opposite,* with Tim Matheson, *Agnes of God* (1985), *Masquerade* (1988) and *Valmont* (1990).**

Below: **Jane Fonda sought Burt Lancaster to play *The Old Gringo* in 1989, but Lancaster could not get the proper insurance to act in the production and was replaced by Gregory Peck, who had not made a movie in nearly a decade. Here Fonda and Peck pose with television's Jimmy Smits; director Luis Puenzo; and Carlos Fuentes, who wrote the novel of *Old Gringo.***

her movies. After *On Golden Pond*, and then the flop of a financial thriller called *Rollover*, she was away from the screen for four years, operating her exercise empire (by 1989, her personal worth was estimated at $60 million), and supporting the political career of her husband at the time, Tom Hayden.

By the time she returned to work in 1985 to star in *Agnes of God* and *The Morning After* (1986), action pictures and comedies dominated the movie business. Good parts were harder to come by than ever. "It's very difficult to find already-written scripts that are right for me at this time of my life," she said. She responded by producing her own version of an action picture — *The Old Gringo* (1989) came complete with gunfire and a social conscience. Audiences could not have cared less. Besides, there were other actresses who had learned the lessons Jane Fonda taught. None learned them better than a former model named Jessica Lange, and a television actress named Sally Field.

"I FEEL *EXTREMELY* LUCKY," SHE SAID IN 1989. "I'VE been in the right place at the right time, several times . . . I mean, some roles I've had, people wait a lifetime for. They have one role in a career, and I've had a couple."

But if Sally Field now found herself in the right place, it had taken her an awfully long time to get there. She had begun her professional life a very long way from the right place, in that low-rent region of show business known as television. She had a high, squeaky voice, and was pert, wholesome, pug-nosed and cheerful throughout the sixties, first as *Gidget*, then as *The Flying Nun*. She seemed forever typecast as the pleasantly likable TV cupcake. She was on television, and no one expected her to act. No one thought she *could* act.

But beneath that good-natured cheerleader exterior she wore in public lurked something else, a quality that most producers missed: anger. "Anger has been my best friend," she would later say. "It comes from an accumulation of years of letting myself be treated disrespectfully. I'm still kind of afraid to let go, to laugh, to just be Sally without worrying. I'm so intense. And for years, I was doing my best acting off stage."

Sally Field with Paul Newman.

She had made some headway changing the perception of her abilities, playing the bruised sexpot in Bob Rafelson's movie *Stay Hungry* and on television as the multi-personality *Sybil*. But it was that simmering anger that director Martin Ritt noticed when he looked at her for the role of the union organizer Norma Rae in the movie of the same name. "It's so shocking that someone who looks like you can have so much anger," he told her during filming. The movie, released in 1979, won her an Academy Award for best actress, and the unlikely story of how TV's *Gidget* grew up to win an Oscar became part of endlessly repeated movie folklore.

Norma Rae had been followed by a clutch of movies that — with the exception of *Absence of Malice*, in which she was paired with surprising effectiveness with Paul Newman — had inspired neither box office receipts nor critical accolades. Her one attempt at romantic comedy, *Kiss Me Goodbye*, opposite Jeff Bridges, had flopped badly. Then the director and screenwriter Robert Benton appeared. He was looking for someone to play an indomitable Texas widow

Rosanna Arquette was another of the young, beautiful actresses who tended to be used as set decoration in movies. Arquette at least brought an offbeat edge to the decoration in *Desperately Seeking Susan* (1985), *After Hours* (1985) and *Eight Million Ways to Die* (1986).

Young starlets with great bodies posing in bathing suits did not completely disappear in the eighties. They tended to show up in the dozens of teen exploitation movies that were produced during the decade. Here Teal Roberts demonstrates why it was appropriate that she would appear in a movie titled *Hardbodies* (1984).

A lot of actresses who were hot stars in the seventies did not fare so well in the eighties. Ali MacGraw was a box office star in the seventies thanks to *Goodbye Columbus*, *Love Story* and *The Getaway*. In the eighties, she appeared in *Just Tell Me What You Want* (1980), then virtually disappeared from the screen.

Below: Candice Bergen, the daughter of the comedian Edgar Bergen, made infrequent movie appearances, most notably in *Rich and Famous* (1981), then retreated to television where she found a whole new career and popularity in the situation comedy *Murphy Brown*.

Right: Sally Field with Danny Glover and the kids in *Places in the Heart* (1984).

named Edna Spalding in a new film he had written called *Places in the Heart*. The film was to be based on stories he had heard about his grandmother. As far as he was concerned, there was only one actress who could portray Edna.

"Among the good actors in America, there are only a few who can truly disappear into a part," he said. "That's what I wanted. And I mean this as the most profound compliment to Sally when I say that's what she does. She is an actor of the highest order."

By the time *Places in the Heart* was released in 1984, Field was 37 years old, and there were lines under her eyes. Even though the heart-shaped face retained the pertness that launched all those high

Nielsen ratings when she was *The Flying Nun*, it was a face now clouded by a constant wariness. There was a suggestion about her that she was no one's fool and was not to be treated as such. Stardom had made the deep strength Benton had discovered more evident than ever.

Still, she could let her guard down, as she did the night she won her second Academy Award for *Places in the Heart*, and blurted out, "You like me, you really like me." When the incident was mentioned later, she was defensive, but unrepentant. "It was how I was feeling at the time," she said. "I just said what I felt."

Even after *Places in the Heart*, however, Field was under no illu-

Farrah Fawcett was briefly a phenomenon of the seventies in TV's *Charlie's Angels*. In the eighties, she shed her TV blonde image, and transformed herself into a respected actress, mostly in movies for television. Occasionally, however, she appeared in movies such as *Cannonball Run II* (1984) and much more notably, in *See You in the Morning* (1989).

***Bottom*: Missouri-born Janet Jones attracted notice playing Matt Dillon's country club girlfriend in *The Flamingo Kid* (1984). She had a shot at stardom in *American Anthem* (1986), but her best-known role came in real life when she became the wife of Canadian hockey star Wayne Gretzky.**

Above: **Jack Nicholson discovered Mary Steenburgen in 1978. She later played the novelist Marjorie Kinnan Rawling in Martin Ritt's *Cross Creek* (1983).**

Below: **Helen Slater was cast as *Supergirl* in 1984. It bombed, but Slater survived to play a starring role in *The Legend of Billie Jean* (1985).**

Opposite: **Actress Frances Farmer, whose career flared briefly in the late thirties and early forties, was a classic example of how Hollywood uses and abuses women. Farmer was all but forgotten until Jessica Lange brought her to the screen in *Frances* in 1982.**

sions. "It's a male-oriented society, that's the truth . . . In my business there are more men producing, writing and directing . . . It's unusual and out of the norm for a male writer to write about women and for a writer and producer to really connect and want to make that film. It just means that project has to be so much better than the norm, you have to work three times as hard, and there is little or no room for failure."

AT ONE POINT, IT LOOKED AS THOUGH JESSICA Lange would amount to little more than a reminder of the sort of female stardom prevalent in another time — the blonde bimbo snatched from nowhere in order to adorn a big-budget Hollywood epic. In this case, the epic was a 1976 remake of the classic *King Kong*, and Lange was the model chosen to play the old Fay Wray part by producer Dino De Laurentiis after the usual exhaustive search. Not that De Laurentiis initially was all that impressed. "Here was a girl with nothing at all," the Italian producer recalled in *People* magazine. "But I was getting desperate now, so I say, 'Okay, give her a screen test.' A few hours later, director John Guillermin calls me and says, 'Dino, get to the screening room. One of these girls is sensational on camera.' He was right."

Lange was supposed to sit in Kong's paw and look pretty while screaming. The scenario called for her to emerge into the limelight just long enough to have her photograph taken, receive lots of publicity for the film, then disappear again, the way so many legions of blonde starlets before her had disappeared. But Jessica Lange wasn't about to play that game.

Jessica Lange in *King Kong* (1976).

"People put a lot of limitations on me I didn't feel myself," she said later. "It's a real frustrating situation when people have an idea of you that really has nothing to do with what you are, what you're capable of."

Lange was born in a small town called Cloquet, Minnesota. Al Lange, Jessica's father, moved around constantly, working at a variety of jobs, everything from selling cars to teaching high school physical education. Ultimately, he settled down to work for the Burlington Northern Railroad. She remembered a sense

Susan Sarandon struggled throughout the eighties for a major stardom she was never quite able to attain. She appeared in everything from *Atlantic City* (1980) to *Tempest* (1982) and *The Hunger* (1983). She came closest to stardom in 1988 playing the spunky, independent baseball groupie in *Bull Durham*, one of the best female roles of the eighties, for which, curiously enough, she was not even nominated for an Oscar.

***Below*: Kelly McGillis had made her movie debut in *Reuben, Reuben* (1983) but she was waiting tables in New York when she was cast as the Amish widow opposite Harrison Ford in *Witness* (1985). Subsequently, she co-starred with Tom Cruise in *Top Gun* (1986).**

of loneliness, of being filled constantly with a yearning that she could never quite identify. She decided eventually that it was something that was just there, part of her and the rural countryside in which she grew up. That yearning, however, appeared to go unnoticed by her peers. When she was a teenager, her high school yearbook described her as "artistic, dramatic and fun." She escaped the Midwest via the state university in Minneapolis, where she met a handsome guest professor named Paco Grande, a 24-year-old Spaniard who, she said later, swept her off her feet.

In 1970 she married Paco at her parents' home in Wisconsin. But neither her marriage nor her nomadic lifestyle was fulfilling enough for her. She was looking for something else. She took mime classes in New York and waited tables at a bar called The Lion's Head. By 1974, she was separated from Paco Grande and was working as a model for the Wilhelmina agency, her hair tinted blonde, wearing braces to correct an overbite. It was then that De Laurentiis found her for *King Kong*.

AFTER KONG, SHE APPEARED BRIEFLY AS THE Angel of Death in Bob Fosse's *All That Jazz*, but otherwise the only work she did was in a flop 1980 comedy called *How to Beat the High Co$t of Living*. Her breakthrough came when she got the role of Cora, the restless waitress in Bob Rafelson's remake of *The Postman Always Rings Twice*. The next year she did *Frances*, the tragic story of actress Frances Farmer. She found the experience as intense and draining as anything she had gone through in her life. Needing something less demanding, she took the supporting love-interest role in Sydney Pollack's *Tootsie*, a movie she originally turned down. She didn't think a lot about *Tootsie*, it was just a job.

But that year she ended up being nominated for best actress for *Frances* and best supporting actress for *Tootsie*. It was the first time an actress had been nominated in two categories the same year since Teresa Wright had done it four decades before. She won for *Tootsie*, the movie she could not have cared less about.

By then, Lange had developed a reputation for being remote and distant while working on a film. She filmed a television production of Tennessee Williams' *Cat on a Hot Tin Roof*, with Tommy Lee Jones playing Brick. A reporter from *TV Guide* caught the tension and remoteness she often brought to the set: "On the small set they usually said little to one another . . . Jones stared vacantly . . . Lange lay on a bed, pressed her index fingers to her temples, and closed her eyes. Five minutes later, she still had not moved . . . Then someone spoke. A grip murmured something about the play. Lange wheeled around and seemed to stare right through him."

And she had problems with her directors, clashing with Taylor Hackford on *Everybody's All-American* ("I was totally fucked," she said) and quarreling with Paul Brickman during the making of *Men Don't Leave.*

"Paul Brickman says I'm drawn to grief, you know," she told journalist Bart Mills. "I suppose there is that side of me. Maybe it comes from my heritage, or growing up in the woods of Minnesota, maybe it instills a certain sense of despair and loneliness in you, I'm not sure. But yeah, I do find those are the things that move me."

When *Music Box* was released at Christmas 1989, Jessica Lange had to point out to usually adulatory journalists that, despite all the attention she received, almost none of her movies had made any money. "They keep telling me I have to have a hit." She laughed and shrugged. Her next movie after *Music Box* was *Men Don't Leave.* It didn't make any money either. She appeared to take no notice.

Not everyone took the business of acting quite so seriously, however.

Beauty and Brains: The Survival of Sensuality

KATHLEEN TURNER, UNLIKE MANY OF HER contemporaries, refused to take herself too seriously or to hide her sexuality. Of the small number of other actresses who were like her, including Glenn Close, Kim Basinger and Michelle Pfeiffer, none was more adored than Kathleen Turner.

Vanity Fair magazine lauded her for refusing to play a farm wife, when farm wives were all the rage that year (Jessica Lange, Sally Field and Sissy Spacek all played them). "She has the sensuality and high wit of Carole Lombard and Jean Arthur," the magazine noted.

When Kathleen Turner heard this, she laughed delightedly, blew more cigarette smoke across the room and curled the best legs in movies beneath her. "Someone said to me, 'Sex is not funny.' I said, '*What?* You can be incredibly funny and sexy at the same time. In fact it makes it delightful. To add the laugh is to add the joy to it."

She sent another cloud of cigarette smoke swirling around her. "I don't see why finding the comic aspects of something devalues what you do. I don't see that at all. I think a lot of things are funny, actually. I'm often awkward and I bump into things. When I think I'm most glorious, I usually tend to do something pretty stupid, like split my pants or something."

Maria Conchita Alonso, petite, dark-eyed and Latin, played opposite Robin Williams in *Moscow on the Hudson* (1984), and was thereafter usually wasted as the girlfriend in action movies such as *The Running Man* (1987) and *Extreme Prejudice* (1987).

***Below*: Nastassia Kinski became every director's fantasy woman for much of the eighties. The German-born daughter of actor Klaus Kinski was dating Roman Polanski when he cast her in *Tess* (1980). Thereafter, she appeared in a string of European and American movies such as *Cat People* (1982), *One from the Heart* (1982), *Hotel New Hampshire* (1984) and *Revolution* (1985).**

Sex Symbols: *Left*: Bo Derek, who had become something of a sensation as the girl of Dudley Moore's dreams in *10*, tried to revive the sex symbol in the eighties with some help from her husband, photographer and director, John Derek. But she was never very successful; she wasn't much of an actress, and her movies, *Tarzan, the Ape Man* (1981) and *Bolero* (1984) were terrible.

Opposite page left: Mariel Hemingway's big chance came when she had her breasts enlarged and convinced director Bob Fosse to allow her to play the murdered *Playboy* playmate Dorothy Stratten in *Star 80* (1983).

Opposite page: Pia Zadora was one of the oddities of the eighties. A petite, charming singer who desperately wanted to be a movie star, she married a multimillionaire who financed two movies for his wife, *Butterfly* (1981) and *The Lonely Lady* (1983), movies only a millionaire husband would want to see.

This page: Jamie Lee Curtis, daughter of actress Janet Leigh and actor Tony Curtis, started out in horror pictures such as *Halloween* (1978) and *Prom Night* (1980), before graduating in the eighties to more respectable work in *Trading Places* (1983), *Perfect* (1985) and *A Fish Called Wanda* (1988).

Michelle Johnson came out of nowhere to co-star opposite Michael Caine in *Blame It on Rio* (1983). After the comedy came out, she quickly returned to nowhere.

Below*: Julie Andrews, one of the most popular stars of the sixties and early seventies, survived with good humor in the eighties, usually in the movies of her husband, director Blake Edwards. In *S.O.B.* (1981) she bared her breasts, and in *Victor/Victoria* she was a girl playing a boy playing a girl. None of it helped; to the public she would always be Mary Poppins and Maria, the singing nun in *The Sound of Music.

Turner's father was a diplomat in the foreign service and the family moved around all over the world. She says she was 14 years old and living in London when she decided to become an actress. When her father died, the family moved back to Missouri, where she had been born. She attended Southwest Missouri State College and the University of Maryland before heading for New York. Her first break came in New York playing the ingénue-vamp on the television soap opera *The Doctors*. Eighteen months later, she went to read for a part in a *film noir* thriller titled *Body Heat*. She walked in wearing a slit skirt and spiked heels, and she *was* Matty Walker, the sexually duplicitous gold digger. As soon as the screenwriter and director, Lawrence Kasdan, heard her read in that low sexy rasp of a voice, he knew he had found the actress he was looking for. "You're not too smart, are you?" Matty snaps when she is hit on by William Hurt as the small-town Florida lawyer she will encourage to murder her husband. "I like that in a man."

Kathleen Turner with Jack Nicholson in *Prizzi's Honor* (1985).

"I was scared," Turner remembered. "I had never seen myself as being a very powerful woman sensually. I was kind of scared that I would throw this smoldering look at Bill Hurt and everyone would start to giggle."

Nobody giggled. *Body Heat* established her sensuality, but it was *Romancing the Stone* (1984) that established her stardom, as well as her sense of humor. It also established her toughness. When it came time to make the inevitable sequel, this one titled *Jewel of the Nile*, she balked. Turner felt the spirit of the character of Joan Wilder created by the screenwriter, the late Diane Thomas, had been lost somewhere inside the word processors of two male writers. She refused to do the movie. Lawsuits were threatened. Then the script was rewritten to her satisfaction. "I don't like being told what to do in terms of somebody ordering me to do something," she said. "I like it to be my choice. It's not that I want everyone to do what I say. It's that I don't want to be somebody's puppet. We all want that, don't we, really?"

Turner held onto her independence and her stardom, not to mention her sense of having a sexy, sassy good time, whether she was playing a hit woman in love with dumb gangster Jack Nicholson in *Prizzi's Honor* (1985), the housewife who becomes a teenager again in *Peggy Sue Got Married* (1986) or giving wondrous throaty voice to the astonishing cartoon curves of Jessica Rabbit ("I'm not bad. I'm just drawn that way.") in *Who Framed Roger Rabbit* or as the willful, embittered Barbara Rose fighting to save her dream house from the clutches of her estranged husband, Michael Douglas, in *The War of the Roses* (1989). Even when the movie was very bad, as *Switching Channels* was, Kathleen Turner could be very good. At the end of the decade she was wowing Broadway audiences in the role she may have been born to play — Maggie the Cat in a revival of Tennessee Williams' *Cat on a Hot Tin Roof.*

By now, she was only too aware of the effect she had on journalists and on audiences, and she loved playing to her tough, seductive image — her passion to win. "I can't help it. I don't like failing."

Kelly LeBrock was a former model married to the producer of *The Woman in Red* (1984). That probably at least partially explained how she landed the role of the object of Gene Wilder's desires. The photograph probably explains the rest of it.

GLENN CLOSE CHANGED HER IMAGE MIDWAY through the eighties, and became second only to Meryl Streep as the most respected actress in film. Close, unlike many of her contemporaries, did not try to produce her own movies, and managed to appear in some hits. As well as being serious, she was also popular.

Close was born in Greenwich, Connecticut, into an aristocratic family that could trace its roots right back to the founding of the town. She grew up on her grandfather's 500-acre estate with three sisters, and regarded herself as "a wild little tomboy" who dreamed someday of being discovered by Walt Disney. That never happened, perhaps because her father, an eminent surgeon, opened a clinic in what was then the Belgian Congo (now Zaire), and moved his family there.

Later, Close traveled in Europe with the singing group Up with People, then majored in drama at William and Mary College in Virginia. Throughout the seventies, she acted on the Broadway stage and in various regional repertory companies. But it was while performing in the musical *Barnum* on Broadway that she was noticed by director George Roy Hill, who, in 1982, was preparing the film version of John Irving's best-selling *The World According to Garp.* He signed her to play nurse Jenny Fields, Garp's mom. "I noticed in Glenn a remarkable quality," Hill said later, "a combination of dignity, warmth and extremely rare serenity." It was those qualities, plus the sense of innate decency that she brought to the screen, that helped her win her first Oscar nomination, and tended to typecast her for future movie roles. In her next movie, *The Big Chill,* she was Sarah, the strong den mother to the ensemble cast. In *The Natural*

Originally, the producers of *Fatal Attraction* (1987) offered the role of the publishing executive who becomes psychotic after a weekend fling with lawyer Michael Douglas to Debra Winger. She turned it down. They next tried to get Barbara Hershey, but she wasn't available. Only then was Glenn Close, who was noted for her rather sexless, down-to-earth portrayals, considered. By now everyone knows the final sequence was refilmed so that Close met her end in a bath tub, but not however, in the one pictured in the photograph *above*.

(1984) while Robert Redford was out running around with glamorous blonde Kim Basinger, Close stayed home and loyally waited for her childhood sweetheart to return. She was always, in the movies at least, such a *good* little girl. She began to feel trapped by her image.

She played a more glamorous role as the attorney defending suspected wife-killer Jeff Bridges in *Jagged Edge.* The thriller established her as an actress who could carry the weight of a movie. But she was still looking for something more, something that would release her as an actress. She knew as soon as she read James Dearden's script for *Fatal Attraction* that she had found the part she needed — as a beautiful publishing executive whose emotions become enraged after a weekend fling with Michael Douglas. Innate decency went right out the window.

"People have always said, 'Oh, yeah, but can she be sexy?'" Close said. "I thought, I'll show you sexy!"

The movie, released in 1987, became one of the most popular dramas of all time and was number-two at the box office that year. Its subject matter — male infidelity, female obsession and revenge — also made it one of the most controversial American films in years. "I was reading a commentary that said *Fatal Attraction* pretended to have 'feminist pretensions.' We did not set out to do that — I didn't read the script, and say, 'Oh, boy this is a feminist statement!' It wasn't even on my mind. Maybe that's bad, but I'm an actor first and foremost. If I read a project that's a good acting challenge, politics go way down on the list."

Fatal Attraction led to the role of the conniving Marquise de Merteuil in *Dangerous Liaisons* (1988). "She's wonderfully powerful, and I loved wearing those costumes," Close said. "She's very controlled, but there's a violence about her, a danger. She's kind of a nice combination."

She remained pleasantly surprised by her success. "I mean I'm just astounded a lot of the time that I'm even doing what I'm doing, because I don't think I have the body. I look at this, and *this* is the stuff movie stars are made of?"

KIM BASINGER LOOKED EXACTLY LIKE THE stuff movie stars were made of. She was perched on a log on location outside Vancouver, British Columbia, in 1980, distant and unapproachable, her sleek long-maned blonde beauty quite startling, set off against the surrounding wilderness. She was a former Ford model and one-time Breck girl who had attracted notice in the TV mini-series *From Here to Eternity*. Now she was in the woods outside Vancouver shooting an outdoor adventure movie directed by Charlton Heston titled *Mother Lode*.

As she sat on the log, she worried about the effect her background as a model would have on a film career. It turned out her concerns were well-founded. When she returned to Los Angeles after completing *Mother Lode*, her career stalled. Nothing happened until, curiously enough, she posed for *Playboy* magazine. A *Playboy* layout was not exactly the proven route to stardom, but in Basinger's case, it worked. After the nude photos appeared in 1983, her phone began to ring, and she started to land roles that played heavily on her looks. She was every leading man's dream girl come to life on the screen, and she was featured opposite just about everyone: Sean Connery in *Never Say Never Again*, Burt Reynolds in *The Man Who Loved Women*, Robert Redford in *The Natural*, Sam Shepard in *Fool for*

Faye Dunaway, one of the most powerful female stars of the seventies following the success of *Bonnie and Clyde*, frankly admitted that her decision to play Joan Crawford in *Mommie Dearest* (1981) almost destroyed her career. For a long time after that, Dunaway was a campy joke, confined to playing powerful bitch roles. She made something of a comeback in 1987, playing a non-bitchy skid row alcoholic in *Barfly*.

Femmes Fatales: British actress Rachel Ward, *above*, lured Burt Reynolds in *Sharky's Machine* (1981) and Jeff Bridges in *Against All Odds* (1984).

***Below:* Sean Young appeared in *Dune* (1984), but she was best remembered in the eighties for steaming up the back of a limo with Kevin Costner in the thriller *No Way Out* (1987). She subsequently hit a streak of bad luck, losing leading roles in *Batman* (1989) and *Dick Tracy* (1990).**

***Opposite*: Kim Basinger inherited Young's part in *Batman*. But she gained notoriety in the eighties co-starring with Mickey Rourke in *9 1/2 Weeks* (1986).**

Love, and Richard Gere in *No Mercy*. She was usually a combination of the victim and the hero's girlfriend; sultry and desirable, but guileless at the same time. The combination of vixen and victim worked most controversially in *9 1/2 Weeks*, where she was sexually manipulated by Mickey Rourke. The movie failed utterly in North America, but was a huge hit in Europe.

Director Robert Benton, who cast her in the title role of *Nadine* in 1987 called what she previously was doing "decorative roles." She laughed when she heard the description. "He would call them that," she said. "I've been through that sort of thing, and I'm not gonna say I fought 'em tooth and nail, 'cause I didn't. It was just another step with me. I knew I'd never be stuck there, and I was determined. I'd love of course to do juicier pieces, things I could really stick my teeth into."

She landed what was probably the decade's ultimate girlfriend role in *Batman*, when actress Sean Young was injured in a fall from a horse. Basinger, at the last minute, was called to London to portray Vicki Vale, the girl reporter who falls for millionaire Bruce Wayne. "I was sort of the light between these two dark characters (Batman and the Joker), and, at the same time, I had to bring some reality to the piece," she explained. "My character got psychologically strange as well. Her love of bats — I mean, I share that with the character. I mean, I love all animals, but I really do like bats. . ."

I THINK THAT SOME DIRECTORS JUST BELIEVE THAT perhaps a beautiful woman is not appropriate for the part," Michelle Pfeiffer said. "It's like the way an actor looks plays a crucial part in whether you're right for something." Pfeiffer was lovely, and she was from California, so perhaps it was only natural that she would win a beauty contest (Miss Orange County) and grow up wanting to be an actress. She performed plays in her back yard as a child and pretended she was Elvis Presley. In high school she took theater classes in order to avoid taking English. "But I never thought I would really pursue acting until I was 19 or 20. It was just so removed from my environment. I mean, I had never even met a movie star, you know?"

She looked like a Miss Orange County — precisely even features, the sort of sweet, blonde beauty that met guest-starring roles on episodic TV. She was "the Bombshell" on *Delta House*, the short-lived TV version of *Animal House*. The producer Allan Carr "discovered" her in the course of his exhaustive search for an actress to co-star in his 1982 production of *Grease II*. The movie went nowhere, but Pfeiffer survived the experience and landed the role of Elvira, Al Pacino's mistress in Brian De Palma's remake of *Scarface* (1983).

"There are all sorts of turning points, and I guess I would have to say that was a major one. Everything started to turn in a different direction after that."

By the end of the decade, she had established her credentials in a series of diverse roles that increasingly challenged her abilities as an actress, without taking anything away from her beauty. She played a princess in *Ladyhawke*, a gum-cracking gangster's widow in *Married to the Mob*, and the virtuous Madame de Tourvel in *Dangerous Liaisons*. In *The Fabulous Baker Boys* (1989), she got her best role ever, as the bruised ex-hooker turned nightclub singer. The part won her a second Academy Award nomination and ensured her membership in the exclusive club of major film actresses.

Make Them Laugh, Ladies: Women and Comedy

GOLDIE HAWN WAS UNUSUAL AMONG ACTRESSES on the modern screen in that she wasn't afraid to make people laugh.

She was the bird-brained gamin from TV's *Rowan and Martin's Laugh-In*, who had gone on to win a supporting Oscar in her very first movie in 1970, the otherwise totally unremembered *Cactus Flower*. In 1980, she had the biggest hit of her career with *Private Benjamin*, a comedy about a self-absorbed Jewish American princess who finds her real self after she enlists in the United States Army. The movie grossed $110 million, put its star on the cover of *Newsweek* magazine, and established Goldie as perhaps the only female star whose name above the title could attract an audience. It was worth noting that she did it with comedy. For women as well as men in the eighties, laughter was the fastest route to box office success. But audiences were much more comfortable with men making fools of themselves than women. With the exception of Goldie, none of the great television comediennes of the fifties, sixties and seventies had made a successful transition to the big screen.

Goldie Hawn.

Private Benjamin was at once the best thing that ever happened to Goldie Hawn, and the worst. She was a major superstar, with more power than she'd ever had in her life. There was now a career

***Opposite*: Michelle Pfeiffer played Elvira, the coke-snorting mobster's moll in *Scarface* (1983). But when she portrayed a former hooker turned lounge singer in *The Fabulous Baker Boys* (1989), she created one of the most memorable scenes of the eighties, singing "Making Whoopee" sprawled across a piano while co-star Jeff Bridges played the accompaniment.**

***Above*: A hit on stage with her one-woman comedy shows, Lily Tomlin never enjoyed the kind of movie stardom of other comediennes. Her most popular film in the eighties was *All of Me* (1984) with Steve Martin.**

***Below*: One of the few teen comedies that attempted to do a little more than merely exploit women in bikinis was *Fast Times at Ridgemont High* (1982), directed by Amy Heckerling. That was not to say there were no women in bikinis: Phoebe Cates, and Jennifer Jason Leigh.**

When *Private Benjamin* was released in 1980, Goldie Hawn became one of the few actresses ever to carry a movie that made over $100 million at the box office. Until Bette Midler came along, no other female star was able to command that kind of clout with the public. However, Goldie's moment of superstardom was fleeting. She was unable to attain the same kind of box office success throughout the remainder of the decade.

to nurture, an image to protect, a large audience out there that had to be placated. Movies became carefully manufactured vehicles designed for her, and that led to trouble.

After *Private Benjamin* came a World War II comedy drama titled *Swing Shift* (1984), about the Rosie the Riveter women who went to work in U.S. defense plants. Goldie was said to have forced director Jonathan Demme to reshoot scenes so as to give more emphasis to her character and less to the character played by actress Christine Lahti. Demme was furious. "He did it, not very well," Goldie

recounted a year after the release of *Swing Shift*. "He just sort of sat there. In all respect for him, he didn't believe he needed it. Instead of saying 'I'm bowing out now, I don't like what you're doing,' he stuck with it, and he embarrassed himself and all of us by doing that. It was very, very difficult."

By the time she made *Protocol*, about a cocktail waitress who gets mixed up in Washington politics, she, like other female stars, had established her own production company. *Protocol* also ran into trouble. "It was a long gestation period," she said. "Lots of blockades." Charles Shyer and Nancy Myers, who had written *Private Benjamin*, left angrily because, they said, Goldie would not listen to them. "We wrote a script that was thrown out," Nancy Myers said. Buck Henry, who had written *The Graduate*, was brought into the project. But even with the return of the cute, daffy Goldie that the public seemed to demand, *Protocol*, released in 1984, was not a success. Neither was her next comedy, *Wildcats*, about a single mother who coaches a high school football team.

WHEN SHE ARRIVED IN WASHINGTON, D.C. to promote *Wildcats* in 1986, she was pregnant with her third child, this one fathered by her lover, actor Kurt Russell, her co-star in *Swing Shift*. Dressed in leotards and a vast black knit sweater, she settled back on a sofa, and belched. "You'll have to excuse me," she said. "I'm going to be belching throughout this conversation, because I'm pregnant, and this first trimester is not the best." She threw back her head and roared with laughter. "What a *crude woman!*"

She was 40 years old, and the endearingly goofy, gamin-like qualities that had helped make her so popular over the years were still in evidence. Kurt Russell had said that what surprised him most upon meeting her was how sexy she was, and that was certainly evident. But the sexuality had an unexpected maturity to it. Although she could still bubble with the happy, unself-conscious charm that was practically her trademark, she said she did not even recognize the kid on *Laugh-In*. It was now impossible for her to reproduce the high-pitched voice that helped to make her famous.

The *Laugh-In* kid was now a Hollywood veteran, a star who knew she was in trouble if she could not come up with a hit. "I wish all my movies could go through the roof," she stated. "But in fact, most movies don't. But what do you know? Nobody knows. There are so many variables in making a movie."

Her next comedy, *Overboard* (1987), was an even bigger disap-

Whoopi Goldberg was from San Francisco and became a sensation with her stand-up comedy act. When Steven Spielberg decided to turn Alice Walker's best-selling novel *The Color Purple* into a movie in 1985, he cast Whoopi as Celie. It was her first movie and she won an Academy Award nomination. After that, Hollywood didn't know quite what to do with her. She starred in a couple of lame comedies, and by the beginning of the nineties was playing a supporting role in *Ghost*.

The daughter of comedian Tommy Chong, Rae Dawn Chong gained notice without saying a word as a cave woman teaching man how to make love in the missionary position in *Quest for Fire* (1982). She also appeared briefly in *The Color Purple* (1985), and gave Arnold Schwarzenegger a run for his money in *Commando* (1985).

Dark-eyed, husky-voiced Demi Moore, seen with Rob Lowe in ***About Last Night*** (1986), came from New Mexico. She left high school in her senior year in order to pursue a career as an actress. She modeled, appeared on the cover of ***Oui*** magazine, and even worked for a collection agency before landing a role on a TV soap opera that led to her movie debut in ***Blame It on Rio*** (1983).

Below: Everyone remembers Shelley Long in the hit television comedy series, ***Cheers***. But who recalls her co-starring in a very unfunny caveman farce titled ***Caveman***, released in 1981? That's former Beatle Ringo Starr looking delighted to share her embrace.

Opposite: Melanie Griffith co-starred with Harrison Ford, and Sigourney Weaver in Mike Nichols' ***Working Girl*** (1988), one of the decade's best romantic comedies.

pointment at the box office. By the end of the decade, she had signed a seven-picture deal at Touchstone, the studio that had revived a number of failing movie star careers. Meanwhile she had stopped trying to carry a movie all by herself and was co-starring with Mel Gibson in an action comedy called *Bird on a Wire.*

"Sure, as you get older you get more concerned about longevity," she conceded. "However, if I think about it, it only lasts a little while. If it's time to step down and let someone else reign, then that's the natural order of things."

GOLDIE'S REPLACEMENT AS THE TOP FEMALE AT the box office was the least likely of movie stars. At the beginning of the decade, there was no reason to suspect Bette Midler even had a future in films. Midler had grown up in Honolulu, Hawaii. "When I was a little girl, all my friends and neighbors, everyone I went to school with, had their roots in some romantic place or other — China, Japan, Malaya, the Philippines — while my folks hailed from New Jersey," she wrote in her best-selling *A View from a Broad.* "My father had moved out to Hawaii during the Depression, not so much to find work as to find a proper setting for my mother, whom he always thought too beautiful and delicate for prosaic Passaic (New Jersey)."

From the time she was a kid, Midler dreamed of being an actress. She attended the University of Hawaii, then landed a job as an extra in the movie production of *Hawaii.* She went back to Los Angeles with the production, ending up in New York, where she played Tzeitel in the original Broadway production of *Fiddler on the Roof.* While she was doing the show, she was approached by Stephen Ostrow, the owner of the newly redecorated Continental Health Club. Ostrow hired her to sing in the baths, a venue where, if the customers didn't like an act, they threw their towels. No one ever threw a towel at Bette. It was here that the Bette she chose to present to the world began to emerge, the Divine Miss M, the campy eccentric possessed of the sweet voice and the lacerating wit. In 1979, director Mark Rydell chose her to play the Janis Joplin-like rock star in *The Rose.* She was nominated for an Oscar for her performance, but then the problem: What to do with Bette? She could sing, write and act. She was brassy, loud, vulgar and very, very funny, but those were not qualities that played well for a woman in movies. And somehow she didn't *look* like a star. Women like Bette Midler went to the movies and dreamed; they did not act in them. Besides, she had spent a great deal of time mocking the sort of people who were in movies. "Art always deals with tragic issues, show business doesn't," she said.

A Bronx-born graduate of the High School of Performing Arts, Ellen Barkin was once described as having a nose "that looks like it was broken in a schoolyard boxing match." Few people noticed her nose in two steamy thrillers in the eighties, *The Big Easy* (1987) and *Sea of Love* (1989). The movies helped establish a reputation for on-screen sensuality that Barkin said she found surprising.

Actress Ally Sheedy was best known as one of the female members of the so-called "Brat Pack" of young actors who hung out together in the eighties. She appeared with her pals in movies such as *The Breakfast Club* (1985), *St. Elmo's Fire* (1985), and *Oxford Blues* (1984), in which she got to hose down Rob Lowe.

"I think I'm a sendup of a show business person. Show business really irritates me, art never does."

In 1980, there was a concert film called *Divine Madness*, based on her stage show. After that, she made a disastrous comedy, *Jinxed*, fought with its director Don Siegel and came away with such a bad reputation that no one would hire her. ("I'd let my wife, children and animals starve before I subjected myself to something like that again," Siegel said.)

Bette was brokenhearted, but she kept going, keeping busy with singing tours, records — and waiting. Then, one day, director Paul Mazursky telephoned to ask her to play the role of a rich, spoiled Beverly Hills housewife in a new comedy he was preparing called *Down and out in Beverly Hills*. Midler later would give Mazursky the credit for rescuing her movie career: "He was the one who literally gave me a hand up." *Down and out in Beverly Hills*, released in 1985, adroitly answered the question of what to do with Bette: let her be funny. If she didn't look like anyone's idea of a movie star, well, neither did Mae West. Both actresses possessed the same brassy, bawdy, nasty but somehow lovable sensibilities. Jeffrey Katzenberg, head of production at Disney, took her career in hand and created around her a series of carefully formulated comedies — *Ruthless People*, *Outrageous Fortune* and *Big Business* — that had no reason for being other than to give Bette an opportunity to make audiences laugh at the way she was so lovably hateful. "Very few people have ever done in a leading role what Bette has done in those comedies," commented Lily Tomlin, her co-star in *Big Business*. "She's played characters that are not particularly likable in the conventional sense — they're ballsy, strong, and pushy — yet Bette makes them totally appealing."

Richard Dreyfuss with Bette Midler.

In addition to unexpectedly rediscovered stardom, there was a new husband, Martin von Haselberg, and a baby daughter. Midler was as happy as she ever had been. "I can only say these must be the seven fat years, because the seven lean years were just before this. I think it's just a cycle. I don't think I'm doing anything different than I was doing. My heart is the same; my soul is the same.

My *clothes* are the same. Maybe the scripts got better, or my type came into demand, I really don't know, and I don't really try to examine it deeply, because I don't want it to go away. I'm having a wonderful time, and that's all that counts."

And yet, by the end of the decade, with another hit in movie theaters, this one a weeper titled *Beaches*, and a remake of *Stella Dallas*, released early in 1990, she was becoming more cynical about success. "I really don't pay much attention to it anymore," she admitted. "It's sort of lost its magic for me. I try to do good work. I'm very interested in creating and making things that people will enjoy and find beautiful, and that's a greater reward actually than physical success. It sounds pompous I think, but when you're making something, it's transporting. You become someone else, and you drift away, and it's a very exciting feeling."

THERE WERE OTHER ACTRESSES LEARNING THE value of laughter at the box office. Sigourney Weaver shook up her rather stiff, blue-blooded image by co-starring in *Ghostbusters*. "They thought of me as Sarah Bernhardt or something," laughed the actress, who had become famous dispatching the monster in *Alien* and making love to Mel Gibson in *The Year of Living Dangerously*. "It was really flattering; it was, 'Hey, you know what? We got a real legitimate actress in our film.' And they still have it. They still think I legitimized their movie or something." She did a serious movie, *Gorillas in the Mist*, then did a hilarious send-up of the corporate Brahmin bitch goddess in *Working Girl*. Both roles got her nominated for Oscars in 1988, although she didn't win for either.

Melanie Griffith was the daughter of actress Tippi Hedren, best remembered as the former model discovered by Alfred Hitchcock and cast in his film *The Birds*. Griffith had wandered into acting at the age of 18, playing nymphets in two 1975 private-detective movies, *Night Moves* and *The Drowning Pool*. "All I was doing was reading my lines and playing myself," she said. "I didn't have any desire to be an actress."

No one paid much more attention to her until Brian De Palma cast her as the porn actress Holly Body in *Body Double* (1984), his *homage* to Hitchcock's *Rear Window*. That was followed by *Something Wild*, in which Griffith was very wild and very amusing — and abruptly she was being taken seriously as a funny actress. But it was Mike Nichols who allowed Griffith to finally turn her usual breathless bimbo role into someone possessed of brains and ambition in *Working Girl*.

Robert Redford cast Elizabeth McGovern as Timothy Hutton's girlfriend in *Ordinary People* (1980). Thereafter the chipmunk-cheeked actress played in everything from Milos Forman's *Ragtime* (1981) to Sergio Leone's *Once upon a Time in America* (1984) to *She's Having a Baby* (1988). Here she co-starred with Dudley Moore in a romantic comedy called *Lovesick* (1983).

The idea for the famous orgasm scene in *When Harry Met Sally ...* (1989), came out of a conversation director Rob Reiner had with the movie's writer, Nora Ephron. She told him women often faked orgasms, and a few weeks later Reiner incorporated the scene in which Meg Ryan informs Billy Crystal of this fact in a restaurant, then proceeds to show him how it is done. It was Rob Reiner's mother who, after watching Ryan, nods to a waiter and says, "I'll have what she's having."

MEG RYAN HAD PLAYED EVERYONE'S CUTE, pert girlfriend in movies such as *Innerspace* and *Presidio*. Then, in 1989, Rob Reiner cast her as Sally, the girl Harry (Billy Crystal) only wants to be friends with in *When Harry Met Sally . . .* Ryan got to play the most talked-about movie scene of the decade — when she demonstrates for Billy Crystal how women fake orgasms, and does it in a crowded restaurant (actually Katz's Delicatessen in New York City). "Women love me now," she said, shortly after the movie was released. "Mostly women over 30. I mean they *lo-o-ove* me! They'll talk to me about anything. In aisles, and check-out lines in grocery stores and drugstores and stuff, they corner me and reveal the most personal things."

Andie MacDowell also got to talk about sex in a deadpan funny way as the repressed southern wife in *sex, lies, and videotape* (1989). Before she agreed to make the movie for novice director Steven Soderbergh, she was best known as the model whose body appeared in *Greystoke: The Legend of Tarzan, Lord of the Apes* but whose voice in that movie had been dubbed by Glenn Close. "When I read the script for *sex, lies, and videotape*, I thought, 'Oh, I know this woman,' she recounted. "I know that feeling of trying to do everything perfectly . . . I just knew I wanted to be in it."

JULIA ROBERTS WAS A NATIVE OF SMYRNA, Georgia, 22 years of age, tall, possessed of a loveliness that was almost ethereal. Her older brother, Eric Roberts (*The Coca-Cola Kid, Star 80*) was also an actor, but Julia said that, as a child, she had been more interested in becoming a veterinarian. "I wouldn't say I had a tough adolescence," she said. "I had a good time, but I was a very rugged individualist at 13 years old." She decided to move to New York at the age of 17 to pursue an acting career."

In 1988, she played Daisy, a hard-boiled waitress in her first film, the low-budget *Mystic Pizza*. "There came a point where I almost forgot about it," she said. "And then it came out, and it was so shocking, and people really liked it."

Julia Roberts in *Steel Magnolias*.

The critical reaction to her performance led to her being cast as the dying southern belle in *Steel Magnolias* (1989). Abruptly, she found herself surrounded by some of the strongest women in film: Sally Field, Shirley MacLaine, Dolly Parton and Olympia Dukakis. Roberts remained undaunted and discovered an unanticipated strength in herself. "I just found the work to be completely challenging. It was just something I was consumed with all the time. It was not the kind of job where I went home and it was over." Perhaps because it wasn't, she received her first Academy Award nomination for what was only her second film. By then she was on to a romance, *Pretty Woman*, playing the not-so-hard-bitten whore who picks up Richard Gere on Sunset Boulevard. Early in 1990, it was a hit, and Roberts held the promise of stardom in her dark beauty, in the warmth of her laughter, and in the strength of her determination.

Debra Winger was one of the most serious and outspoken actresses of the eighties. She made no bones about the fact that she hated working with Richard Gere in *An Officer and a Gentleman* (1982) or that she intensely disliked the experience of making *Legal Eagles* (1986). She even fought with co-star Shirley MacLaine while filming her biggest hit, *Terms of Endearment* (1983). She played Emma Horton, a role that originally was intended for Sissy Spacek.

Before she was 18 years old, Molly Ringwald briefly became the biggest teenaged female star of the eighties, working in such John Hughes-directed comedies as *Sixteen Candles* (1984) and *Pretty in Pink* (1986). But her career floundered after she had a falling out with Hughes, and the older she got, the less audiences seemed to want to see her. Movies such as *The Pick-up Artist* (1987) and *Fresh Horses* (1988) were all but ignored.

PANAVISION
PANAFLEX

THE DIRECTORS

FIGHTING TO KEEP IT PERSONAL

Robert Redford made his debut behind the camera when he decided to direct ***Ordinary People*** (1980), a family drama taken from Judith Guest's best-selling novel. It won the Academy Award for best picture, and Redford was awarded the first Oscar of his career for best direction. In addition, young Timothy Hutton won an Oscar for best supporting actor. Redford took his time about working again as a director. His next film, ***The Milagro Beanfield War, left***, was not released until 1988.

Caught somewhere between the power of the stars and the commercial demands of the film companies, the movie director in the eighties often felt the squeeze — unless he was Steven Spielberg or one of his disciples. Personal films made by young mavericks who wanted to bring their own vision to the screen fell out of fashion after the commercial failures of Michael Cimino's Heaven's Gate, Martin Scorsese's Raging Bull and Francis Coppola's One from the Heart. Directors could make very expensive movies, but they had to be large, impersonal commercial ventures. The young turks, influenced originally by Francis Coppola, who were going to take over Hollywood, instead found themselves being taken over by Hollywood. It became vital to make money, and a director was only as bankable as his last picture. There were exceptions to this, but those directors tended to work either on the edge of the mainstream or outside it entirely, and they worked on shoestring budgets. The decade's most original and individualistic filmmaker seemed unconcerned by any of this, however. He worked in New York, and, in the winter of 1985, he was preparing to have lunch . . .

Woody Allen's most frequent co-star during the eighties was actress Mia Farrow, who was also the woman he lived with and who fathered his child. The two met when he cast her in *A Midsummer Night's Sex Comedy* (1982), and thereafter she appeared in nearly all his pictures, including *Zelig* (1983), *Broadway Danny Rose* (1984), *The Purple Rose of Cairo* (1985), *Hannah and Her Sisters* (1986), *Radio Days* (1987), *September* (1987), *Another Woman* (1988) and *Crimes and Misdemeanors* (1989).

IN FEBRUARY 1985, WOODY ALLEN WAS TAKING A break in the beige interior of a Manhattan editing room where he was putting the finishing touches to his latest movie, *Hannah and Her Sisters*. Allen was 49 years of age, and *Hannah* was his 17th film since he had evolved from a stand-up comic and actor into a director.

His method of working was unlike that of any other American filmmaker. He held to the side of the mainstream of American film, part of the business, but away from it, working in New York rather than Los Angeles, and making small, intensely personal movies that he wrote himself. Most American directors talked about *auteurism*, the authorship of their films, but Woody Allen was America's only true *auteur* filmmaker. Sandy-haired, sallow-faced, bespectacled, he occupied his own turf, mostly unconcerned with the commercial obsessions of Hollywood — he argued that, "most of what comes out of the United States is junk" — or with its propensity for handing out awards. In 1977, when *Annie Hall* won the Academy Award for best picture, and Allen himself won two awards for best director and best screenplay (along with co-writer Marshall Brickman), he didn't even bother watching the ceremonies on television. Instead, he spent the evening playing his clarinet at a lower Manhattan club called Michael's Pub.

His ambition was as pure as it was uncomplicated: he wanted to make movies. Sometimes those movies were classics — *Annie Hall, Manhattan*, and the film he was currently finishing, *Hannah and Her Sisters.* Sometimes they were fascinating and original sketches, such as *Zelig*, *Broadway Danny Rose* and *The Purple Rose of Cairo.* And sometimes they were just plain mistakes, dull dramas verging on parodies of Ingmar Bergman, Woody's favorite director; *September* and *Another Woman* were examples of a great director failing at his art.

Whatever they were, Woody Allen went to work each day of his life writing and directing. He disdained the development and the deal-making that preoccupied other directors. He had a long-term arrangement with Arthur Krim, who headed Orion Pictures. He made his movies for little cost, and without fuss, so that even if they lost money, which they often did, they did not lose much money. New York was his personal back lot, and he almost never left the lot (although he insisted, the evidence of *Annie Hall* notwithstanding, that he did not hate Los Angeles), living on the Upper East Side of Manhattan, not far away from the editing room where he worked. He made movies his own way, and when he felt scenes didn't work, his budget was arranged in such a way that he could reshoot them. He decided the actor Michael Keaton wasn't the right lead after he started to shoot *The Purple Rose of Cairo.* He stopped production and recast Jeff Daniels in the lead. He didn't like *September* after he finished the movie, so he scrapped the entire film, recast it and shot it again — a practice almost unheard of in the history of movies. He remained aloof and distant while he worked, and although he denied he was as reclusive as the press made him out to be, he did not easily make friends. In his fifties, he would become a father for the first time, and his relationship with the actress Mia

***Above*: Woody Allen on the set of *Another Woman* (1988) with Gena Rowlands and Philip Bosco. Allen always said that his films were not widely popular, and that was particularly true when he opted to do straight drama. *Another Woman* was released in only a handful of North American cities before it disappeared.**

***Below*: Allen contributed a straight comic segment to *New York Stories* (1988) titled *Oedipus Wrecks*. Woody played a lawyer with a dominating mother. The mother was played by former vaudeville performer Mae Questel, who for years had provided the voice of cartoon character Betty Boop.**

While Woody Allen continued to work behind a camera, making the kind of movies that appealed to him, few other American directors had the same freedom to bring their personal vision to the screen. One of them who was able to do this was Barry Levinson, *below*. Levinson started out as a screenwriter, then wrote and directed *Diner* (1982), an autobiographical account of young men coming of age in Baltimore in 1959. By the end of the decade, he was one of Hollywood's most respected directors, having won an Oscar for *Rain Man* (1988).

Farrow seemed secure. Nonetheless, he was not happy and insisted that he suffered from a condition called anhedonia, an inability to enjoy life.

Movies were his joy and his salvation. "As a kid," he recalled, "I retreated into movie houses and sat there endlessly. I hated school and spent a lot of time in movies."

He was born Allen Stewart Konigsberg in Brooklyn, New York. He would say later that, as a kid "when we played softball, I'd steal second, then feel guilty and go back." He said he wanted a dog, but his parents couldn't afford one. "So my parents got me an ant. I called it Spot." His one regret in life, he was later to write, was that he "was not someone else."

That image of the put-upon schlemiel, which he cultivated so carefully in his early years as a stand-up comic, was a disguise, like Chaplin's Little Tramp or the miser Jack Benny always made himself out to be. But it was a disguise formed from truth. At Midwood High school, he constantly cracked up his fellow students, and started sending jokes to Broadway columnists such as Walter Winchell and Ed Sullivan under the assumed name of Woody Allen. He was 17 when a press agent signed him to write one-liners for other people. "Every day after school," he remembered later, "I would take the subway to Manhattan and knock out 30 or 40 gags for famous people to say. I was thrilled. I thought I was in the heart of show business."

Woody Allen continued writing jokes for people like Pat Boone and Sid Caesar while attending New York University and City College. He was 19 years old, earning $1,500 a week, and was married to a 16-year-old named Harlene Rosen. The marriage lasted for five years. He used to say his wife was extremely childish. "One time I was taking a bath, and, for no reason at all, she came in and sank my boats."

In 1961, Woody stepped onto a stage in Greenwich Village and reluctantly began performing his own material. His agents, Jack Rollins and Charles Joffe, had to talk him out of quitting a half dozen times. A producer, Charles Feldman, hired him to write his first movie comedy in 1965, *What's New Pussycat.* Allen said the movie didn't make any sense because he dropped the script when he got out of a cab, and the pages were out of order. Nonetheless, the movie was a hit, and led him to *Casino Royale,* in which he played the nephew of 007. He wrote a play (*Don't Drink the Water*); remarried (to actress Louise Lasser); and, in 1969, finally directed his first movie (which he had also written), *Take the Money and Run.*

Woody Allen with Martin Landau.

Yet he was unhappy with making people happy. "It's a question of personal values," he said in 1985, between bites of his turkey sandwich. "When I was a kid, I thought the highest thing one could aspire to was *Duck Soup* with the Marx Brothers, or Charlie Chaplin or George S. Kaufman. And then, as you get older, hopefully, one's feelings about life deepen, and then you see a greater value in deeper and more serious work. When I first started making comedies in film, I only cared about laughs and made films where you would just laugh from beginning to end. But gradually, over the years, I've been sacrificing laughs."

In the seventies, he gave up stand-up comedy completely, and concentrated on making movies. His growth as a filmmaker from *Take the Money and Run* to *Annie Hall,* eight years later, was astonishing. Yet he claimed the public outside of large urban centers never embraced him. "*Annie Hall* was the smallest money-earning Oscar-winner in history. I've never been popular. I was never popular as a nightclub comedian, on television, never. Everyone always thought I would be popular. They would book me into Las Vegas, in Caesar's

Above: James Bridges helped make Debra Winger a star by casting her opposite John Travolta in *Urban Cowboy* (1980). Later, they collaborated on a little-seen mystery titled *Mike's Murder,* made in 1982, but not released until 1984 after Winger's success in *Terms of Endearment.*

***Below*: John Badham was one of the most commercial directors during the eighties. He did everything from *WarGames* to *Blue Thunder* (both in 1983) to *Short Circuit* (1986) and *Stakeout* (1987), and made them all hits.**

The ranks of movie directors were all but closed to most women during the eighties. However, a few managed to break through with varying degrees of success.

Above: Actress Anne Bancroft, took her turn behind the camera in order to make *Fatso* (1980), an unsuccessful comedy starring Dom DeLuise.

Below, centre: Penny Marshall, seen here with Whoopi Goldberg, became a star on television's *Laverne and Shirley*, but like her brother, Garry Marshall, she longed to direct. She finally made her movie debut with *Jumpin' Jack Flash* (1986). It was not a success. Undaunted, she made *Big* (1988), an unexpected comedy success, starring Tom Hanks, that established her as just about the decade's only woman director with a bona fide box office hit.

Below: Barbra Streisand spent 10 years getting *Yentl* (1983) made. She both starred in and directed the musical drama. At the beginning of the nineties, she started shooting a screen adaptation of Pat Conroy's *Prince of Tides*, a drama in which she again directed and co-starred, this time with Nick Nolte.

Opposite: On the set of *She-Devil* (1989), *from left*, Meryl Streep, Roseanne Barr, Sylvia Miles, director Susan Seidelman, Linda Hunt.

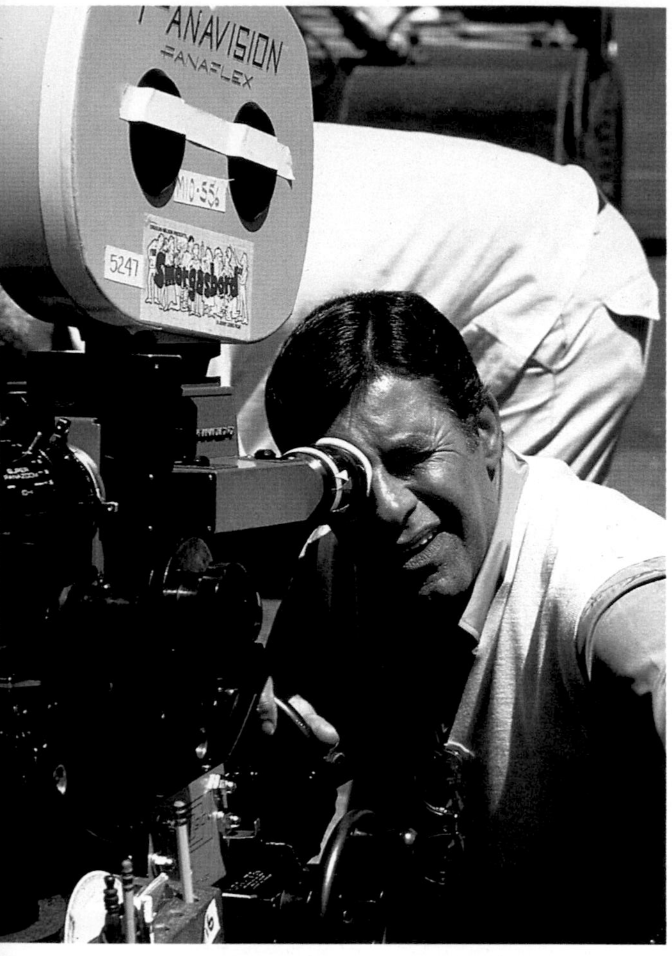

***Above*: The French continued to love him in the eighties, but North American audiences generally ignored Jerry Lewis. He directed a couple of comedies — *Hardly Working* (1981) and *Smorgasbord* (1983), also known as *Cracking Up* — but his best work was as an actor in Martin Scorsese's *King of Comedy* (1982).**

***Below*: Garry Marshall created such hit television comedies as *Laverne and Shirley* and *Happy Days* before switching successfully to feature films with *The Flamingo Kid* (1984). Here he is with the late Jackie Gleason on the set of *Nothing in Common* (1986).**

Palace, and then half the house would be empty. This happened all the time."

In 1989, he made *Crimes and Misdemeanors*, a film about the lack of morality in the eighties, and about the way everything is rationalized to the point where the bad guys end up on top and the good guys are the losers. The film reaffirmed his determination to stretch himself even further. However, he remained unconvinced of his own abilities, and discounted those critics who insisted on calling him a genius. "I haven't done it yet, but I would like to make one picture that I could watch next to *Bicycle Thief* or *Grand Illusion* or *Citizen Kane*, and feel like, gee, I'm playing in that ball game." He said that critics who claimed he already had attained that status were wrong, and did not know films. "I can't kid myself," he said. "I'll know when I do it. I think my films are a group of well-intended, honest failures. I'm trying my best to make something that is genuinely good and original, but I'm not succeeding. They're nice tries, but they're not really there yet."

NEW YORK DURING THE EIGHTIES BECAME something of a safe haven for American filmmakers, a place where a personal vision and a creative edge were still of some value. The veteran Sidney Lumet did not venture outside New York until Jane Fonda lured him out to Hollywood in 1986 to make a thriller called *The Morning After*. Paul Mazursky occasionally was seen under a palm tree, most notably to shoot his biggest hit of the eighties, *Down and out in Beverly Hills*. But he managed to maintain the flinty independence of a New York filmmaker, and by the end of the decade he was back on the Lower East Side shooting *Enemies, a Love Story*, the most critically hailed film of his career.

But next to Woody Allen, the most quintessential of New York directors was a small, dark, intense Italian-American named Martin Scorsese. If Woody Allen had a gently ironic and humorous view of New York life (witness *Annie Hall* and *Manhattan*), Scorsese's view was gritty and frightening, as evidenced by *Taxi Driver*, Scorsese's terrifying masterpiece of the seventies. He was universally celebrated as the prince of urban darkness, a celebration that had reached its apogee with the release of Scorsese's biography of the

Nick Nolte with director Paul Mazursky.

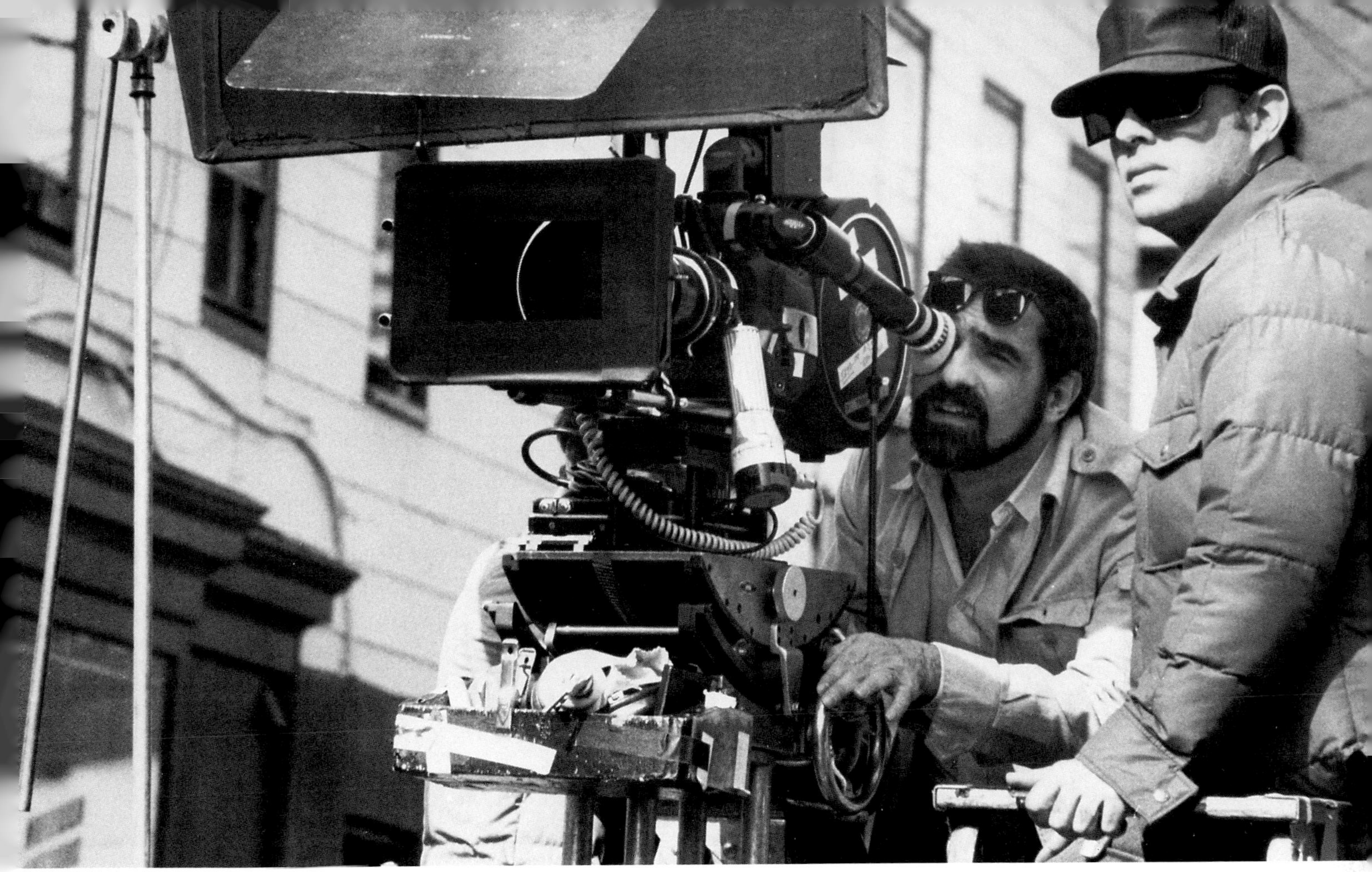

boxer Jake La Motta titled *Raging Bull*, starring his friend Robert De Niro.

At the end of November of 1980, shortly after *Raging Bull* opened in New York, Scorsese, exhausted from editing the film, was not feeling well. "I'm okay really," he said vaguely. "It's just that I've got a cold."

He was lost somewhere beneath the covers, in the bedroom of his apartment high above 57th Street in downtown Manhattan. He was laid out on a vast expanse of bed, swathed in a robe, dark hair straggling away from a pale, bearded face.

Scorsese peered up at a big-screen television situated in a corner off the edge of the bed. On the screen, a young Brigitte Bardot disappeared underwater. "This is *Contempt*," he explained distractedly. "Jean-Luc Godard. They've hacked it up for television."

Scorsese grew up along Elizabeth Street on New York's Lower East Side, in an area known as Little Italy. The family, the Roman Catholic Church and the Mob, those were the influences in the neighborhood. The rest of the world was a long way away. "Elizabeth Street was mainly Sicilian, as were my grandparents, and here we had our own regulations and laws," he was to recall later. "We didn't care about government or politicians or the police: we felt we were right in our way." It was a sensibility that was to be reflected in *Mean Streets* (1973), the first film that gained him real

Above: **Martin Scorsese on the set of *After Hours* (1985).**
Below: **Peter Yates got his start working as assistant director of films such as *The Guns of Navarone* and *A Taste of Honey*. He made his North American debut directing Steve McQueen in *Bullitt* in 1968, creating the classic car chase that is still the prototype for thousands of subsequent imitations. Yates never again exercised quite the same originality of style, but he worked into the eighties, generally on well crafted thrillers such as *Suspect* (1987).**

Richard Donner (*above* with Bill Murray) and Ivan Reitman, *below*, were two of Hollywood's most successful directors during the eighties. Donner broke into movies with *The Omen* (1976), before doing the original — and the best — *Superman* movie (1978). He seemed comfortable with any genre and did everything from comedy (*The Toy*, 1982, *Scrooged*, 1988) to fantasy (*Ladyhawke*, 1985) and action (*Lethal Weapon*, 1987, *Lethal Weapon II*, 1989).

Ivan Reitman got his start in the movie business producing low-budget horror movies in Canada, often for director David Cronenberg. His breakthrough in Hollywood came when he produced *National Lampoon's Animal House* in 1978. He directed Bill Murray's first movie, *Meatballs* (1979), and thereafter specialized in comedies (*Stripes*, 1981, *Ghostbusters*, 1984).

***Opposite*: Robert De Niro in *Raging Bull* (1980).**

recognition.

He attended the film school at New York University, made student shorts, and directed his first feature in 1968, *Who's That Knocking at My Door*, on a budget of $70,000. The film brought him out to Hollywood the next year, where he worked with his friend Michael Wadleigh, director of the feature documentary *Woodstock*, who employed Scorsese to help edit the film — the beginning of Scorsese's career-long love of music that brought him to film the final performance of the rock group The Band, for a documentary titled *The Last Waltz*.

In the early seventies, while Scorsese was working as an editor, he got to know George Lucas, Francis Coppola, Brian De Palma and Steven Spielberg, directors who would play a big part in shaping the films of both the seventies and the eighties. They all seemed to be in trouble. Warner Bros. hated Lucas's first feature, *THX-1138*, produced by Coppola. Brian De Palma was in the process of being thrown off a movie called *Get to Know Your Rabbit*. Spielberg was unhappily shooting television shows.

It was Roger Corman, the mogul of the B-movies, who gave Scorsese his next shot at directing. *Boxcar Bertha* was intended to be another low-budget exploitation gangster film, and it was, except anyone who saw it when it was released in 1972 knew, despite its awesome violence, that the schlock material was in the hands of a very unusual director. Nonetheless, John Cassavetes berated him for making exploitation movies, and encouraged Scorsese to go ahead with *Mean Streets*, the movie which changed his professional life and led to his only truly mainstream Hollywood movie, *Alice Doesn't Live Here Anymore*. After that came *Taxi Driver*, the film Scorsese shot in 1975, from a script by Paul Schrader. It was the movie that made Robert De Niro a star, and for which Scorsese to this day remains best known. (After seeing *Taxi Driver*, John Hinckley became obsessed with Jodie Foster, who played the 12-year-old prostitute, and was inspired to shoot President Ronald Reagan.)

It was De Niro who gave Scorsese a copy of *Raging Bull*. At the time, the director was in hospital recovering from depression caused by the bad reviews and poor box office for his movie musical, *New York, New York* (1977), the most ambitious and expensive project he had undertaken.

United Artists, the studio with whom Scorsese was associated at the time, was not at all happy with the director's determination to turn *Raging Bull* into a movie. Today, the project probably would have been turned down flat. But in the late seventies, major directors with personal vision and passion were being treated with a bit more care. Even so, United Artists executives were anxious to talk

Above: **At the age of 80, George Cukor, one of Hollywood's most esteemed old masters, was still working. Cukor was always known as a "woman's director," and true to form, the beginning of the decade found him guiding two women, Candice Bergen and Jacqueline Bisset, through a high-toned soap opera titled *Rich and Famous* (1981), which was actually a remake of John Van Druten's play called *Old Acquaintance*. It turned out to be Cukor's last film. He died in 1983 after a career that spanned five decades of film.**

Below: **Sam Fuller never gained Cukor's pre-eminence in film, but through the forties and fifties he gained a following as a no-nonsense craftsman of hard-boiled, low-budget crime melodramas. In 1980, he got the chance to turn his personal experiences during the Second World War into a movie titled *The Big Red One*, which starred the late Lee Marvin.**

him out of doing the movie. They met at Scorsese's spartan apartment with its movie posters and state-of-the-art video equipment.

The encounter provided some insight into what happens when Hollywood executives are confronted with difficult material by noted filmmakers. ". . . As fortunate as we felt to have inherited the *Raging Bull* deal from the previous management," wrote Steven Bach, who, at the time, was vice-president and head of worldwide development for United Artists, "we were convinced the script was unmakable. It was brutally depressing and depressingly brutal; the production would be extremely difficult, calling for De Niro at mid-point to gain 60 pounds, necessitating a four-month production shutdown . . ."

United Artists was upset not only by the language of the script ("There must be more fucks in this script than have actually taken place in the history of Hollywood"), but also by the character of Jake La Motta. His anger would infuse the entire film; he was perhaps the most unlikable character ever to be the subject of a major American film. David Field, the United Artists production executive who attended the meeting with Steve Bach described La Motta as "a cockroach."

But Scorsese's passion prevailed at the studio whose executives had also allowed Michael Cimino to go off with $36 million and make *Heaven's Gate*. *Raging Bull* was made for a lot less money ($14 million) and a great deal more artistry. Scorsese took 10 weeks to film the fight scenes, and nine weeks to shoot the dramatic stuff, with four months off in between so De Niro could eat his way through France and Italy and put on 60 pounds to look right as La Motta after he was finished boxing.

NOW, AS SCORSESE LAY IN BED TRYING TO shake his cold, *Raging Bull* was in limited release to qualify for Academy Award consideration. Critics were hailing it as a masterpiece, and many of them at the end of the decade would choose it as the best movie of the 1980s. It is dark and primitive, at times almost impossible to watch, La Motta's domestic violence often much more unsettling than anything that goes on in the ring. Nothing quite like it had been made before in America, and nothing quite like it has been made since.

But Scorsese, as he watched Godard's *Contempt* late into the afternoon, had little inkling of the reaction to the movie. "I don't know too much about the reaction." He was speaking so low you could hardly hear him. "I guess it's been good, but I don't know. I've been here."

Mike Cimino had just pulled *Heaven's Gate* out of release and everyone was talking about it. Scorsese seemed to sense what it was going to mean for the independence of filmmakers within the studio system. "What they are doing is killing off American filmmakers before they can get a chance to work," he said with some passion. "You make one mistake and you fall so far that you never get a chance to do another film. They give a guy all sorts of awards, then they destroy him a year later. You can't create artists and destroy them like that."

By the beginning of 1982, Scorsese more clearly understood the meaning of his own words. He was in trouble. *Raging Bull*, although it was accorded practically unanimous acclaim and had won De Niro an Oscar for best actor, was a box office failure. Scorsese's next film, *King of Comedy*, a black but very funny view of celebrity in America, played poorly and in only a few major cities. *King of Comedy* was supposed to be followed by Scorsese's adaptation of Nikos Kazantzakis' *The Last Temptation of Christ*, but at the last minute, Paramount got cold feet. "Paramount's policy at the time

Veteran Billy Wilder did not fare well during the eighties. He made *Buddy, Buddy* (1981) with Jack Lemmon and Walter Matthau, but it failed commercially, and Wilder, in his seventies, was unable to get another project off the ground.

***Below*: Martin Scorsese on the set of *King of Comedy* (1982) with Robert De Niro.**

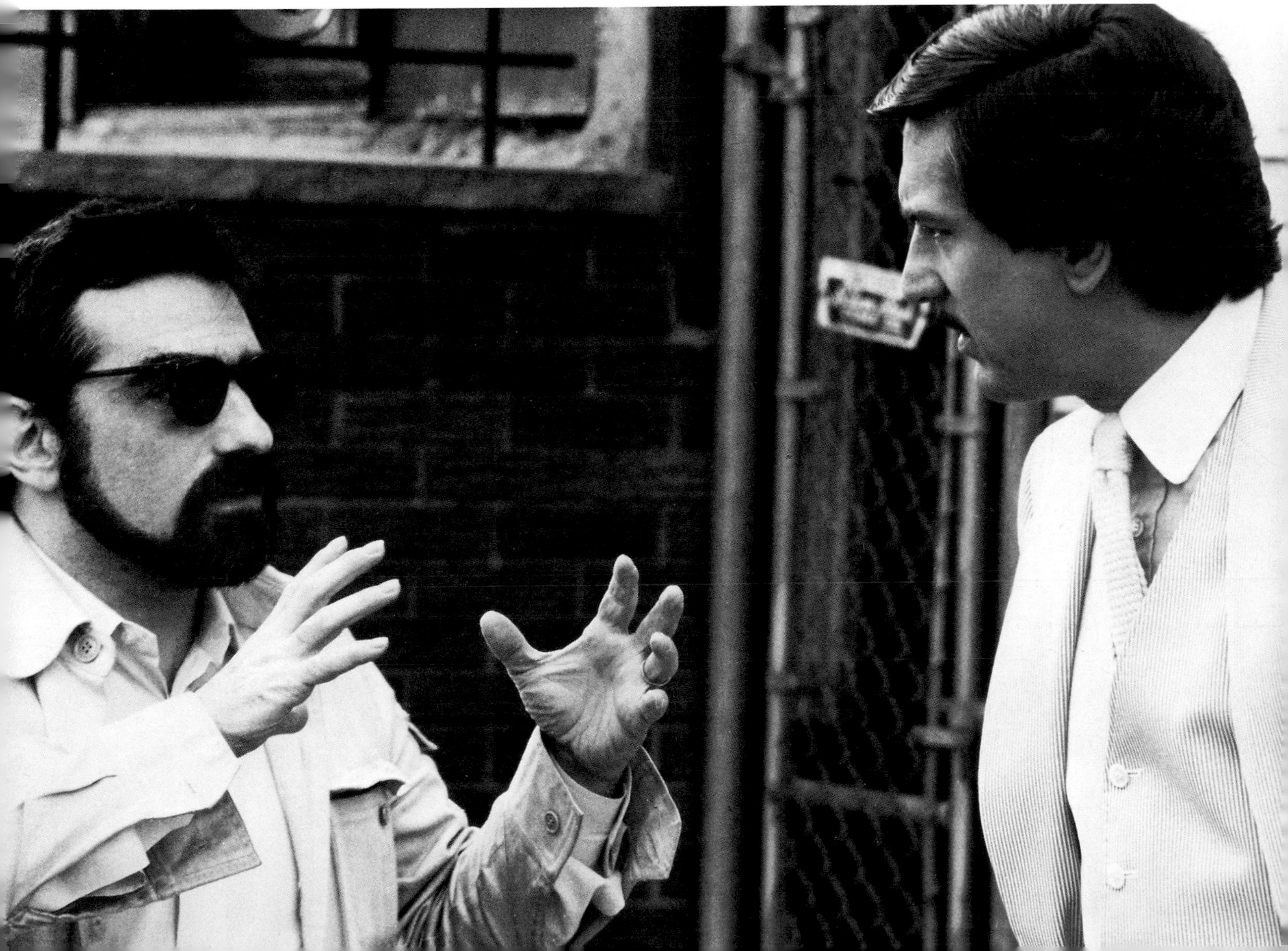

Stars as Directors: After 14 years in the hit television series *M*A*S*H*, Alan Alda concentrated on working behind a movie camera, making urban comedy-dramas in the style of Woody Allen. He wrote and directed *The Four Seasons* (1981), and it was a surprise box office success. But his subsequent films did not do as well, either commercially or critically.

Sidney Poitier, *below* with Richard Pryor and Gene Wilder, all but gave up acting in the eighties, and quietly concentrated on directing commercial comedies such as *Stir Crazy* (1980), *Hanky Panky* (1982) and *Fast Forward* (1985).

Opposite: Martin Scorsese on the set of *The Last Temptation of Christ* (1988).

was to be wary of 'name' directors going way over budget and shooting outside Hollywood," Scorsese said, "basically because they were all extremely frightened by the *Heaven's Gate* affair."

Instead, Scorsese would make another comedy, *After Hours* (1985), on which he virtually was a director for hire. Brian De Palma gave an interview and stated that Scorsese could not get a film made in Hollywood. Scorsese was offended by the comment, but he would not truly redeem himself, at least in the eyes of Hollywood, until he collaborated with two big box office stars, Paul Newman and Tom Cruise, in order to make *The Color of Money* (1986). A sequel to Newman's 1961 pool hall drama, *The Hustler, The Color of Money* finally won Newman an Oscar after nearly 30 years of nominations. It was, to put it mildly, the tamest film Scorsese shot during the decade.

Nonetheless, he once again was hot, and he employed that heat to finally make *The Last Temptation of Christ*. Not surprisingly, it became the most controversial — though least seen — film of his career. Scorsese's view of Christ's life, particularly the sense of Christ as mortal man prone to the same temptations of the flesh as everyone else, caused outrage. When the film opened in the late summer of 1988, religious groups picketed the small number of theaters in which it was shown. *The Last Temptation of Christ* was a victory for Scorsese. Despite the increasing pressures on American filmmakers to make big, mindless, crowd-pleasing movies, Scorsese had resisted. He was as uncompromising when he left the decade as he had been when he had entered it. Others were not quite so fortunate.

Playing the Commercial Game: Why the Young Turks Gave Up

IN FEBRUARY 1982, FRANCIS COPPOLA SAT PLUMP and rumpled-looking in a straight-backed chair in a Toronto hotel suite and talked energetically about his new movie, a love-story-cum-musical set in Las Vegas titled *One from the Heart.* "It's a very simple, sweet movie in content," he earlier told a crowded press conference. "It's my experience if you go and let it happen, you'll find a lot of enjoyment."

Already, at the age of 42, Coppola was a legendary film maverick, the movie guru who had encouraged the careers of a whole corps of movie brats, and who had begun fighting the system almost as soon as the system noticed him. The son of a first flute player with the NBC symphony orchestra under Toscanini, Coppola was the most famous graduate of the University of Southern California Film School. He turned his master's thesis from UCLA into a movie called *You're a Big Boy Now*, and Warner Bros. gave

During the eighties, Francis Coppola endured a great deal of personal misfortune, including bankruptcy, and the death of his 23-year-old son, Gian-Carlo, in a motorboat accident while Coppola was shooting *Gardens of Stone* (1987). Nonetheless, he kept working, if only to pay off his debts.

him an overblown movie version of *Finian's Rainbow* to direct. When it flopped, Coppola set up his own production company, American Zoetrope, in San Francisco in 1969, convincing Warner Bros. to finance it. The first Zoetrope movie was *THX-1138,* directed by George Lucas. The studio hated it, canceled the deal, and Coppola found himself $300,000 in debt. He bailed himself out the way he would any number of times over the years — by taking the first directing assignment that came along. It was a cheap gangster movie called *The Godfather.* The movie, released in 1972, grossed over

$285 million. He made *The Conversation*, then, in 1974, *The Godfather, Part II*, which, if anything, was better than the original. Coppola's reputation and clout had reached proportions so awesome that even he was suspicious of them. "Every year there's a hot director," he said at the time of the release of *Godfather II*. "And if he falls from grace with the critics or the public the next year, he often loses his balance and confidence in his own talent. I've lived in a state of anxiety the last 12 years . . . But I want to keep rocking the boat. Taking chances is what makes you strong, makes you wise."

His wisdom once again would be questioned when he set out to make a film about Vietnam based on Joseph Conrad's *Heart of Darkness.* Shooting *Apocalypse Now* in 1978 in the Philippine jungles nearly cost Coppola his health and his sanity. But, as the eighties began, the movie, with Martin Sheen and Marlon Brando, was a huge international hit. Coppola once again had been vindicated. Now there was no stopping him. Now he would do what he originally intended — he would take on Hollywood itself, and perhaps forever change the style and nature of moviemaking, bring it back to what it once had been, while at the same time leading it into the 21st century.

His plan was to develop his production company, Zoetrope, on a much grander scale. It would be run the way the old studios used to run, with full-time technicians, and stars under contract, and big sound stages on which to film. Coppola would attract the best of the old Hollywood and discover the brightest of the new. There was, not surprisingly, some skepticism about Coppola's intentions. "He's a fine writer and director," observed Ray Stark, one of Hollywood's most powerful producers. "His problem is that he wants to be a mogul. I tell him, 'Francis, there hasn't been a mogul in 20 years . . . the age of the great producer is over.'"

One from the Heart was the combination of the old and the new that Coppola was after — "electronic cinema" he called it. The movie, at a cost of $23 million, had been shot totally on sound stages, which included designer Dean Tavoularis's eye-catching recreation of downtown Las Vegas. Coppola employed state-of-the-art video equipment, and choreographed everything from a large van parked behind the set.

Electronic cinema, however, cost a lot of money, and the fledgling mogul had run out midway through filming. The picture had been finished with the help of an infusion of capital from a Calgary millionaire named Jack Singer. The movie was finally screened at New York's Radio City Music Hall in January of 1982, and soon after, Paramount, the studio that was supposed to release the film, decided not to do it.

Below: Actor Leonard Nimoy often felt trapped by his role of the Vulcan Mr. Spock, in the _Star Trek_ television series, and in the subsequent movies. But he was able to parlay Paramount's desire for a third _Star Trek_ movie into an opportunity to step behind the camera. Nimoy directed _Star Trek III: The Search for Spock_ (1984) and _Star Trek IV: The Voyage Home_ (1986), and both films were successful enough that when Touchstone had to bring in a director at the last moment to do a comedy titled _Three Men and a Baby_, Nimoy was chosen for the job, and thereafter found himself in the enviable position of being one of Hollywood's most sought after directors.

William Shatner, _above_, was not so fortunate. The actor, who played Captain Kirk on the television series and in four movies, decided that he wanted to direct the fifth. He got the job, but _Star Trek V: The Final Frontier_ (1989) was the least successful of the series.

Don Bluth was a disgruntled Disney animator who felt the studio was neglecting the kind of traditional animation it was famous for. He left to make his own animated features, and they did very well, beginning with *The Secret of Nimh* (1982), and continuing with *An American Tail* (1986) and *All Dogs Go to Heaven* (1989).

Below: Disney meanwhile revived its animation division, and made one of the most innovative films of the eighties, mixing animation and live action in *Who Framed Roger Rabbit* (1988), directed by Robert Zemeckis, *below,* with Roger, the movie's star.

One from the Heart: Francis Coppola with Nastassia Kinski and Frederic Forrest.

A month later, Coppola was in Toronto, and *One from the Heart* had a new distributor. But the man who wanted to control everything didn't seem able to control much of anything. Still, Coppola exuded a grandiose confidence. Other Zoetrope projects were going ahead, and Coppola was convinced the public would now flock to *One from the Heart.* Sitting in his hotel suite, he had had nothing but disdain for the Hollywood studio system. "I think this is true of every industry in general," he said. "The power of an industry is created by mavericks and nuts like Eastman and Ford. What people like them, and people like myself, establish is then inherited by Harvard Business School types. How much are these people spending on the development of talent? Nothing. How much on new technology? Nothing. These guys are not interested in the long term.

"Zoetrope is bidding to become the American Motors of the movie industry," he continued. "If we get a foothold, these guys aren't going to be able to compete."

It was not to be. A year later, Zoetrope, the old studio with the new ideas, was all but ruined. The Zoetrope movies that followed *One from the Heart* were all flops. Coppola himself was deeply in debt, embittered, flailing out at the media he said didn't understand him. Yet he refused to desert either his ambition or his idiosyncratic sense of film. In the midst of his financial problems, he proceeded to film two S.E. Hinton novels. The first of these, *The Outsiders,* was shot like a teenaged *Gone with the Wind.* The second, *Rumble Fish,* was practically a European art film. Neither movie made any money, and Coppola hired on to direct the ill-fated *Cotton Club,* one of the decade's great financial disasters. After that he again was a director for hire, this time on *Peggy Sue Got Married,* a delightful fantasy that was Coppola's most commercial Hollywood movie of the eighties, and, ironically enough, his only hit.

At the end of the decade, he was doing what he swore he would never do, what he said he detested: he was making another sequel, the $45-million (and climbing) continuation of *The Godfather* saga, from a script he wrote with his old collaborator Mario Puzo. As usual, he was in trouble. As he started shooting *Godfather, Part III* in Rome in January of 1990, Coppola declared bankruptcy, and listed liabilities of $28.9 million.

As COPPOLA STRUGGLED, SUCCESS HAD changed the direction of the very people the director's maverick ways had lured into the industry in the first place. In 1973, shortly after he made *American Graffiti*, George Lucas told the Modesto, California chamber of commerce that the future of movies lay with independent filmmakers. He said he and other young filmmakers were "forging ahead on the rubble of the old industry." By 1989, now one of the most successful filmmakers in Hollywood history, his view had changed substantially. Now there was no rubble on the horizon. "My direction has changed," he conceded. "When I was younger, I was pursuing more esoteric work, and as I've become more successful, I've drifted into the more popular arena."

Brian De Palma and George Lucas had worked together casting their movies, De Palma looking at young actors for *Carrie* while Lucas interviewed people for *Star Wars*. Beginning in the late sixties, De Palma directed a series of low-budget films that became progressively darker and more macabre — *Greetings, Hi, Mom!, Sisters, Phantom of the Paradise, Obsession, Carrie* and *Dressed to Kill*. He was often compared to Hitchcock, and his films did not sit easily with some audiences and film executives. In the eighties, he horrified everyone with his remake of *Scarface*, but then comfortably assimilated himself into the Hollywood structure, most notably with his direction of *The Untouchables*, a film that gave vent to his tremendous visual skills, particularly where violence was concerned, while still being com-

Brian De Palma with Michelle Pfeiffer.

Bob Fosse was one of the most original and innovative forces on the American musical stage. A former dancer who became a choreographer and then a director on Broadway, his movie career was more problematic. He won an Oscar for his direction of *Cabaret* in 1972, and *All That Jazz*, his semi-autobiographical drama about a director living on the edge, obsessed with a fear of death, was one of the most widely discussed movies of 1979. But his only film in the eighties was *Star 80* (1983), a dark, depressing drama about the life of *Playboy* model Dorothy Stratten that was not widely released. Fosse died of the heart attack he always feared in 1987.

Above: **Brian De Palma on the set of *Casualties of War* (1989) with actors Michael J. Fox, *right*, and Thuy Thu Le, *left*.**

Below: **John McTiernan attracted notice with a low-budget science fiction film called *Nomads* (1986), then landed the assignment to direct *Predator* (1987), in which Arnold Schwarzenegger did battle with an alien creature in the jungle. His biggest success came when he directed Bruce Willis in *Die Hard* (1988), one of the decade's best action pictures. He followed it up early in 1990 with the screen adaptation of Tom Clancy's best-selling *The Hunt for Red October*.**

mercial enough to appeal to a huge audience. *The Untouchables* became the biggest hit of his career. He followed it up in 1989 with another in an increasingly long line of Vietnam films, *Casualties of War*, which co-starred the unlikely combination of Michael J. Fox and Sean Penn. At the beginning of the nineties, now comfortably part of the filmmaking establishment, he began work on the movie adaptation of Tom Wolfe's best-selling novel *The Bonfire of the Vanities*, co-starring Tom Hanks, Melanie Griffith and Bruce Willis.

The young turks from the UCLA film school who sat around eating hamburgers at Bob's Big Boy, sneering at the Gucci crowd lunching at Ma Maison, plotting how they were going to take over Hollywood and make films differently, had not only failed to take over Hollywood, or make films differently, but inadvertently had made the industry more conservative than ever, and less open to change.

Everything became much more commercial, everything had to appeal to the widest possible audience. You were as good as the last picture you made that grossed over $100 million. This preoccupation with the huge profits provided by commercial adolescent entertainments left a lot of great talents floundering. Arthur Penn, who made *Bonnie and Clyde* in the sixties, could do no better in the eighties than an action picture called *Target*. Robert Altman, one of the most prolific and innovative directors of the seventies, after the failure of *Popeye* in 1980, made mostly low-budget adaptations of stage plays. John Schlesinger, the British director who did *Darling* and *Midnight Cowboy* in the sixties could find no place for himself in the Hollywood of the eighties. His attempt to bring his talents to a commercial horror film, *The Believers,* was a dismal failure. Roman Polanski, who made *Rosemary's Baby* and *Chinatown,* had to flee to Paris in order to escape charges of having sex with a minor. Far away from Hollywood in the eighties, he could do no better than a lovely adaptation of Thomas Hardy's *Tess of the D'Urbervilles,* and then a large-budget adventure, *Pirates,* that misfired, followed by a modern-day thriller, *Frantic,* that failed to attract audiences despite the presence of Harrison Ford. Even Blake Edwards, the veteran comedy director (the *Pink Panther* comedies, *10*) who had survived numerous Hollywood fire fights, appeared wearied in the eighties. In over 40 years in Hollywood, he had made close to 50 movies, and in 1982, he managed to score with *Victor/Victoria.* But trouble followed. There were three box office flops in a row: *Trail of the Pink Panther, Micki and Maude* and *A Fine Mess.* He sued MGM/UA, a studio with whom he had fought a number of times

Blake Edwards on the set of *Victor/Victoria* (1982) with Julie Andrews.

over the years, for $146 million. MGM/UA then countersued claiming he had misspent the budget for *Victor/Victoria.* He began directing *Kansas City Jazz,* co-starring Clint Eastwood and Burt Reynolds, then had a falling-out with Eastwood, and left the project. The movie was finished by director Richard Benjamin and released under the title *City Heat.* Blake Edwards' screenplay credit read "Sam O. Brown" — *S.O.B.,* the title of his 1981 satire about Hollywood.

When Edwards turned 60, he suffered a late mid-life crisis, then turned the experience into a movie, *That's Life!* He then proceeded to make two more failures, *Sunset* and *Skin Deep.* The roller coaster ride of the eighties left him rueful: "My wife (the actress Julie Andrews)

John Hughes started as a screenwriter (*Mr. Mom,* 1984) but quickly became the decade's most successful director of teen-oriented comedy dramas (*Sixteen Candles,* 1984, *The Breakfast Club,* 1985, *Pretty in Pink,* 1986). By the end of the decade he had successfully moved away from teenagers into more adult-oriented comedy.

***Below*: George Roy Hill, seen here with Robin Williams, was one of the most powerful directors of the seventies. In the eighties his power waned. He did carefully mounted adaptations of two bestsellers, *The World According to Garp* (1982) and *The Little Drummer Girl* (1984), neither of which was successful. Incongruously, he then directed a comedy titled *Funny Farm* (1988).**

Above: Ridley Scott, with Michael Douglas, made his feature debut with _The Duellists_ in 1977, but it was his direction of _Alien_ in 1979 that established his visual style. He worked throughout the eighties in a series of action pictures — _Blade Runner_ (1982), _Someone to Watch over Me_ (1987) and _Black Rain_ (1989) — that had more to do with style than with substance.

Below: Arthur Penn, with actor Matt Dillon, directed the classic gangster movie, _Bonnie and Clyde_ in 1967, and was one of the most respected directors in the business. But in the eighties, the best he could do was an action thriller called _Target_ (1985).

keeps a diary, and one day I said, 'Jeesh, why do I feel like this? Really miserable.' And she said, 'I'll tell you why. Let me read.' And she read over the past year, and when you read it condensed, I mean, my God! It's a wonder I didn't jump off a roof somewhere."

The British director David Lean, who made two of the greatest epics of modern cinema, *The Bridge on the River Kwai* (1957) and *Lawrence of Arabia* (1962), lay quiet for 15 years after *Ryan's Daughter* did not fare well in 1970 with either the critics or the public. Finally, in December 1984, at the age of 76, he was back on the screen with an adaptation of *A Passage to India*, E.M. Forster's 1924 novel. He wrote the screenplay, directed it on arduous locations

Peter O'Toole in _Lawrence of Arabia_ (1962), re-released in 1989. _Opposite_: David Lean on the set of _A Passage to India_ (1984).

in India, then edited the whole film himself. The movie was extravagantly received by critics; old slights were forgotten; and Lean was fashionable again, particularly after the re-release of the restored and re-edited *Lawrence of Arabia*. At the age of 80, Lean was planning a new movie, Joseph Conrad's *Nostromo*.

THERE WERE DIRECTORS WHO THRIVED WITHIN the confines of the Hollywood system. Their vision of things came from innocence and old movies; their abilities evolved from a willingness to meticulously utilize the various wonders of technology to rework what already had been done. Mostly they were young, male, and usually either inspired or hired — or both — by Spielberg and Lucas: Robert Zemeckis (*Back to the Future, Who Framed Roger Rabbit*), Joe Dante (*Gremlins*), Ron Howard (*Cocoon, Parenthood*), Tim Burton (*Beetlejuice, Batman*), Rob Reiner (*Princess Bride* and *When Harry Met Sally . . .*), John Hughes (*Sixteen Candles; Breakfast Club; Planes, Trains and Autombiles*), and, a trifle older than the others, Richard Donner (*Ladyhawke, Lethal Weapon, Scrooged*) and John Badham (*WarGames, Blue Thunder, Stakeout*).

The veteran Sydney Pollack, a throwback to the old style of commercial director, who in the eighties made *Tootsie* and *Out of Africa*.

CAM 17

***Above*: Sydney Pollack, on the set of *Out of Africa* (1985) with Meryl Streep.**

***Below*: Sergio Leone established a name for himself with the so-called spaghetti westerns of the sixties. He spent years putting together the financing for what was to be his epic gangster movie, *Once upon a Time in America*. When the film was finally completed, Warner Bros. completely re-edited it for North American release in 1984. Leone died in 1989.**

Pollack had an unabashed love of movie stars and star-driven vehicles. "I am lazy," he said. "I read a picture and I see a movie star. Maybe if I'd started differently, I'd have developed differently. But the first movie I ever did had two stars in it. To me, growing up in Indiana, everybody in the movies was a movie star. Debra Paget was a movie star in South Bend."

IF THERE WERE *AUTEURS* DURING THE EIGHTIES, they could often be found among the stars themselves, who increasingly turned to directing. The trend started with Robert Redford, usually snubbed as an actor, who got an Oscar in 1980 the first time he stepped behind the camera to bring *Ordinary People* to the screen. The urge to give actors Oscars for directing spilled over into the following year when Warren Beatty, whose acting talents for the most part went unnoticed, was given an Academy Award for *Reds.*

Danny DeVito, having established himself as one of the decade's most popular comic actors (in *Romancing the Stone*, *Jewel of the*

Nile and *Twins)* made an impressive debut with *Throw Momma from the Train*, then followed it with the even more impressive *The War of the Roses*.

Even Eddie Murphy decided to get in on the act. "Directors have egos, and really big directors have huge egos," Eddie Murphy said, explaining why he directed *Harlem Nights*. "Most directors, when they become stars, don't want to work with big, big actors, and I want to get a big director and get moving fast, these directors aren't available for three years. Only schleppers are available. Rather than get a half-assed job, I figured I might as well do it myself."

Oliver Stone and the Return of the Maverick

NOT QUITE ALL WAS LOST IN THE EIGHTIES. There remained tough, iconoclastic directors, who delighted in jabbing and tilting at the strait-laced commercialism of movies, who worked the edges of the system and made the movies they wanted to make. Nobody was a more committed maverick than a former screenwriter named Oliver Stone. One morning, in the fall of 1985, he sat eating breakfast. He had recently returned from the Philippines where he had been shooting a movie called *Platoon*, about his Vietnam experiences.

He laughed and poured himself some coffee, recalling the first movie he ever directed, a low-budget horror flick called *Seizure* which he did for producer Roger Corman.

"It was in 1972, outside Montreal in the lake country," Stone said, as he put down the coffee pot. "It was a film with Martine Beswick from the Hammer films and Herve Villechaize from *Fantasy Island*. And we shot it for nothing practically; we ended up running out of money, and giving the film away for some cash. It was one of those tax shelter deals in Canada. They were just interested in taking the loss, so it was never really distributed."

Stone was friendly, but nevertheless, there was something dangerous and threatening about him. His thinning black hair flopped across his forehead; his beard was a constant five o'clock shadow; his eyes were dead pools, flashing occasional hints of deep-seated anger. He had been born in New York City. His father was a wealthy Jewish stockbroker; his mother was Catholic. His father, he later said, raised him as a Republican and instilled in him a fear of and loathing for Communism. He dropped out of Yale university, ended up spending time as a Catholic schoolteacher in Saigon in 1965, then worked as a merchant seaman to earn his way back to the U.S. He returned to Yale, only to drop out again, and this time

Above: **Mark Rydell, with Katharine Hepburn, was a former actor turned director. He didn't work much in the eighties, after he directed Hepburn along with Henry and Jane Fonda in *On Golden Pond* (1981).**

Below: **Feisty Martin Ritt, with actress Sally Field, was also a former actor. In his seventies and in ill-health, Ritt nonetheless kept working during the eighties, making *Cross Creek* (1983), *Murphy's Romance* (1985) and *Stanley and Iris*, released early in 1990.**

Danny DeVito was from Ashbury Park, New Jersey and grew up hiding the fact that he wanted to be an actor. He made his movie debut when producer Michael Douglas cast him in a small role in *One Flew over the*

Cuckoo's Nest (1975). He finally scored on the hit TV series, *Taxi* playing the nasty dispatcher Louis DePalma. He had a role in *Terms of Endearment* (1983), but he became a recognizable star name during the eighties — the little guy you loved to hate in hits such as *Romancing the Stone* (1984), *Ruthless People* (1986), *Tin Men* (1987) and *Twins* (1988). He made his debut as a director with *Throw Momma from the Train* (1987), but it was with his next picture, *The War of the Roses* (1989), *insert,* that he demonstrated a particularly dark streak of comic genius.

Actor Dennis Hopper made *Easy Rider* (1969), the pivotal film of the counter-culture era. Thereafter, his addiction to drugs and alcohol nearly cost him his career as well as his life. In the eighties, he pulled himself together, and got a chance to direct a gritty thriller called *Colors* (1988). It was a success, and Hopper found his career revived.

***Below*: Oliver Stone in the Philippines on the set of *Platoon* (1986).**

enlisted in the army. He would fight the good, patriotic fight against the communist menace. He was sent to Vietnam in 1967, was shot in the neck and won a Bronze Star for blowing up a machine-gun nest. His emotions were contradictory and confusing. "I saved a girl from rape and getting killed once," he said later, "and then, at the same time, I'd be furious and want to kill some old man. At first, I was completely paralyzed when I saw the enemy. At the end, I got to be a good soldier. But I was just trying to get out in one piece."

Back in the States, 14 months later, he was "very mixed up, very paranoid, very alienated." Against his father's wishes, he enrolled in New York University's film program, where one of his instructors was Martin Scorsese. He wrote ten unproduced scripts before anyone took any notice of him. In 1972, Stone directed the schlock-horror *Seizure*. In 1978, he wrote the screenplay for *Midnight Express* and won an Academy Award. After that, he got a second chance to direct, another horror film called *The Hand* (Michael Caine being chased around by the title character — a dead hand). When *The*

Hand failed critically and financially, he wrote more screenplays: *Conan the Barbarian*, *Scarface* and *Year of the Dragon*. His scripts were scary, intense, violent. Stone never brushed the audience's shoulder; he clubbed it over the head or opened fire on it with a machine gun. He never hesitated to take everything over the top, and then some. Even in those days, you could not mistake his work for anyone else's. Oliver Stone was never going to be everyone's cup of tea. Sidney Lumet took one look at his *Scarface* script and refused to direct it.

Even as he became one of Hollywood's most successful screenwriters, Stone was not satisfied. He wanted to direct his own movies. Michael Cimino read one of the scripts Stone had written when he was trying to get started. It was titled *Platoon*, and Cimino was impressed enough that he made an arrangement with the producer, Dino De Laurentiis, whereby if Stone would write the movie adaptation of *Year of the Dragon* for the director, De Laurentiis would ensure that Stone could direct *Platoon*. In the summer of 1984, he was in the Philippines scouting locations when De Laurentiis announced that no American distributor would touch *Platoon* and he was dropping the project.

Stone was brokenhearted, but undaunted. He met an out-of-work journalist named Richard Boyle who was just back from the civil war in El Salvador. He and Stone wrote a script about the journalist's experiences in the country, called it *Salvador*, then persuaded a British producer named John Daly, who headed an independent production company called Hemdale, to finance it and allow Stone to direct. "I'd had it with the system, so to speak," Stone said. "Waiting around to do a movie the studios probably wouldn't have wanted to do anyway. I decided I just would do what *I* wanted to do, which was something extreme and radical."

Salvador, released in 1985, was harsh and enthralling — the civil war in El Salvador filtered through the red-rimmed eyes of a couple of doped-out freelance journalists: James Woods playing Boyle, and James Belushi as his disbelieving partner. *Salvador* was the promise of uncompromising things to come.

Hemdale, the British company that financed *Salvador*, decided to back Stone again, this time to make his dream movie — *Platoon*. One year later, in 1986, Stone was the hottest director in Hollywood, and *Platoon*, the film he had shot in the Philippines and based on his own experiences in Vietnam, had become a phenomenon, featured on the cover of *Time* magazine. Stone wasn't just another Hollywood director making a war movie; he was the real thing, a Vietnam vet who'd been there, and this was his voice telling (mostly) his story. As Steven Spielberg noted, *Platoon* was like being in Viet-

Age and failing health could not stop the legendary John Huston in the eighties. He directed everything from big glossy entertainment such as *Victory* (1981) and *Annie* (1982) to smaller more personal films, such as Malcolm Lowry's *Under the Volcano* (1984) and *Prizzi's Honor* (1985). He directed his last film at the age of 79, sitting in a wheelchair, attached to an oxygen tank. The movie was an adaptation of James Joyce's famous short story, *The Dead* (1987), and it was a wondrous, enchanting finale to a long and colorful career. Huston's legacy lived on, however, in his daughter, Anjelica, a highly respected actress, and in his son, Danny, *below*, who took his own turn at directing *Mr. North* (1988).

John Waters worked far from the mainstream of American film in order to create *Pink Flamingos* (1973) and *Polyester* (1981). After the release of *Polyester*, Waters slipped a little closer to the mainstream with *Hairspray* (1988), starring the transvestite, Divine, in his last role before he died, as the chubby girl who finally gets the man of her dreams. That was followed by *Cry-Baby*, released in 1990, starring Johnny Depp from television's *21 Jump Street*. It was described as "the ultimate juvenile delinquent story." As usual the casting was, to say the least, unique, featuring former porn star Traci Lords and kidnap victim Patty Hearst.

nam, and it made you feel like you never wanted to go back.

There had been other successful films about Vietnam (*The Deer Hunter*, *Apocalypse Now*) but *Platoon* somehow validated the war as a subject for the movies. Whereas Dino De Laurentiis only a few years before could not interest anyone in distributing *Platoon*, now everyone was planning their own Vietnam picture, among them, *Hamburger Hill*, *Full Metal Jacket*, *Gardens of Stone*, *Off Limits* and *Casualties of War*.

STONE ACCEPTED HIS OSCAR FOR BEST PICTURE of 1986 for *Platoon*, then went right out and shot another movie. This time he was taking on the greed and malaise of the eighties in *Wall Street*. "I wanted to go right away," he said, after the movie was completed. "Finally I got a shot here to make pictures my way — I don't have to compromise. This is the time to make pictures that normally cannot get made." In 1988, he directed a lacerating movie version of Eric Bogosian's off-Broadway success *Talk Radio*. Then he was back in the Philippines once again trying to come to terms with Vietnam, directing Tom Cruise in *Born on the Fourth of July*, based on the true story of a Long Island kid named Ron Kovic who was wounded in Vietnam and left paralyzed and confined to a wheelchair. *Born on the Fourth of July* was another of the scripts he previously couldn't get filmed. The movie had been four days away from production in 1978 with Al Pacino starring, when the financing fell apart. *Born on the Fourth of July*, released in 1989, won him his second Oscar for best director. "They say I'm unsubtle," Stone told the *New York Times*. "But we need, above all, a theater that wakes us up: nerves and heart.

Eric Bogosian in Oliver Stone's *Talk Radio* (1988).

"I'm in the face all the time," he continued. "Always in your face . . . I put my passion out there, my honest feelings, that's all I do. Some people like that, and some people feel it's too strong."

Stone remained proof that it was still possible to work against the grain in American film, but he was one of the few who could. The studio system could tolerate the odd iconoclast — but just barely.

DAVID LYNCH EXISTED UNEASILY WITHIN THE movie establishment. He was lanky, sandy-haired, fresh-faced, a disconcertingly average native of Missoula, Montana, who happened to see things a little differently. Mel Brooks described him as "Jimmy Stewart from Mars." *Newsweek* magazine reported, "He's fascinated by human organs; when one of his producers underwent a hysterectomy, he made her promise to send him her uterus."

But there was, thankfully, more to Lynch than his bizarre fascination with the uterus. His low-budget independently made *Eraserhead*, a surrealistic black-and-white movie that became a cult sensation in 1977, was such an astonishing debut that Mel

Above: Director David Lynch on the set of _Dune_ (1984).

Below: The Coen Brothers, Joel, _left_, and Ethan, _right_, raised the money they needed to make their first movie, _Blood Simple_ (1984). It was a cult hit, and led to the brothers' next film, a comedy titled _Raising Arizona_ (1987). In 1990, the brothers turned out a gangster movie titled _Miller's Crossing_.

Above**: Ron Howard was another actor turned director. Best known as Opie on TV's *****The Andy Griffith Show*****, Howard got his start directing low-budget movies for Roger Corman. He graduated to bigger and better things with *****Splash***** (1984), *****Cocoon***** (1985) and *****Parenthood***** (1989). He's seen here with George Lucas and members of the cast of *****Willow***** (1988).**

Below**: Richard Benjamin, standing with actor Peter O'Toole, starred in such successes as *****Goodbye Columbus***** (1969) and *****Portnoy's Complaint***** (1972), before turning to directing during the eighties. His best picture was a comedy titled *****My Favorite Year***** (1982).**

Brooks immediately gave him a chance to direct *The Elephant Man.* The 1980 movie, also shot in black and white, was based on the life of the horribly disfigured John Merrick, who became known in Victorian London society as "The Elephant Man." It was a success, and Lynch found himself nominated for two Academy Awards (best director and best screenplay adaptation), a sure sign of acceptance by the Hollywood establishment. In Hollywood, acceptance is rewarded with trust, and trust means money and a very big picture. Sure enough, Lynch was hired by producer Dino De Laurentiis to direct the $50-million film version of the science fiction epic *Dune*. Released in 1984, *Dune* was a disaster of such immense proportions that it was to haunt Lynch for the remainder of the decade. "That was a dark time for me" he remembered later.

But he got right back behind a camera. Using a comparatively minuscule $5 million of De Laurentiis's money, Lynch retreated to what he knew best and made *Blue Velvet* (1986), one of the most bizarrely original pictures in years. It was a dark, unsettling detective story set in a small all-American town called Lumberton ("so get those chainsaws out," encourages the local DJ). Lynch had an uncanny ability to draw the most bizarre images from the most middle-class values of American life. The more normal things seemed, the more peculiar they became in his hands. The movie featured one of the weirdest performances ever seen from Dennis Hopper as he played a sadomasochistic bad guy, Frank, who liked to inhale from an oxygen mask and call out for his mommy each time he forced sex on Isabella Rossellini. Rossellini, the daughter of the late Ingrid Bergman, played perhaps the most battered and traumatized woman ("Hit me! Hit me!") in the history of movies. For years she could not do an interview without being asked, often in some horror, about the role (Rossellini took the questions in stride, in part because she was, by that time, involved in a relationship with Lynch).

Kyle MacLachlan and Isabella Rossellini in *****Blue Velvet*** (1986).**

After *Blue Velvet*, Lynch should have been off and running with one of the most interesting careers of the era. But De Laurentiis went bankrupt, tying up several of Lynch's scripts. He wasn't able to get another film underway until the end of the decade, when he produced an ABC television mini-series, *Twin Peaks*, that became something of a phenomenon in the spring of 1990; and a new feature film, *Wild at Heart*, described by co-star Nicolas Cage as "Elvis and Marilyn in hell."

SPIKE LEE SEEMED TO HAVE NO TROUBLE AT ALL getting his films made. He was the decade's most controversial and successful African American filmmaker. ("To a whole lot of black folk," wrote Greg Tate in *Premiere* magazine, "Spike Lee is more than merely a filmmaker. He's a *cause célèbre.*" Lee was a good example of what could still be accomplished at arm's length from Hollywood. His first feature, *She's Gotta Have It*, a delightful comedy about a young woman who kept three increasingly jealous lovers in a state of agitation with her free-spirited lifestyle, was shot on Lee's home turf in Brooklyn Heights, with an all-black cast, on a budget of just $150,000. When it was first shown at the Cannes Film Festival in 1986, it became the most talked-about American film at the festival. Lee did his next movie, *School Daze*, for a major studio, Columbia Pictures, and, despite the fact the studio refused to give the picture much of a release, it still managed to become its most profitable picture of 1988.

Lee's most contentious film was released in the summer of 1989. *Do the Right Thing* was an investigation of the roots of racial violence in a ghetto neighborhood. The film was inspired by an incident in New York's Howard Beach in which a gang of whites chased three black youths. One of the youths was killed. "I was pissed. I was angry," Lee told journalist Bart Mills. "Here was 1989, in what's supposed to be the most liberal city in the world, New York City, and here are these three young black men, and they got attacked because they were in the wrong neighborhood."

Do the Right Thing was just about the only film made during the eighties that tried to deal with the race problem in the United States. Despite its controversial subject matter — or perhaps because of it — it became an unexpected hit in the summer of 1989. "I have the best of both worlds, because I'm an independent filmmaker, but I don't have to scrape around for money," he said. "I go directly to Hollywood for my financing. It doesn't mess with my creativity because I have the final cut and the control that I would have had if I raised the money all by myself. I'd still have to go to Hollywood

Above: Jim Henson brought Kermit the frog, Miss Piggy and the Muppet gang from television to the movies in the eighties, beginning with _The Great Muppet Caper_ (1979), and continuing with _The Muppets Take Manhattan_ (1984). Henson was less successful with such non-Muppets movie ventures as _The Dark Crystal_ (1983), although he was involved in the making of _Teenage Mutant Ninja Turtles_ at the time of his death early in 1990, at the age of 53.

Below: The veteran Fred Zinnemann (_High Noon_, _From Here to Eternity_) made only one movie during the eighties, a curious drama called _Five Days One Summer_ (1982), about an older man's lust for a young woman during a climbing holiday in the Swiss Alps in the 1930s.

for distribution anyway — there's just no way I'm going to reach the people I want to reach carrying a film can under my arm and going from theater to theater across the country . . . The studios want to make as much money off you as possible, basically just pump you. Yet it is possible to keep your agenda and make films too."

At the 1989 Cannes Film Festival, Lee's *Do the Right Thing* was unexpectedly overshadowed by another independent American film that became one of the most dramatic examples of how a filmmaker could work outside the system, not spend a lot of money, and still attract a lot of attention.

Sex, lies, and videotape had been shot by a 26-year-old filmmaker, Steven Soderbergh from Baton Rouge, Louisiana, who had never shot a feature before, and was made on a budget of just $1.2 million. The movie dealt with a philandering lawyer (Peter Gallagher), his beautiful but miserable young wife (Andie MacDowell) and the

Peter Gallagher and Andie MacDowell in *sex, lies, and videotape* (1989).

ways that their lives are disrupted by the arrival of an old friend (James Spader) who is impotent and who likes to videotape women talking about the intimate details of their sex lives.

"I went through a period of my life where I behaved very much like the Peter Gallagher character," Soderbergh admitted. "Once I got clear of that, I became obsessed with how and why that happened." The screenplay for the film took shape, he said, during an eight-day drive from Baton Rouge to Los Angeles.

To everyone's surprise, Soderbergh's movie won the prestigious Palme d'Or at Cannes, beating out, among others, *Do the Right Thing.* Lee was furious, but it made no difference: Soderbergh, rightly or wrongly, was the flavor of the moment. Back in North America, *sex, lies, and videotape* grossed nearly $25 million, which, considering how little it cost to make, was a huge profit. The whole experience left Soderbergh in a daze. "Nobody involved in the movie could have predicted this," he said.

Michael Moore mortgaged his house in order to make *Roger and Me* (1989), about his search for General Motors president Roger Smith, and it became the most successful and controversial documentary ever released by a major studio.

***Below*: Paul Newman stepped behind the camera to direct *Harry and Son* (1984), and a film adaptation of Tennessee Williams' *The Glass Menagerie* (1987).**

***Opposite*: Spike Lee on the set of *Do the Right Thing* (1989).**

MONEY AND GREED

THE BUSINESS OF MOVIES

Wall Street **(1987), the quintessential 1980s movie about big business, money and greed, featured Michael Douglas as a modern-day robber baron named Gordon Gekko. Director Oliver Stone and his co-writer Stanley Weiser drew on a number of Wall Street traders, including Michael Milken and Ivan Boesky, both of whom, like Gekko, ran afoul of laws against insider trading, the major business sin of the decade.**

The business of Hollywood had always been business, but never did that business receive so much attention as it did in the eighties. Everyone became preoccupied with how much movies cost, how much stars earned, and who was in and who was out in the corporate hierarchy. The Hollywood power brokers — the men who headed the studios, the independent producers who brought scripts to the studios for financing, the agents who put their stars, directors and writers together with the studios — these people became celebrities who were often written about as much as the actors appearing on the screen. Corporate Hollywood became a never-ending game of musical chairs during the decade: studios were bought and sold to high-rolling entrepreneurs who ran huge international conglomerates. Everyone complained about how much movies cost to make, and how much stars cost to hire, and how few profits there were after the bookkeepers were finished, but nobody did much about it. One movie executive did try, and the story of how he failed is also the story of money and greed, and Hollywood business in the eighties. . .

Make My Day: Clint Eastwood, playing the Dirty Harry role, *below*, that audiences liked him in best, may have been the richest actor in Hollywood in the eighties. While filming *Paint Your Wagon*, a mega-budget musical adaptation of the Lerner and Loewe Broadway hit, Eastwood was appalled at what he considered the waste of money going on around him. Determined to take his destiny more firmly in his hands, he formed his own production company, Malpaso, and produced his own movies (usually released through Warner Bros.). He directed much of his own material, kept his budgets low, shot fast, and at the end of the day retained ownership of his movies.

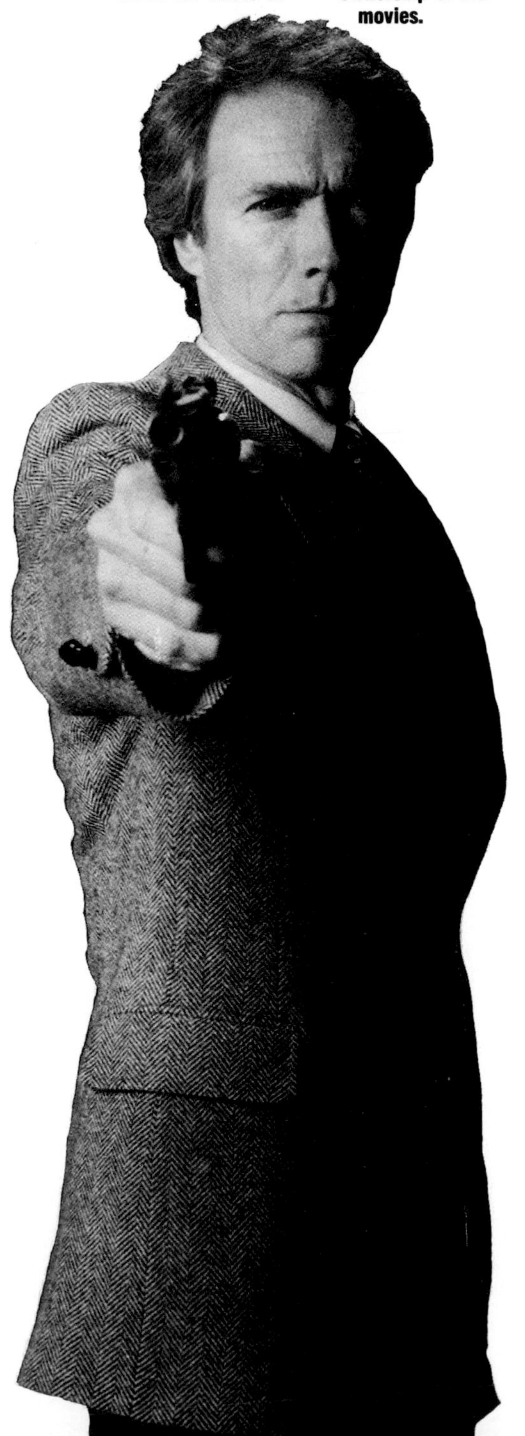

IN MAY OF 1986, THE BRITISH PRODUCER DAVID Puttnam sat in his hotel suite at the Cannes Film Festival, promoting not only his latest production, a $25-million epic titled *The Mission*, but also his views on Hollywood and what was wrong with it. He disliked intensely the way Hollywood did business. The escalating cost of movies and their stars, the huge international profits some movies were capable of generating, was attracting increasing attention. Hollywood was as famous for its greed and its profligacy as it was for its hit movies.

Puttnam, at the age of 45, looked more like a gentle English professor than a successful international film producer. He was small, bearded, and quietly outspoken. He had developed something of a reputation as a walking time bomb, possessed of a tongue that could explode at any time. His talent and determination had produced the sort of ambitiously high-minded pictures that Hollywood ordinarily shunned. Puttnam had made *Midnight Express* in 1978 about a young American imprisoned in a Turkish jail, and it had become an international hit, although he later was to denounce the film and the way he said it glorified violence. As a kind of antidote to *Midnight Express*, he produced *Chariots of Fire*, about two British runners, one a Scottish Christian and the other a British Jew, at the 1924 Olympics — not exactly the sort of subject matter considered to be surefire at the box office. To everyone's surprise, not only did *Chariots of Fire* become a hit (thanks in no small part to the film's evocative score by the composer Vangelis), but it quite unexpectedly won the Academy Award for best picture in 1981. Puttnam next had gone on to make *The Killing Fields* (1984), about a *New York Times* reporter searching for a friend in war-torn Cambodia. Now, as he sat in his hotel suite overlooking the harbor at Cannes, he had just completed work on his most ambitious film yet. *The Mission*, directed by Roland Joffe (who had also done *The Killing Fields*), dealt with the relationship between a Jesuit missionary, played by Jeremy Irons, and a Conquistador, portrayed by Robert De Niro, against the background of the Spanish and the Portuguese and their colonization of South America. It wasn't exactly Eddie Murphy as

Producer David Puttnam.

a cop in Beverly Hills. But then, David Puttnam did not make the movies other people made — mostly because David Puttnam did not *like* most of the films other people made, and he did not hesitate to say so.

"I know the ideas I live with and by," he said, sitting beside *The Mission's* co-producer, Fernando Ghia, "and the ideas that have stimulated just about everything in my life, I gained in the cinema between the ages of 10 and 18. And they were rich. They were the ideas given to me by Kazan and Rossellini and Renoir. The meal that was offered to me was fantastic. I feel sorry for kids of the last decade, because I think their diet has been very restricted, and I think they will have a lot of problems understanding the richness we took for granted."

The Mission had been a decade in the making, Puttnam maintained, because it did not follow any of the formulas. "I remember the week immediately following (the Oscar win of) *Chariots of Fire*, there was chaos in Hollywood — *chaos*, I'm happy to say — because they couldn't understand it. It didn't fit anywhere. Why were people seeing this movie? Instead of being thrilled, they were puzzled.

The Mission **(1986) was the sort of plodding, well-meaning big budget effort that Hollywood avoided during the eighties, but foreign producers were willing to spend years getting them off the ground. The Italian producer Fernando Ghia became fascinated with the clash between the Spanish and the Portuguese in 18th-century South America. He hired screenwriter Robert Bolt (*Lawrence of Arabia*) to write a slow but literate screenplay, then failed to raise financing for the next 10 years until he became involved with the British producer David Puttnam. He helped get the movie made, with Roland Joffe directing, and featuring Robert De Niro, *above, left*, as a conquistador and slave trader named Mendoza. The movie was seen as a well-meaning, liberal-minded follow-up to *The Killing Fields*, also produced by Puttnam and directed by Joffe. *The Mission* managed to win the prestigious *Palme d'Or* at the Cannes Film Festival, and although it came weighted down with importance, it did not do particularly well at the box office, and did not encourage Hollywood to make more period epics.**

Chariots of Fire (1981) was one of the phenomenons of the decade. It was David Puttnam who originated the idea for a film based on the true story of the Scottish missionary Eric Liddell, who competed against the Jewish Harold Abrahams at the 1924 Olympics. He persuaded Canadian film financier Jake Eberts to put up the $50,000 development money for the script, then brought in billionaire Mohammed El Fayed to finance actual production of the film. Even so, *Chariots of Fire* was produced on a limited budget. It's director, Hugh Hudson, had directed commercials but had never before done a feature film, and the movie's two stars, Ben Cross, *insert*, and Ian Charleson, were newcomers. To the amazement of everyone, the movie not only grossed over $30 million at the North American box office, a record for a foreign picture at the time, but went on to win the 1981 Academy Award for best picture.

***Above*: Even the presence of big box office stars did not always guarantee the success of a picture. *Family Business* (1989) starred the supposedly surefire combination of Sean Connery, Matthew Broderick and Dustin Hoffman, as three generations of crooks.**

***Below*: Francis Coppola talked for over two decades of making a movie based on the true story of the inventor who took on the Big Three automakers of Detroit in the late forties, and was, according to Coppola at least, destroyed because he dared to be a maverick. Coppola finally realized his dream to make *Tucker: The Man and His Dream* in 1988, thanks to his friend George Lucas, who acted as producer and insisted on taking on a rather unconvincingly happy ending to the story. It turned out, however, that no one was interested in Coppola's dream.**

It was very inconvenient."

Puttnam didn't believe that the success of a *Chariots of Fire* or *The Killing Fields* was persuading Hollywood to make more films of substance — all those successes were doing was causing Hollywood to hire the people who made them. "So buy the person, and you solve the problem."

The words proved to be prophetic. Moments later the telephone rang, and David Puttnam rose to take the call. "I'm sorry," he said. "I've got to take this. We've been ringing each other for three days." He slipped into an adjacent room and picked up the receiver. David Puttnam was in the process of being offered a job as the head of a Hollywood studio. As the new chairman and chief executive officer of Columbia Pictures, he would not only shake up his own admittedly rather complacent life, but briefly shake up the entire American film industry as well.

MOVIES IN THE EIGHTIES WOULD ESCALATE from an average cost of $10 million in 1980 to more than $23 million in 1989. An intricately mounted, star-driven action picture of the sort that became an industry staple during the decade cost anywhere from $40 to $50 million. Movie star salaries became astronomical: Sylvester Stallone received $12 million to star in an arm-wrestling picture called *Over the Top*. In 1989, *Forbes* magazine would estimate Eddie Murphy's income at $57 million. But that was nothing compared to director Steven Spielberg, who was making $105 million and was, next to singer Michael Jackson, the second-highest-paid entertainer in America. Jack Nicholson was said to be receiving $60 million as his share of the licensing and merchandising profits from his Joker character in *Batman*. Even a leading man such as Dennis Quaid,

Dennis Quaid and Jessica Lange in *Everybody's All-American* (1988).

with no hits to his credit, was earning $2 million a picture. Chevy Chase, in something of career slump toward the end of the decade, nevertheless got $6 million for *National Lampoon's Christmas Vacation*. Robert De Niro and Jane Fonda, two stars without box office hits through most of the eighties, received $4 million and $3 million respectively for *Stanley and Iris*, a drama about a schoolteacher teaching a blue-collar worker how to read. "We've got a lot of stars who are making $3 million to $7 million a picture," said Gary Lucchesi, president of Paramount Pictures, "and they will normally be attracted to a director who's making $2 million. If your screenplay works quickly, your screenplay and producer cost another $1 million altogether. Otherwise, it's a million dollars for the screenplay alone if it needs lots of revisions. Cast a second lead, and you may be at $18 million before you even start shooting."

If movies had never been more expensive to make, conversely, they had never been more profitable, although not necessarily at the box office, which, on average produced only about one-third of a movie's revenues. The rest came from ancillaries such as video

Above: Cannon Films paid Sylvester Stallone a record $12 million to star in a movie about, of all things, arm-wrestling. _Over the Top_ (1987) didn't even earn back Stallone's salary, let alone go over the top.

Don Simpson and Jerry Bruckheimer became one of the hottest production teams in Hollywood after the release of _Flashdance_ (1983) and _Beverly Hills Cop_ (1984). But they didn't always hit the bull's-eye. _Thief of Hearts_ (1984), _right_, starring newcomer Steven Bauer, fizzled at the box office.

and television. Even so, getting your money back was often a long, slow process. If the average movie cost $20 million, then by the time marketing (average $7 million) and studio overhead ($3 million) were added, the cost had risen to $30 million. On average, a film made about $30 million at the box office, and the studio got to keep a little less than half, or about $13 million of what are known as rentals. Distribution outside the North American market might bring in another $6 million. That meant that the $11-million shortfall would have to be made up by the ancillary sales: an average of $9 million from a video sale, and a further $2 million from cable television. Given all that, real profit for the $30-million movie would not occur until one of the American networks, three years or so down the line, kicked in with $3 million. That's a wait of almost five years from the inception of the project. Little wonder then that only the major studios with their fat credit lines could afford to play that kind of waiting game.

Consequently, the major studios increasingly made fewer movies, but made them bigger, concentrating on blockbuster hits that could rake in over $100 million at the box office. Hollywood bookkeeping, always suspect, remained arcane and duplicitous. A movie could earn hundreds of millions of dollars at the box office, yet the brilliance of accounting could keep it safely in the red. When the humorist Art Buchwald sued Paramount Pictures, claiming the studio had stolen an idea that eventually became *Coming to America* (1988), and not paid him properly, the studio argued that, even though the Eddie Murphy comedy had grossed $350 million worldwide, it had yet to show a profit. Hardly an eyebrow was raised at the news. Hollywood business was being conducted as usual. The American movie industry was, after all, a small, elite club of about 25,000 members. There were only eight major studios (Columbia, Disney, MGM/UA, Orion, Paramount, Twentieth Century-Fox, Universal and Warner Bros.), and although various independent producers had tried to challenge the majors over the years, and the studios themselves had been bought and sold and broken up and glued back together with a ferocious regularity, that essential truth had not changed since the 1920s. The major studios controlled the all-important distribution. Although they often acted more as bankers than the big entertainment factories most of them had started out as, very little was distributed without their say. In 1988, the studios produced fewer than a third of the movies released, yet these films accounted for 80 percent of the box office receipts. What's more, studio product predominated in movie theaters around the world. Membership in the movie club did not come easily. There was a way of doing things, and no one was anxious to change those ways.

Above: Cannon Films made some very curious decisions during the eighties. For example, it made two versions of a book titled _52 Pick-up_ by American crime novelist Elmore Leonard. One version was called _52 Pick-up_ (1986) and starred Ann-Margret and Roy Scheider.

Opposite: Jane Fonda and Robert De Niro co-starred in _Stanley and Iris_ (1990), a movie about a woman teaching a man how to read. The cost of the lessons was high: De Niro earned $4 million, Fonda took home $3 million.

Below: Next to _Heaven's Gate_ (1981), the movie that stood most for a Hollywood disaster in the eighties was _Ishtar_ (1987), starring Warren Beatty and Dustin Hoffman.

Universal studios was founded in 1912 by Carl Laemmle. In the thirties it was known for its horror pictures, in the forties for Arabian nights adventure pictures, in the fifties and the sixties for a series of slickly produced bedroom farces, and in the seventies for big budget disaster movies. In the eighties, however, the studio's image became less certain. Under Frank Price, Universal produced a big budget hit like *Out of Africa* (1985), *below*, starring Meryl Streep and Robert Redford. But it was also responsible for one of the decade's major disasters, *Howard the Duck* (1986), *opposite, below*. The movie's failure caused Frank Price to lose his job and inspired this classic *Variety* headline: "Duck Cooks Price's Goose." When a former lawyer named Tom Pollock took over the studio in 1986, Universal's fortunes began to improve. Among the hits Pollock helped to green light was *Uncle Buck*, *opposite, above*, a John Hughes comedy that became a sleeper hit in the late summer of 1989.

It was one thing to say movies cost too much to make — everyone agreed that was true — it was another thing entirely to do anything about it, particularly since the club members made astronomical amounts of money from the very movies that cost too much.

Hollywood was in love with money and power. If greed was good in American business during the eighties, greed had never been better in Hollywood. Everyone wanted more, not less. David Puttnam wanted to give everyone in Hollywood precisely what they didn't want — he wanted to give them less.

Puttnam's appointment as chairman/CEO of Columbia Pictures was made in late June of 1986. He did little to allay anyone's fears at his first press conference. He made no bones about the fact that he still thought movies cost too much to make, and that the movie audience was being ill-served by Hollywood. "Maybe I'm being naive, maybe I'm going to get the most terrible shock in the coming years, but I do trust the audience. I think if you give them good films, they'll respond."

IN HOLLYWOOD, THE PEOPLE WHO RAN THE STUDIOS were known as "picture pickers." It was their job to say yes or no to the dozens of producers who arrived with scripts they wanted the studio to invest millions of dollars in to see turned into movies. How good a picker a studio boss turned out to be meant the difference between a studio's success or failure. For example, when a former lawyer named Tom Pollock became the picture picker at Universal studios in 1986, he was 46 years old and had little experience on the so-called creative side of running a studio. Universal, which was owned by the Music Corporation of America (MCA), had huge hits with *E.T.* and *Back to the Future.* For some years, it had not enjoyed nearly the same number of hits as were being produced at other studios in town, and had lived on profits from its film library. Although it had produced *Out of Africa,* Universal was better known recently as the studio that made *Howard the Duck* — a flop of titanic proportions. In the next two years — about the time it took for a new studio head's influence to be felt — Pollock turned Universal around, giving the go-ahead for the production of such 1988-89 successes as *Twins, Parenthood, Field of Dreams, Sea of Love* and *Uncle Buck*. Pollock, despite expectations to the contrary, had turned out to be a pretty good picture picker.

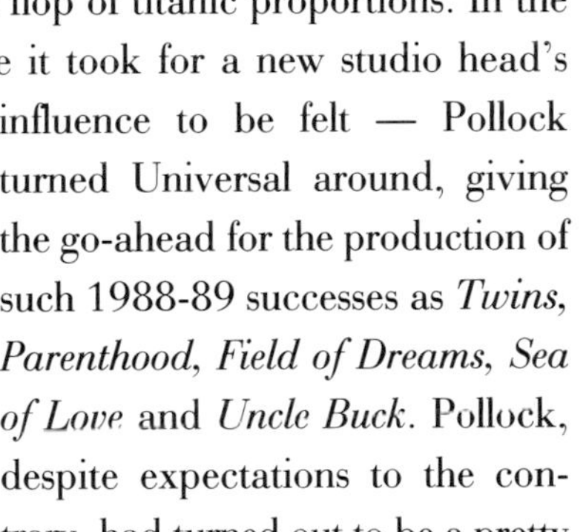

If David Puttnam knew anything when he arrived in Hollywood, he should have known that, whatever happened, he was not going to last long as the boss of a studio — a picture picker. No one did. The games of corporate musical chairs seemed as endless as they were unnecessary. For all the talk of a town gripped by the fear of failure, it didn't seem to matter on the executive level whether you succeeded or not. Either way, events — or a new owner — soon conspired to unseat you. In Hollywood, as the *Los Angeles Times* once pointed out, everybody fights everybody sooner or later.

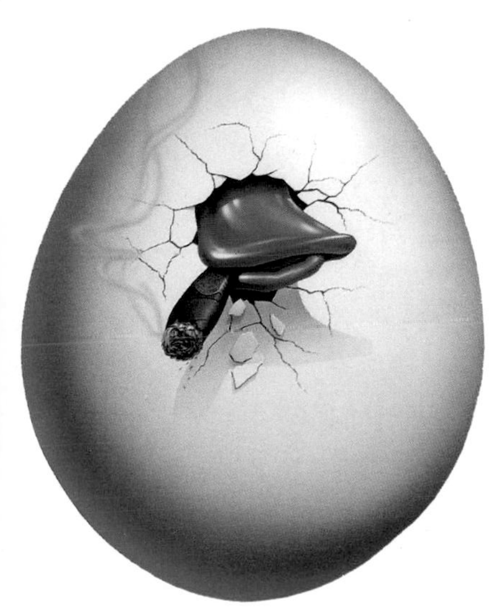

Above: One of the best commercial hits produced by the Disney studio was _Stakeout_ (1987), starring Richard Dreyfuss and Emilio Estevez.

Below: When the studio broke away from the comedy-action formula it tended to take the same chances as everyone else. Disney's Touchstone Pictures released _Blaze_ at Christmas of 1989, and not even the prospect of Newman doing the first steamy love scene of his long career could induce audiences to see it.

Below**: Anthony Hopkins played a more kindly Captain Bligh in yet another remake of *****The Mutiny on the Bounty***** story, this one titled *****The Bounty***** (1984), and co-starring Mel Gibson as Fletcher Christian. The movie was produced by Dino De Laurentiis, who originally intended to make two movies out of the story, both of them directed by David Lean, and written by Robert Bolt. But then De Laurentiis ran out of money, as he has a number of times throughout his long production career, and the two movies became one, directed not by Lean but by New Zealand's Roger Donaldson. It flopped at the box office.**

Opposite**: Tanya Roberts had co-starred in the final year of TV's *****Charlie's Angels***** before being cast in the title role of *****Sheena, Queen of the Jungle***** (1984), the first movie green lighted by Guy McElwaine when he arrived at Columbia Pictures. Sheena was supposed to ride a zebra in the movie, but unfortunately no zebra had ever been ridden, so a little horse had to be properly painted.**

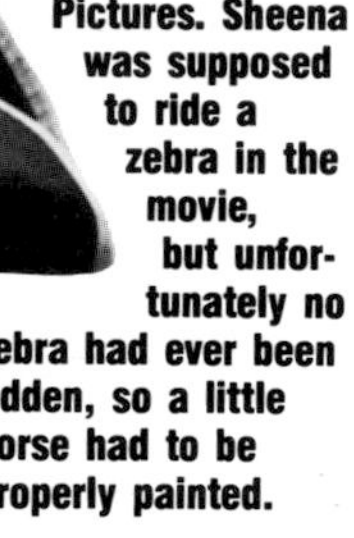

Columbia had come to Puttnam via a long and complicated road which began in 1977, when it was discovered that David Begelman, the production executive credited with turning the troubled studio around, had embezzled $10,000. The resulting scandal shook Columbia, resulted in Begelman's resignation, and the firing of Alan Hirschfield, the president and chief executive officer of Columbia Pictures Industries. Hirschfield was to become the hero of *Wall Street Journal* reporter David McClintick's book on the scandal, *Indecent Exposure: A True Story of Hollywood and Wall Street.*

In 1982, Coca-Cola, the soft-drink conglomerate, bought Columbia Pictures Industries for $750 million. A year later, Frank Price, the production head who had overseen *Ghostbusters*, the biggest hit in the studio's history, resigned, feeling that his power as studio chief was being eroded. He was replaced by a former professional baseball player and agent named Guy McElwaine, who decided to make something called *Sheena, Queen of the Jungle.* McElwaine somewhat redeemed himself with *The Karate Kid*, and he formed strong alliances with filmmakers such as Lawrence Kasdan, Norman Jewison and Warren Beatty. Even so, by early 1986, McElwaine was gone, and the search was on for a new studio chief. Shortly after Puttnam had been chosen for the job, he made it clear that he wasn't going to be like other movie executives. He stated that if they had come to him with a proposal to make *Rambo II*, he would have turned it down flat. At this point, the foot-shuffling started, the nervous coughing commenced. What was Hollywood to do with a man who wouldn't make *Rambo II*?

The Karate Kid **(1984): Ralph Macchio and Pat Morita.**

EXECUTIVES IN HOLLYWOOD MIGHT NOT KEEP their jobs long, but that wasn't to say they didn't find other executive positions. David Begelman was a good example of what happened. If he could find another job, then presumably anyone could. Sure enough, the ousted and shamed production executive at Columbia hopped across town to MGM, where he became head of production. Shortly thereafter, MGM's controlling shareholder, Kirk Kerkorian, after failing to take control of Begelman's old studio, Columbia Pictures, purchased United Artists, which was still reeling from *Heaven's Gate*. The company that brought Hollywood its biggest

British television and movie producer Lord Lew Grade (he became known as "Low Grade") made a bid for international movie respectability via an independent production company called ITC whose North American distribution arm was known as Associated Film (AFD). Instead of gaining respectability, however, Grade ended up turning out some of the decade's biggest turkeys.

Above: Neil Diamond made his movie debut in a remake of *The Jazz Singer* (1980), in which he reprised the old Al Jolson role with Laurence Olivier, of all people, playing his father.

Right: Jason Robards didn't sink the Titanic he merely held it in *Raise the Titanic* (1980), a megabudget adventure-disaster picture, based on a best-selling novel by Clive Cussler. The author was so upset by the resulting movie that he refused to allow any more of his books to be filmed.

Remember the singing group known as The Village People? If you do, then perhaps you were among the unfortunate few who saw *Can't Stop the Music* (1980). The disco group who sang "YMCA" co-starred with actress Valerie Perrine, *center*, in ITC's attempt at a big budget musical, produced by Allan Carr, the man who brought *Grease* to the screen. The whole thing was a mess, featuring disco-oriented music that was out of fashion before the picture was released.

Finally, ITC tried its hand at a comic strip movie, this one a western titled *The Legend of the Lone Ranger* (1981), *below*. Tonto was played by a native American named Michael Horse while the Masked Rider was played by an unknown 25-year-old named Klinton Spilsbury, who had acted only twice before in his life. His voice turned out to be so inadequate that it had to be dubbed by actor Stacy Keach.

Not all box office flops during the eighties were artistic disasters. Under David Begelman, MGM turned *Pennies from Heaven* (1981) into a big budget musical directed by Herbert Ross and starring Steve Martin, whose only previous film had been a lowbrow comedy titled *The Jerk* (1979). *Pennies from Heaven* was a darkly original musical, but Martin's audience was completely unprepared for their idol's startling transformation, and stayed away.

disaster and the man who created its biggest scandal were now together. Neither one was doing very well. Kerkorian eventually amalgamated the two companies into a single entity: MGM/UA Entertainment Company. David Begelman, meanwhile, had put together an unprecedented string of box office flops (*Pennies from Heaven, All the Marbles, Cannery Row*, among them). Begelman was finished at MGM/UA, not because he was crooked, but because he couldn't make profitable pictures.

MGM/UA stumbled along through most of the eighties, until finally, Kerkorian, in early 1990, tried to sell it off for a whopping $1.2 billion, to a man named Giancarlo Parretti, described by *Variety* as "the Italian-born mystery man." Parretti, who said he started out washing plates, had already appeared on the Hollywood scene to buy the Cannon group, the troubled independent film company, and change its name to Pathé Communications.

At one point during a press conference at his home town of Orvieto, Italy, Parretti introduced one of his Pathé partners, Yoram Globus, to the press. He joked, "The thing me and Yoram have in common is that we're both from the Mafia." The comment was met with dead silence. Less than a month later, Parretti was convicted in an Italian court of fraudulent bankruptcy, a felony, and sentenced to a jail term of 46 months. Observers said his conviction was not likely to prevent him from taking possession of MGM/UA. They said it with a straight face. However, by mid 1990 Parretti was still trying to secure the deal, and in the meantime, a major Hollywood studio floundered as it never had before in its history.

MEANWHILE, ALAN HIRSCHFIELD, WHO HAD been squeezed out at Columbia in the wake of the Begelman scandal, soon reappeared at Twentieth Century-Fox, where he was named president of the company.

It quickly became apparent, however, that Hirschfield did not get along with Dennis Stanfill, Fox's chief executive officer. Texas oilman Marvin Davis inadvertently solved the problem when he purchased Fox for $722 million. Stanfill, fed up, resigned, leaving Hirschfield to become the company's chairman and chief executive officer.

In 1985, Davis brought in another high flyer, Australian press magnate Rupert Murdoch, to co-own the studio. Shortly thereafter, Murdoch bought out the entire studio, and Davis was gone. So, too, was Hirschfield. He was replaced by Barry Diller, who once ran Paramount Pictures. Diller, in turn, hired as production chief in 1986 a television producer named Leonard Goldberg. He lasted four years, and was replaced by Joe Roth, an independent producer (the successful Morgan Creek Productions) who was also a director, one of the few times in the history of Hollywood that a creative person had actually run a studio. As for what happened to Dennis Stanfill, there was speculation at one point that he would take over the troubled Disney organization, but the stiffly formal business executive was not that studio's sort of guy. The job of saving Disney would go to someone else.

Movies featuring stars on ships did not do well during the eighties.
***Above*: Roman Polanski launched *Pirates* in 1986 with Walter Matthau as a blustery Long John Silver-type varmint. The movie was shot under arduous conditions in Tunisia, with Polanski and Matthau fighting constantly. *Pirates* quickly sank with all hands on board.**
***Below*: Dino De Laurentiis brought a hilariously bad version of James Clavell's best-selling *Tai-Pan* to the screen in 1986, with Australian actor Bryan Brown in the lead. It became one of the big budget flops that helped drive De Laurentiis into bankruptcy by the end of the decade.**

Something Wicked This Way Comes (1983), starring British actor Jonathan Pryce, was one of a number of failures Disney suffered in the early eighties, in its efforts to launch a hit movie that would revitalize the studio. *Something Wicked* was based on a famous novel by Ray Bradbury about a mysterious carnival that threatens a small town at the turn of the century. It was a dark, moody film directed by Jack Clayton and audiences, by now scared off by Disney's name on the marquee, were not interested.

Paramount Pictures maintained a sometimes uncanny ability for turning out hits during the eighties, even when it was least expected. *An Officer and a Gentleman* (1982), *below*, was a love story starring Richard Gere and Debra Winger that took off unexpectedly at the box office. *Flashdance* (1983), *below, right*, starring Jennifer Beals, became a phenomenon in the early part of the decade and was responsible for the aerobic-dancing trend.

How Disney Did What David Puttnam Couldn't Do

COULD MICKEY MOUSE BE SAVED? THAT WAS THE question some Disney studio executives were asking themselves at the beginning of the decade. Walt Disney Productions had not been in so much trouble since Walt Disney arrived in Los Angeles from Kansas City in 1923 and began drawing crude cartoons for local movie houses.

The story of Disney in the eighties actually begins at Paramount Pictures. As was almost always the case at the major studios, even when things were running well, which they certainly were at Paramount, corporate executives looking to solidify their own power or jealous of someone else's, conspired to mess things up. Paramount was the hottest studio in town at the beginning of the eighties. Charles Bluhdorn, the chairman of Gulf and Western, the company that owned Paramount (later it would become Paramount Communications) hired a former television programmer named Barry Diller (he is credited with originating the idea of made-for-TV movies) as the studio's chairman in 1974. Diller was 32 years old at the time. In turn Diller hired his friend, Michael Eisner, the same age, who also got his start in television, as the studio's production head. Those two men, along with Jeffrey Katzenberg, were responsible over the next eight years or so for producing an awesome string of hits: *Saturday Night Fever*, *Raiders of the Lost Ark*, *Flashdance*, *An Officer and a Gentleman*, *Terms of Endearment*, *48 HRS* and *Star Trek — The Motion Picture*. The reputations of Eisner and Diller grew to the point where, following *Terms of Endearment's* huge success in 1984 (it won five

Oscars), *New York* magazine dubbed the two "Hollywood's hottest stars." But Bluhdorn had died the year before, and Eisner in particular felt as though he had lost a close friend, someone he could confide in when he and Diller got into a particularly nasty fight, which was often. Bluhdorn had been succeeded as Gulf and Western chairman by Martin Davis (who was no relation to *Marvin* Davis, over at Fox). The tension that had always existed between New York and Los Angeles was now exacerbated, and, despite their amazing successes, "Hollywood's hottest stars" were quietly in the marketplace looking for new jobs. Diller went first. He called Eisner to tell him he had accepted a job as chairman of Twentieth Century-Fox. Eisner was more convinced than ever that it was time to depart Paramount. There was a job offer over at the beleaguered Disney studio.

THE TROUBLE AT DISNEY, IN EFFECT, HAD started with the death, in 1966, of its founder and driving creative force, the domineering and manipulative Walt Disney. The Disney theme parks in Anaheim and Orlando were huge money-makers, and there was plenty of continuing revenue from the re-release of its animated classics. But the movie side of things was floundering badly. The studio had released *Mary Poppins* in 1964, and it had become the most successful live-action film in the company's history. But, by the seventies, the studio was making lame formula comedies that had less and less appeal to a young audience growing increasingly more sophisticated. Disney was particularly shaken up by the success of *Star Wars* over at Fox in 1977. That year, while *Star Wars* cleaned up, revenues at the Disney film division, which had once amounted to more than half the studio's income, had fallen to a mere 20 percent of it. *Star Wars* was the sort of picture Disney should have made. Filmmakers like Steven Spielberg and George Lucas, who had grown up on Walt Disney films, were now doing the kind of magical, innovative things Walt himself would have appreciated, but they were doing them at other studios. Kids now thought Disney was old hat. Walt's name over the title of a picture once ensured that kids would flock to it. By the beginning of the eighties, it ensured they would stay away in droves. Disney executives commissioned a study that quoted one 19-year-old as saying he "wouldn't be caught dead" at a Disney movie. By 1984, Disney had a new executive, Richard Berger, who had come over from Twentieth Century-Fox to run a new, more adult film division called Touchstone. A mermaid comedy called *Splash* was to be Touchstone's first offering. The movie contained

You could spend little during the eighties, and end up making a lot. Or you could spend a lot, and end up making nothing.

***Above*: *Porky's*, for example, was a low-budget teen-exploitation comedy written and directed by Bob Clark, who claimed to have experienced much of what went on in the movie. It became a huge success in 1982, and inspired dozens of imitations.**

***Below*: Jack Nicholson co-starred with Meryl Streep in *Ironweed* (1987), about a couple of Depression-era bums trying to survive in Albany, New York. It was based on a highly respected novel by William Kennedy, but it was not exactly surefire material at the box office.**

some adult language and a fleeting glimpse of Daryl Hannah's breasts. No matter. *Splash* became the biggest hit in the company's history.

Even so, the value of Disney's stock had fallen below the value of the company's assets, which made it a prime target for corporate raiders. Sure enough, the most lethal of those raiders, Saul Steinberg, turned up to take a position in Disney, and the company was "in play." Suddenly, it looked as though Walt's magical kingdom, which had endured as more or less a family enterprise for six decades, was about to be taken over. What's more, the people who ran the company, including Walt's son-in-law, Ron Miller, were not at all knowledgeable about Wall Street or the conniving of corporate raiders. Steinberg, despite his chubby, jolly facade, was no one to fool around with. If he got hold of Disney, he planned to strip the company — sell off most of its assets in order to repay the money borrowed to buy the studio. Steinberg would hold onto Disneyland and Walt Disney World, but Walt Disney as America and the world had so long known it, would be no more.

Eventually, Steinberg was shaken off when Disney agreed to buy back the stock the raider had purchased in the company — a process known as greenmailing. The buyback agreement called for Disney to pay Steinberg $325.5 million. In just three months time, the raider had made himself a profit of $31.7 million. The greenmailing left the Disney organization dazed and shaken. That episode — as well as the company's continuing vulnerability, and the return to the board

In 1983, Walt Disney Productions released a movie version of Canadian author Farley Mowat's *Never Cry Wolf, left*, about Mowat's adventures as a young government biologist sent into the north to study the habits of wolves. It did well at the box office. But the next year, Disney introduced its Touchstone Pictures division, in an attempt to change its image.

The first Touchstone release was a comedy titled *Splash* that co-starred Daryl Hannah, *below*, as a mermaid who falls in love with Tom Hanks. It became the biggest hit in Disney's history, and helped establish the kind of comedy-action formula it would pursue so successfully throughout the remainder of the decade.

Above: Baby pictures did exceedingly well at the box office during the eighties. One of the most unexpected successes was *Look Who's Talking* (1989), starring John Travolta and Kirstie Alley.

Below: *Glory* (1989) was one of the few movies dealing with the American Civil War ever made by Hollywood. This one concerned the history of the union army's first black regiment, and although it was filmed with great visual beauty by director Edward Zwick, and featured Matthew Broderick, Morgan Freeman and Denzel Washington (who won an Oscar for his performance), the movie failed to draw audiences.

of directors of Roy E. Disney, Walt's nephew who had retired out of frustration over the way Disney was being run — finally led to drastic action. Ron Miller was gone as chief executive officer. Roy Disney moved to install Michael Eisner as the new boss at Disney.

WITH EISNER RUNNING DISNEY, THE TRANSformation was as quick as it was miraculous. Eisner wasted little time in bringing Jeffrey Katzenberg from Paramount, and installing him as president of Disney's movie and television divisions. Shortly thereafter, the company announced its first project, a comedy written and directed by Paul Mazursky titled *Down and out in Beverly Hills.* It would be R-rated. The film, which starred Bette Midler, Richard Dreyfuss and Nick Nolte, was released in December of 1985 under the Touchstone banner. It surpassed the success

Down and out in Beverly Hills **(1985): director Paul Mazursky.**

of *Splash.* The new management was on its way. In the next five years, Disney's share of the box office would increase from 3 percent to 20 percent, as it churned out a succession of hits, mostly through its Touchstone division. Most of those successes drew on a carefully constructed formula of adult comedies, starring names that, while still potent, had suffered a downturn in their careers, and thus were less expensive than other so-called 'hot' stars. The formula rejuvenated the careers of not only Bette Midler (who became something of a Disney contract player), but also Richard Dreyfuss and Tom Selleck (*Three Men and a Baby*).

The studio quietly set about changing the ways in which Hollywood conducted business. Eisner and Katzenberg were notoriously tight-fisted with a dollar (Walt, who never liked to pay anyone very

much of anything, would have been pleased). Disney pictures cost about 30 percent less than the Hollywood average. If major changes were required, then they were made at the far less expensive script-writing stage of the movie. Once a film was in production, a financial spy was attached to make sure that costs stayed in line. Despite grumbling about stinginess, the studio for the most part refused to put up with overpriced stars or play along with the upward spiral of the costs of producing blockbusters (although by 1989 even Touchstone was making exceptions, and *Dick Tracy*, its most expensive picture yet, was in production at a cost of over $30 million, directed by and starring Warren Beatty). Over at Columbia, David Puttnam was trying to accomplish many of the same things as Disney, but he was being much less quiet about it — and much less successful.

It was Paul Mazursky who cast Bette Midler in his comedy for Touchstone Pictures titled *Down and out in Beverly Hills* (1985). However, it was Jeffrey Katzenberg at Disney who signed Midler to a long-term contract, and shaped her career so that by the end of the decade she had become America's favorite comic actress. Such was Disney's influence, that when Katzenberg wanted her to do another remake of *Stella Dallas* in 1990, Midler went along despite reservations about the material. Bette was right: *Stella* bombed at the box office. By the end of 1990, however, she was working once again for Paul Mazursky under the aegis of Disney, who had pulled off one of the great casting coups, pairing her with Woody Allen in a comedy titled *Scenes from a Mall*.

The demise of the animated feature was often predicted, but in the eighties it actually enjoyed a revival thanks largely to the efforts of Walt Disney, the studio whose history was, of course, based on the pen and ink creations of its founder, *above, far right*. The revival began in 1985 with the release of *The Black Cauldron*, *opposite*, Disney's most ambitious and expensive animated feature of that time. The movie was the first created by a new generation of animators who replaced the "Nine Old Men," who did all the animation since Disney produced its first animated feature, *Snow White and the Seven Dwarfs* in 1937.

The Disney animation department had suffered a setback when several animators, including Don Bluth, walked out protesting what they said was a lack of quality animation. Despite all the fuss over The Black Cauldron, it was one of Disney's least successful animated features. ***The Great Mouse Detective**, far left*, released in 1986, was much more successful. However, with the release of ***The Little Mermaid*** in 1989, ***above***, Disney animation was back in full glory. ***The Little Mermaid*** was the best animated feature made by the studio since the heyday of Walt. Not only was it good, but it did the kind of box office business usually reserved for live action movies. By the end of the decade, Disney had dedicated itself to turning out a new animated feature every year and a half.

***Below*: When David Puttnam was running Columbia Pictures, he got a script written by playwright John Patrick Shanley originally titled *Moonglow*, and quickly passed on it. Miffed, the project's director, Norman Jewison, took it over to MGM/UA who decided to make it. *Moonstruck* (1987), starring Cher (*below* with Vincent Gardenia), about a widow who falls in love with her fiance's brother under a full moon, became the biggest hit of Jewison's long career. When Cher won an Academy Award for her performance, she remembered to thank her hairdresser, but failed to thank Jewison, who talked her into being in the movie in the first place.**

PUTTNAM KEPT ANNOUNCING OVER AND OVER again that movies cost too much, stars' salary demands were too high, and agents too powerful. He refused to get involved with so-called "package" deals, whereby an agent put together the star, the script, and the director, usually from a list of his clients, then brought it to the studio. Thus, he alienated Hollywood's most powerful agent, Michael Ovitz of Creative Artists Agency. He also alienated Ray Stark, the independent producer, and a major Columbia stockholder. Stark wanted to make a movie titled *Revenge*. Puttnam wasn't interested. Norman Jewison showed him a script called *Moonglow*. Puttnam turned it down, and Jewison was

***Opposite*: Bill Murray had to be talked into doing a reprise of the 1984 comedy hit *Ghostbusters*. By the time David Puttnam had left Columbia, the studio was in desperate need of a hit. Dawn Steel, the new head of production, immediately gave *Ghostbusters II* the go-ahead, then proceeded to give away large portions of the film's potential grosses in order to lure back Murray and other members of the original cast. When the completed film opened in the summer of 1989, it earned $100 million, less than half of what the original did, and because of what was given away to the actors, the movie was considered a flop. *From left*: Dan Aykroyd, Harold Ramis, Sigourney Weaver, Bill Murray, Ernie Hudson.**

gone from Columbia. *Moonglow* was finally produced at MGM/UA where it became *Moonstruck*, a huge hit.

Because he didn't like sequels, Puttnam refused to make *Jagged Edge II.* More seriously, he angered superstar Bill Murray by suggesting during a luncheon speech that, for all the money he earned, "you don't see people — for example Bill Murray — putting back any dollars made from *Ghostbusters.*" Thus, abruptly, the prospect of making a sequel to Columbia's most profitable picture ever was in doubt.

Warren Beatty and Dustin Hoffman were angry at Puttnam over his refusal to have anything to do with *Ishtar*, a $49-million comedy featuring the two stars, that was in production by the time Puttnam

STANTZ
ENGLER

***Above*: Nobody could make a flop bigger than Dino De Laurentiis. *Dune* (1984) was one of his biggest.**

***Below*: Bernardo Bertolucci's epic, *The Last Emperor* was released in 1987, after David Puttnam had left Columbia. Despite the fact that the movie was an immediate success at the box office, Columbia did not open it as broadly as it could have. Rightly or wrongly, it was speculated that the studio did not want a Puttnam picture to succeed.**

arrived at the studio. Bill Cosby was furious at the way his movie for Columbia, *Leonard Part VI*, was being handled by Puttnam's choice of an English director who didn't know anything about American movies or Bill Cosby.

Bill Cosby in *Leonard Part VI* (1987).

Within eight months of his arrival at Columbia in 1986, David Puttnam had managed to get just about everyone fed up with him: from members of the close-knit Hollywood community, to Francis T. (Fay) Vincent Jr., chairman of Columbia Pictures Industries, to the people who ran Coca-Cola itself. It was only a matter of time until he was gone.

The end came when Coca-Cola, without consulting Puttnam, announced that it was merging Columbia Pictures with another one of its subsidiaries, Tri-Star Pictures. The new company would be called Columbia Pictures Entertainment, and Victor Kaufman from Tri-Star would head it up. Puttnam would remain where he was, but effectively he was running a company that didn't exist anymore. Shortly thereafter Puttnam stood up before Columbia employees and told them he was resigning. As the announcement was made, some of the people present broke into tears.

What did he leave behind? A lot of pictures that didn't make any money. He also left *The Last Emperor*, Bernardo Bertolucci's film about the life of Pu Yi, the last emperor of China, which won nine Academy Awards in 1987, including best picture (although no one, Bertolucci included, made any mention of Puttnam. He had already become a non-person in Hollywood). The big, glitzy commercial pictures he did not want to make, including *Ghostbusters II*, *Revenge* and *Jagged Edge II* (it was called *Physical Evidence*) all eventually were made, but in their own way failed as badly as any of the films Puttnam greenlighted.

Did Puttnam finally change anything? The question, in light of what happened after he left, was laughable. The ante was about to be raised to levels beyond anyone's wildest imagination.

The Japanese Come to Town: Money Beyond Imagination

IT WAS 1975, AND JON PETERS WAS SHOUTING. Frank Pierson, the director of *A Star Is Born* was in the bathroom, and Peters, the movie's producer, a former hairdresser who currently was living with the movie's star, Barbra Streisand, was in the bedroom shouting almost incoherently. Pierson, a highly respected Academy Award-winning screenwriter (*Dog Day Afternoon*) had fought with Streisand throughout the location shooting of the film. Now her boyfriend and co-producer had returned from Los Angeles and arrived at his room at midnight. Two hours later he was still carrying on.

"I remember I'm not dealing with reality, and go back to urinating," Pierson was to write later. "He (Peters) talks on and on. I realize that he is here to try to force me to quit. Or did she tell him to fire me? Whatever it is, it seems to have worn him out. Without ever getting to the point of what he came for, Jon blurts out: 'I'm not afraid of your Oscar.' He gets up and leaves."

Pierson wrote about his experiences making, or remaking *A Star Is Born* in the November 15, 1976 issue of *New York* magazine. Until then, the world outside the narrow confines of Hollywood had never heard of Jon Peters. But over the years, as he became better known as one of Hollywood's hottest — and hottest-headed — producers, such stories would proliferate. There was the time, for example, when two workmen came to collect a $110 bill at his place

Hollywood loved to travel back in time during the eighties, whether it was *Time after Time* (1980) or *Back to the Future* (1985). One of the best, but least remembered of the time travel pictures was *Somewhere in Time* (1980). Christopher Reeve played a writer who falls in love with a portrait of a beautiful young woman (played by Jane Seymour) at a resort in northern Michigan and ends up traveling back to the turn of the century in order to meet her. Reeve, who was riding high at the time as Superman, was never more handsome, and Seymour never more beautiful. Nonetheless, the movie was not a success, adding to the perception that as soon as Reeve took off his blue tights, the audience went away. By the end of the decade, Seymour was known as the queen of the television mini-series, and almost never made feature films.

***Above*: *Highlander* (1986), a bizarre science fiction action movie, starring Sean Connery and Christopher Lambert, failed at the North American box office. Yet in Europe where the two stars were very popular, the movie was a huge hit.**

***Below*: Paramount Pictures demonstrated early in 1990 that a high-tech action thriller like *The Hunt for Red October*, starring Alec Baldwin, could gross over $100 million at the box office outside the summer and Christmas releasing seasons.**

***Opposite*: *Rain Man* (1988), starring Tom Cruise and Dustin Hoffman, was not only a huge North American hit, grossing over $150 million, but it went on to be as popular in foreign markets, and grossed another $150 million.**

in Aspen, Colorado. "Mr. Peters came out wearing a bathrobe and carrying an old-style, pearl-handled six-shooter," reported the police officer who investigated the incident. "He proceeded to point it at them, yelling and screaming at them to get off the property." Peters reportedly had to finally settle the whole incident by paying the workmen $60,000.

Peters was not from the sort of background that encourages young men to become movie executives. He was a high school dropout, who also did time in reform school, before becoming hairdresser to the stars. He met Barbra Streisand when he cut her hair. Reportedly *Shampoo*, starring Warren Beatty was based on Peters' life. As the incident in Aspen illustrated, he had a temper. "You do not want to fight this guy, period," his cousin told *Premiere* magazine. "Shoot yourself in the leg and have the ambulance come and get you, 'cause I guarantee you'll be better off."

When Peters produced *A Star Is Born*, everyone laughed. Barbra's boyfriend playing at movies. Then it made $75 million, and suddenly Jon Peters was a producer. He closed down his hairdressing salon, put away his scissors and started making movies. During the filming of *The Eyes of Laura Mars*, he met the former head of production at Columbia Pictures, a man named Peter Guber. Guber was the exact opposite of Peters; he never went to reform school or waved a gun at anyone. That sort of behavior was frowned upon in Newton, Massachusetts, where Guber grew up in an upper-middle-class family. He attended New York University, earned a law degree, and had no ambitions whatsoever to be in film when Columbia Pictures recruited him in 1968 at $450 a week. A few years later, he was in charge of worldwide production.

As just about everyone pointed out, the two men were a study in dramatic contrasts. While Peters blew up, Guber maintained his cool. The two of them became a production team in 1980, and the independent Guber-Peters Company over the next 10 years helped produce such hits as *Flashdance*, *The Color Purple*, *The Witches of Eastwick*, *Rain Man*, and, their biggest success ever, *Batman*, produced for Warner Bros. How much Guber-Peters were actually responsible for the success of any of these pictures was a hotly debated topic around Hollywood. Certainly, they were by no means infallible, as such flops as *Vision Quest*, *The Legend of Billie Jean* and *Six Weeks* demonstrated. It made no difference. After the success

Jack Nicholson with *The Witches of Eastwick* (1987).

***Annie*, based on the long-running comic strip *Little Orphan Annie*, was a Broadway smash musical in the seventies. In 1981, producer Ray Stark made a lavish, old-fashioned movie version of the show, the like of which had not been seen on the screen in years. John Huston was the unlikely choice to direct, and Albert Finney, *left*, played Daddy Warbucks opposite young Aileen Quinn as Annie.**

As the eighties rolled to an end, an average of 500 new films were being released in North America each year. There were so many movies being released that a lot of good ones got ignored. One of them was *True Believer* (1988), starring James Woods and Robert Downey, Jr. as a couple of lawyers trying to establish the innocence of a young Los Angeles gang member, Yuji Okumoto, accused of murder.

of *Batman*, Guber and Peters could do no wrong. They were, for a few moments anyway, film geniuses. Geniuses who shared a dream: they wanted to be moguls. They wanted to run their own studio. Their dream was about to come true.

AFTER THE DAVID PUTTNAM FIASCO, WHICH continued to have repercussions long after he left, Coca-Cola was fed up with the movie business. Dawn Steel, who formerly was at Paramount with Michael Eisner and Jeffrey Katzenberg, was now running Columbia. A native of Great Neck, New York, her original claim to fame lay in successfully marketing upscale toilet paper for yuppies who had everything. She knew how to play the Hollywood game, quickly putting *Ghostbusters II* into production. Nonetheless, Columbia, thanks at least in part to the failure of most of Puttnam's pictures was still hemorrhaging money.

In the middle of 1988, not too long after David Puttnam left Los Angeles, the Japanese arrived in town. Akio Morita, founder of the giant Sony Corporation, was there to look into the prospect of acquiring a studio. Sony wanted "software" to complement its "hardware" — videocassette recorders and television sets. There were those who felt that, if Sony had gotten into the software end of things back in the seventies, its superior Beta system of VCRs might have carried the day, rather than the slightly inferior VHS system. Sony was determined not to make the same mistake twice. It was after vertical integration, the ability to service every segment of the entertainment business.

Chairman Morita was shown around Hollywood by the flamboyant, hard-driving Walter Yetnikoff, the man who convinced Sony to buy the highly profitable CBS Records in 1987 and allow him to run the company. Now he was pushing the idea of Sony owning its own studio. Morita and his president and chief executive officer, Norio Ohga, met with every motion picture executive in town. They took a look at beleaguered MGM/UA, but it quickly became apparent that the biggest "for sale" sign in town was hanging out in front of Columbia's studios. Columbia had a good library of films, something Sony was very interested in acquiring, as well as television holdings and theater screens. An agreement to purchase was negotiated during the summer of 1989, while *Batman*, produced by Guber and Peters, was filling theaters, and everyone was talking about how much money the movies were making. The purchase price was $3.4 billion. The Japanese had no interest in actually running an American studio themselves. They began looking around for someone who could replace Victor Kaufman, who currently headed Columbia. Again it was Walter Yetnikoff who suggested Guber and Peters. You only had to look at the lineups outside *Batman* to know they were the hottest producers around. "Guber, Peters and I have long shared a hope of working together," Yetnikoff stated in court papers. There was only one small problem. Guber-Peters recently had signed a five-year contract with Warner Bros., the company for whom they produced *Batman.*

Throughout the eighties, Warner had remained the most stable studio in town — and one of the most profitable. There had been none of the frenetic management musical chairs that had gone on at the other studios, thanks largely to the steadying hand of Steve Ross, the former funeral business manager who was the likable chairman of Warner Communications. The studio could even afford to play the nice guy every so often. When *Driving Miss Daisy*, a Warner Bros. release, took off at the box office, the studio paid advance profit shares to stars Jessica Tandy, Morgan Freeman and Dan Aykroyd, as well as to director Bruce Beresford and writer Alfred Uhry, a practice unheard of, given the usual state of Hollywood bookkeeping. *Batman*, with help from *Driving Miss Daisy* and *Lethal Weapon II* had made Warner the top studio at the box office for the third time in 10 years. Only Paramount had matched that record.

Weintraub Entertainment was started up with financing of close to $500 million. Yet it couldn't make any hits, and the failure of its most expensive production, *My Stepmother Is an Alien* (1988), starring Dan Aykroyd and Kim Basinger, put the company in financial jeopardy.

Warner Bros. was founded by four brothers named Warner in 1923. It was the Warner brothers who launched the sound era with the release of *The Jazz Singer* in 1927, and throughout the thirties and forties, the studio was known for its tough, hard-hitting melodramas and its acting stable. Throughout the eighties it continued to be one of the most successful studios in Hollywood, and in 1989 was the top studio thanks to hits such as *Batman*, *Lethal Weapon II*, (*above, right*) and *Driving Miss Daisy* (*above, left*).

But in the midst of the calm, Warner was actually putting the finishing touches to a historic merger. After two years of negotiations, Warner Communications was merging with Time Inc. to form the biggest entertainment conglomerate in America. The deal would momentarily be sidetracked by a suit filed by Paramount, and that

The Disney entertainment factory, always quick to pick up on a trend, contributed to the popularity of cop-and-dog movies in the eighties when Tom Hanks co-starred with a big, drooling canine companion in *Turner and Hooch* (1989).

***Young Guns* (1988) was another retelling of the Billy the Kid story, this time with, *from left*, Lou Diamond Phillips, Kiefer Sutherland, Emilio Estevez, Casey Siemaszko, Charlie Sheen, Dermot Mulroney.**

resulted in a turnaround of sorts, whereby Time actually made a $13-billion bid for Warner Bros. By July of 1989, Time Warner, as it was to be known, was a corporate reality (the deal actually closed in January 1990), an empire selling $8.7 billion worth of movies, records, books, magazines and TV shows around the world. This happened just about the time Columbia came looking for Jon Peters and Peter Guber.

There was no suggestion that Dawn Steel would stay on at the studio. *Ghostbusters II* had made money, but not *enough* money. *Karate Kid III* had made no money at all, and neither had *Casualties of War*. Steel did not suffer long, though. Early in 1990, she signed an independent development and production deal with Hollywood Pictures, the new subsidiary of Disney/Touchstone. She was reunited with her old Paramount pals, Eisner and Katzenberg.

Sony agreed to buy out the Guber-Peters company for $200 million and pay the pair a compensation package that included $2.7 million in annual salaries. They were on their way to not only being studio heads but two of the richest producers in Hollywood when Steve Ross stepped in. He was furious over losing the producers who had provided Warner Bros. with *Batman* just as his company was merging with Time. Ross was said to be "crazy because of the Time deal."

By the time the dispute was settled, Sony had agreed to pay Time Warner as much as $500 million in order to release Guber and Peters from their contract. When that figure was added to the $200 million the corporation had already paid for the Guber-Peters Company, then the cost of hiring Jon Peters and Peter Guber as studio heads may have risen as high as $700 million. Even in a town grown rather jaded about big money, this was a stratospheric sum. Despite Sony's adamant denials that they had paid that much, there was little doubt the deal was going to change the face of Hollywood.

THE GUBER-PETERS DEAL SET OFF A FEEDING frenzy the like of which had never been seen. "Overnight the salary structure in Hollywood has begun to crumple," wrote *New York Times* reporter Aljean Harmetz. "Studio heads who make well over $1 million a year are feeling underpaid, and plan to do something about it. The aftershock will eventually force higher the immense salaries already being won by actors, directors and agents."

Jerry Bruckheimer and Don Simpson, high-profile producers working out of Paramount who had made *Top Gun*, *Beverly Hills Cop*, and, like Guber and Peters, also laid claim to the success of *Flash-*

dance, were at least as adroit at making audience-pleasing movies — maybe more so. Even though they recently had produced only a Tom Cruise movie, *Days of Thunder*, the studio quickly signed them to a new deal which reportedly allowed the producers free rein to make five pictures over the next five years and begin receiving revenues from the very first dollar Paramount took in on those pictures. The studio, in full-page newspaper ads, called the agreement "a visionary alliance." Simpson, reflecting the tenor of the times, simply termed it "the biggest deal in Hollywood."

SITTING ON THE SIDELINES AND WATCHING ALL this was David Puttnam. He had wasted little time in returning to London, where he licked his wounds, gave lots of press interviews, then restructured his old company, Enigma Productions. Late in 1989, he was back in production, this time with *Memphis Belle*, a World War II drama based on William Wyler's documentary about the crew of an American B-17 Flying Fortress bomber. Puttnam remained as vocal as ever about Hollywood and the kinds of movies it was making. "I think the films of the eighties have been execrable," he pronounced in the *International Herald*

Matthew Modine starred in David Puttnam's production of *The Memphis Belle* (1990).

Tribune. He continued harping away to anyone who would listen about why he thought Hollywood had failed: "It has tried to tell people that life is simple," he argued. "It's anything but."

That may have been about the only point David Puttnam and the people running the major Hollywood studios in the eighties would have agreed on.

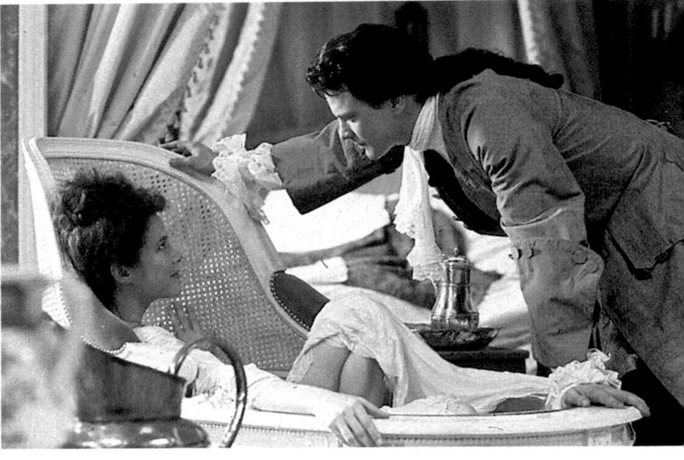

***Les Liaisons Dangereuses*, written by a former French artillery officer named Choderlos de Laclos, was first published in Paris in 1782. Amazingly enough, in the eighties, Laclos' tale of sexual deception inspired not one but two movies, one right after the other. First there was *Dangerous Liaisons*, directed by Stephen Frears, and released in 1988. The next year, director Milos Forman unveiled his version, *Valmont*, *above*, with Colin Firth in the title role and Annette Bening as Marquise de Merteuil. Frears, who got there first, had the hit; Forman had the flop.**

For years Norman Jewison tried to interest Hollywood in making a movie version of William Goldman's fairy tale for adults, *The Princess Bride*. Finally in 1987, Rob Reiner was able to get the movie made, and it was a box office success. Goldman, one of Hollywood's most respected screenwriters, wrote a book titled *Adventures in the Screen Trade*, in which he noted the following: "NOBODY KNOWS ANYTHING. Not one person in the entire motion picture field *knows* for a certainty what's going to work. Every time out it's a guess — and if you're lucky, an educated one."

BEYOND HOLLYWOOD

THE WORLD AND THE MOVIES

***Brazil* (1985), directed by Terry Gilliam, was the kind of movie that could only have been made beyond Hollywood. It was also the kind of movie Hollywood wanted nothing to do with. When Gilliam turned it over to Universal studio, they thought it unreleasable until a public battle ensued.**

American movies increasingly dominated the world during the eighties, and often it was hard to hear anything from a country's filmmakers over the din created by the arrival of the Hollywood blockbusters. But movies beyond Hollywood managed to survive, not always well, and without the vigor and originality of the sixties and seventies. Television and home video reduced audiences in most countries, and there was increasing alarm being expressed at the domination of American movies in most countries, particularly in Canada, which, because of its proximity, was vulnerable to the American invasion. The Americans seemed oblivious to the effect they were having. They couldn't understand why the whole world didn't want to see their movies. They came to Berlin early in 1990 just as the world was opening up . . .

The producers claimed that any number of attempts had been made over the years to stop production of a movie about the John Profumo scandal that rocked Britain in 1963. That may explain why it took until 1989 for the story to come to the screen. *Scandal* turned out to be a tame retelling of the story with Joanne Whalley-Kilmer, *above*, as Christine Keeler, and John Hurt wonderfully appropriate as the osteopath Stephen Ward.

In *Lawrence of Arabia* (1962), Irish-born Peter O'Toole gave one of the finest performances ever put on film. Thereafter, however, he was never quite able to scale the heights of greatness. He worked steadily all over the world in the eighties, in movies ranging from *The Stunt Man* (1980) to *Club Paradise* (1986), *above*, and *The Last Emperor* (1987).

On a February evening in 1990, the bulldozers knocked down the portion of the Berlin Wall between the Reichstag and Checkpoint Charlie. The event caused more excitement at the Berlin International Film Festival than any of the movies being shown. Festival-goers dashed out of packed screenings, rented a hammer for five marks, and began chipping off souvenir pieces of the wall. Meanwhile, East Berliners hurried past, flocking into the West, lugging huge plastic shopping bags with which to carry the goods that, for years, they could only dream about — everyone seemed particularly anxious to purchase bananas. On this, the festival's 40th anniversary, East was meeting West; history was being made. However, the Americans visiting Berlin did not see history. They looked across Checkpoint Charlie, past the East Germans buying bananas and they saw . . . a new marketplace for American movies.

In France, in 1989, American films took 55 percent of the receipts at the box office, an all-time high, while receipts for French films fell to an all-time low of 33 percent. In Italy, more than 70 percent of the box office was dominated by American films, and in Spain only 12 percent of revenues went to Spanish-made films. In Germany, in 1989, only three of the top 10 films were produced locally. In Canada, a country that had never been able to launch much of an indigenous cinema, only three percent of the box office went to Canadian films. In America, this was seen as a good thing; the opening up of new appetites and territories that helped offset the growing production costs of American movies. From the perspective of the world beyond Hollywood, however, the increasing domination of American films, as well as the growth of television and home video was viewed as nothing less than life-threatening.

Britain, like most other European countries during the eighties, was not very successful in staving off the American onslaught, and the situation was not helped by a government no longer interested in aiding the film industry. A number of times, the industry seemed poised to rise or fall on the success of a film such as *Absolute Beginners* or *Revolution*, although British film managed to survive their ultimate failure. There were lots of success stories: Hugh Hudson's *Chariots of Fire* was a huge international success, and won the

Hugh Hudson directing *Revolution* (1985).

Academy Award for best picture in 1981. Sir Richard Attenborough, after trying for two decades, finally filmed *Gandhi,* and this film too was rewarded with an Oscar for best picture, in 1982. *A Room with a View,* based on the E.M. Forster novel, was the most profitable picture ever produced by the production team of James Ivory and Ismail Merchant. The veteran Stanley Kubrick made two highly successful films, both of them produced on his home turf, if only because he refused to travel. Kubrick managed to shoot Stephen King's very American horror novel *The Shining* (1980) in London with Jack Nicholson, and he recreated the Tet offensive in an abandoned factory complex for his Vietnam film, *Full Metal Jacket* (1987).

Despite the huge international success of *A Fish Called Wanda*

Director Richard Attenborough's fight to bring Gandhi's story to the screen for over two decades was often retold during the eighties — usually by Attenborough himself who was tireless when it came to promoting the movie. He cast an unknown 39-year-old actor of Indian descent named Ben Kingsley, *insert*, to portray the 79-year-old Mahatma.

(1988), written by ex-Monty Python member John Cleese, British films continued to prefer dressing up in period costume throughout the decade, flailing away at the idea of Empire while simultaneously celebrating it. Therefore, in addition to *A Room with a View*, there was *A Handful of Dust* (from Charles Sturridge and his partner Derek Granger, who did TV's very successful *Brideshead Revisited*), *The Shooting Party*, *Maurice* (also from Forster by way of Merchant and Ivory) and *White Mischief*.

But it was an angry, offbeat, socially conscious British cinema, often supported by Channel 4 Television, that caused the most fuss internationally. Films such as *The Long Good Friday*, *Mona Lisa*, *Sid and Nancy*, *Withnail and I*, *Wish You Were Here*, *Dance with a Stranger*, *No Surrender* and *Scandal* were tough, uncompromising, critical of the British establishment, and surprisingly popular. No one, however, was more provocative, or more successful in the British cinema of the eighties, than a former TV director named Stephen Frears.

Julian Sands and Helena Bonham Carter in *A Room with a View* (1985).

Frears was born in Leicester, and studied law at Cambridge, before going to work as an assistant director for people such as Karel Reisz and Lindsay Anderson. He made an impressive film debut in 1971 with *Gumshoe*, starring Albert Finney, but then languished in television through most of the seventies before returning to theatrical features with *The Hit* in 1984. It was Frears' work the following year on *My Beautiful Laundrette*, from a screenplay by Hanif Kureishi, that established his reputation. Full of scathing wit and anger, *My Beautiful Laundrette*, was a harsh indictment of Margaret Thatcher's Britain. It became the seminal British film of the mid-1980s and proved that a gritty, contemporary British movie could attract a worldwide audience. Further, it confirmed Frears as a director with a social conscience who could also shoot quickly and cheaply. Kureishi described how Frears liked to work: "He said he wanted to shoot

***Above*: The great Lord Laurence Olivier set out to make a lot of money from the movies in the eighties so that his heirs would be well taken care of after his death. As a result he didn't always pay a lot of attention to what he was appearing in. Here he played Zeus in an awful adventure fantasy titled *Clash of the Titans* (1981). Olivier died in 1989.**

***Opposite*: *A Fish Called Wanda* was a sleeper hit in the summer of 1988. *From left*: Michael Palin, John Cleese, Jamie Lee Curtis, Kevin Kline (who won an Oscar for his performance).**

***Below*: Michael Caine played a comic Sherlock Holmes in *Without a Clue* (1988). Ben Kingsley was his long-suffering Watson.**

Dangerous Liaisons **(1988) was the biggest, splashiest — and most successful — movie Stephen Frears made during the eighties. It was based on Christopher Hampton's successful stage adaptation of the Choderlos de Laclos novel. Glenn Close, *above*, played the conniving Marquise de Merteuil, and John Malkovich, *below*, with Close and director Frears, was Valmont.**

my film in February. As it was November already, I pointed out that February might be a little soon. Would there be time to prepare, to rewrite? But he had a theory: when you had a problem, he said, bring things forward; do them sooner rather than later. And anyway, February was a good month for him; he made his best films then — England looked especially unpleasant, and people worked faster in the cold."

Frears followed *My Beautiful Laundrette* with *Prick up Your Ears*, about the playwright Joe Orton. Then came *Sammy and Rosie Get Laid*, again from a screenplay by Kureishi, and, if anything, even more critical of Britain under Margaret Thatcher than *My Beautiful Laundrette*. "In a ghastly way, she is very much a woman: capricious," he said of Thatcher. "And she sort of falls in love with people, has a cabinet of emasculated men, and is a profoundly repres-

Sammy and Rosie Get Laid (1987).

sive woman. She once said that by the time she was 15 she was through with her mother, and has spent the rest of her life avoiding being her mother."

Frears' work often dealt explicitly with sex — the two male lovers in *My Beautiful Laundrette*, the free-loving couple in *Sammy and Rosie Get Laid* — but Frears himself professed to being resolutely heterosexual and moderate in his personal life. His opportunity to make a big, international picture with an all-star cast and a large budget came when he took on Christopher Hampton's stage success, *Les Liaisons Dangereuses*. Released in 1988 as *Dangerous Liaisons*, it co-starred Americans John Malkovich, Glenn Close and Michelle Pfeiffer. It became Frears' biggest success. "I think it's a film like all my others," he shrugged during shooting. "It's about sex, power, money. They all seem to me identical. But, of course, when I join the scenes up, I may discover I've been laboring under an illusion."

Pauline Collins starred in both the London and New York productions of ***Shirley Valentine***, Willy Russell's play about a working-class housewife who goes on a dream vacation to the Greek Islands. The last thing Collins expected was to be cast in the movie version of the play. But director Lewis Gilbert did choose her, and she was nominated for an Academy Award in 1989 for her performance.

After winning an Oscar for ***Darling*** in 1965, Julie Christie was much in demand, but in the seventies she made fewer and fewer films. Always fiercely independent, Christie concentrated on political activism in the eighties, and only occasionally worked in front of the camera. One of those occasions was ***Miss Mary*** (1986), a film she made in Argentina.

BRITAIN PROVIDED ANY NUMBER OF COMMERcially viable directors throughout the eighties, including the Scott brothers, Ridley (*Blade Runner*, *Someone to Watch over Me* and *Black Rain*), and Tony (*Top Gun*), Hugh Hudson (*Chariots of Fire*, *Greystoke*, *Revolution*), Alan Parker (*Angel Heart*, *Mississippi Burning*), John Boorman (*Excalibur*, *The Emerald Forest*, *Hope and Glory*), Adrian Lyne (*Flashdance*, *Fatal Attraction*), Roland Joffe (*The Killing Fields*, *The Mission*, *Fat Man and Little Boy*), Lewis Gilbert (*Educating Rita*, *Shirley Valentine*) and Mike Figgis (*Stormy Monday*, *Internal Affairs*).

Those directors tended to go after subject matter with wide appeal. Bill Forsyth worked, for the most part, closer to home, and thus was close behind Frears in being the most eccentric and original filmmaker to come out of Britain during the decade.

It was Forsyth's *Gregory's Girl* and *Local Hero* which caused international audiences to sit up and take notice. Forsyth was from Glasgow, and what made his accomplishments all the more noteworthy was that they came out of Scotland, a country with almost no history of, or reputation for, making films. Forsyth appeared to have wandered into a life in film in the same offhand way he made his movies. "I was just a kid of 17," he recalled, "and I just took a job with a film company as an apprentice, because I thought there was money in it." He began to see movies by filmmakers such as François Truffaut and Louis Malle, and the next thing he knew he was so hooked on European films that he was smoking Gauloises cigarettes. He initially made documentaries, even though, he later

***Above*: Albert Finney and Tom Courtenay performed brilliantly in *The Dresser* (1983), adapted from Ronald Harwood's play about a doddering old actor trying to get on stage during the Second World War for one more performance of *King Lear*, and being helped by his long suffering dresser.**

***Below*: Alec Guinness became known to a new generation of moviegoers thanks to George Lucas who cast him as Obi-Wan Kenobi in the *Star Wars* trilogy. Guinness, who was born in 1914, returned to the screen fairly often. He played in David Lean's *A Passage To India* (1984), and he was Amy Dorrit's impoverished father, *left*, in a two-part film of Dickens' *Little Dorrit* (1988).**

David Puttnam produced Bill Forsyth's *Local Hero* (1983).

conceded, he was never very good at non-fiction. His first feature, *That Sinking Feeling*, was shot with a 16-millimeter camera. His next film, *Gregory's Girl*, was shot in 1980 on a budget of just $400,000.

Forsyth said he shot his first movies in Scotland because he was lazy. "I knew Scotland and I knew the people. If I'd gone somewhere else, I'd have had to work harder." The low-key charm of Forsyth's films lay in the Scottish landscape, character, and in the problems of living in a country which shares very little with the British, unless it's the problems of unemployment and social injustice. *That Sinking Feeling*, for example, was about a gang of unemployed youths robbing a plumbing warehouse with highly comic results. *Comfort and Joy* was a shaggy comedy that also managed to become a portrait of a modern Scotland in which everyone is miserable and a bit of a scoundrel. *Local Hero*, about a young American sent to buy an entire Scottish fishing village, dealt with the problems of the pervasiveness of American culture on a little country like Scotland.

BY THE END OF THE EIGHTIES, THERE WAS more grumbling about an unsympathetic government that did virtually nothing to help the film industry. British TV, once a major source of financing, was backing away from movie production, although Granada Television was involved in *My Left Foot*, the story of Irish writer and painter Christy Brown, who suffered from cerebral palsy. In the midst of the gloom and doom over British movies, *My Left Foot*, about Brown's valiant fight to lead a normal life, appeared to come out of nowhere and take everyone by surprise.

Noel Pearson had known Christy Brown while he was alive — the two of them were born within a couple of hundred yards of each other in the Crumlin area of Dublin. Pearson had managed

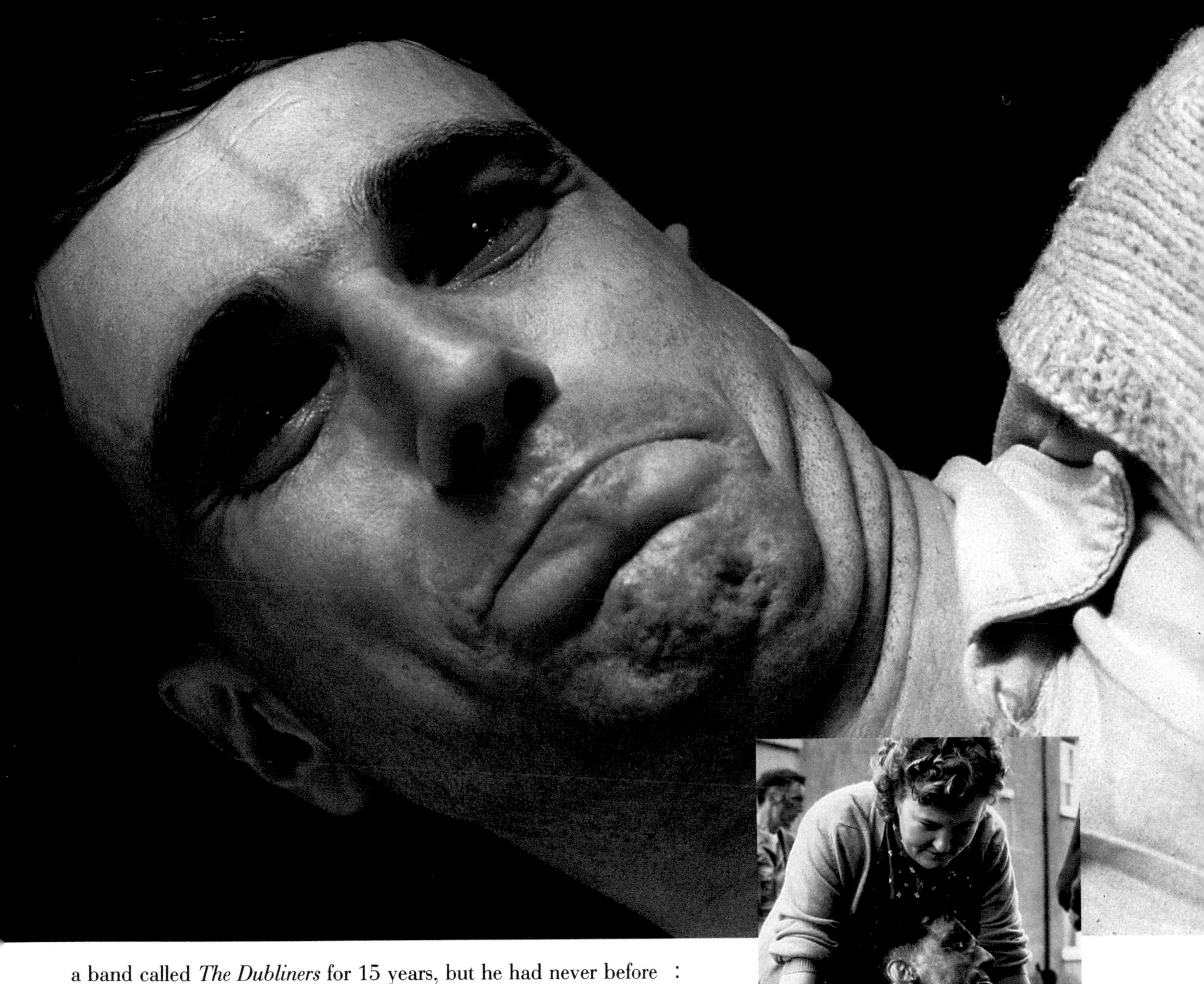

a band called *The Dubliners* for 15 years, but he had never before produced a movie. That was fine: Jim Sheridan, the man who co-wrote and directed *My Left Foot*, was known for his work in theater and had never before written or directed a movie. Daniel Day Lewis, the most talented and charismatic actor to emerge from British film during the eighties, first heard the story of Christy Brown one drunken night at Pearson's house. He was fascinated by the story but thought nothing more of it until the script for *My Left Foot* arrived unannounced on his doorstep a couple of months later.

Daniel Day Lewis's father, C. (Cecil) Day Lewis, once the Poet Laureate of Britain, had been born in Ireland. But Daniel grew up in southeast London before going off to an English public school at the age of 12. By the time he read *My Left Foot* and fell in love with the script, he had attracted immense attention for the diversity of his performances, first as the blond homosexual in *My Beautiful Laundrette*, then as the upper-class prig in *A Room with a View*, and after that as the relentlessly womanizing Czech physician, Tomas,

Even before the film was shown to the critics, those involved in the production of *My Left Foot* (1989) were in awe of Daniel Day Lewis's performance as the Irish literary figure, Christy Brown. For starters, Lewis had to learn to use his left foot to pick up things, the same way Brown did. And then there was the reproduction of that unique Christy Brown voice. Brenda Fricker, *Insert*, who played Brown's mother, won the Academy Award for best supporting actress.

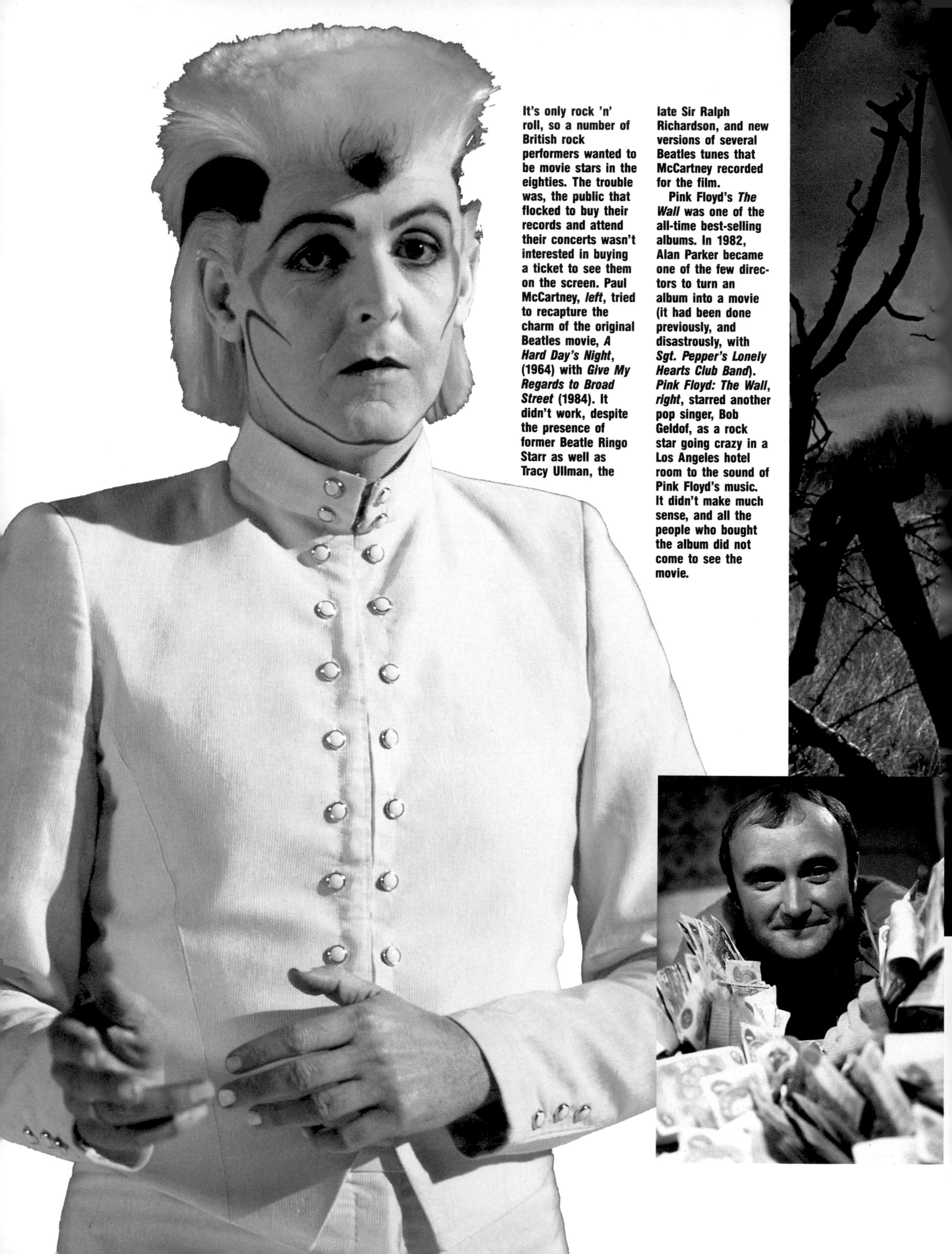

It's only rock 'n' roll, so a number of British rock performers wanted to be movie stars in the eighties. The trouble was, the public that flocked to buy their records and attend their concerts wasn't interested in buying a ticket to see them on the screen. Paul McCartney, *left*, tried to recapture the charm of the original Beatles movie, *A Hard Day's Night*, (1964) with *Give My Regards to Broad Street* (1984). It didn't work, despite the presence of former Beatle Ringo Starr as well as Tracy Ullman, the late Sir Ralph Richardson, and new versions of several Beatles tunes that McCartney recorded for the film.

Pink Floyd's *The Wall* was one of the all-time best-selling albums. In 1982, Alan Parker became one of the few directors to turn an album into a movie (it had been done previously, and disastrously, with *Sgt. Pepper's Lonely Hearts Club Band*). *Pink Floyd: The Wall*, *right*, starred another pop singer, Bob Geldof, as a rock star going crazy in a Los Angeles hotel room to the sound of Pink Floyd's music. It didn't make much sense, and all the people who bought the album did not come to see the movie.

Phil Collins, *far left*, one of the most popular recording artists of the eighties, made his starring debut playing one of the great train robbers in *Buster* (1988). However, audiences were not interested in seeing one of the era's most popular music idols on the screen.

David Bowie began appearing in movies as early as 1967, but did not attract attention until he played the title role in Nicolas Roeg's *The Man Who Fell to Earth* in 1976. In the eighties, he appeared in a wide array of movies and roles including: *Christiane F.* (1981), *Merry Christmas, Mr. Lawrence* (1983), *left, The Hunger* (1983) and *Absolute Beginners* (1986). For all his work, however, Bowie remained much more popular as a singer throughout the decade than he did as an actor.

John Boorman was one of Britain's most prolific and erratic filmmakers. He made his debut as a director in 1965 with a movie starring the pop group Dave Clark Five called *Catch Us If You Can* (known in America as *Having a Wild Weekend*). But his reputation was secured when he directed a stylish Lee Marvin thriller, *Point Blank* in 1967, then did *Deliverance* in 1972. He was capable of being either very bad as he was with *The Emerald Forest* (1985) or quite good as he was with *Hope and Glory* (1987), *below*, his autobiographical film about growing up in London during the Blitz. *Excalibur* (1981), *above*, with Nigel Terry and Cherie Lunghi, in another retelling of the King Arthur story, fell somewhere in between. It was, however, one of his more internationally successful efforts during the decade.

Lena Olin in *The Unbearable Lightness of Being* (1987).

in Philip Kaufman's adaptation of Milan Kundera's *The Unbearable Lightness of Being* (1987). After that movie, however, he did not work for a year. "I sometimes feel very, very old," he explained, "this sense of unbreachable pessimism, this sense of profound weariness that affects me physically as well as it does mentally. I let it take its course like a virus.

"I've always been determined never to work unless I needed to. I'd almost rather do any kind of work than perform just to earn money."

Day Lewis agreed to play Christy Brown, despite the fact that there was no financing for the film, and he had reservations about trying to fake the very real agony of Christy Brown's life. "I had a huge compulsion to be involved in the film. I wasn't sure if it was possible; I wasn't sure it would be practical; and I wasn't sure it would be ethical. There was a sort of obvious hypocrisy involved. I understood the film would only be made if someone had a price, if only a small one, on their heads, and I had that, and I wanted the film to be made. In the end, all my reservations were very forcibly put to one side."

For their parts, Sheridan and Pearson decided not to allow the mere lack of financing stop them. They went right ahead and started shooting anyway. The necessary financing came along.

Daniel Day Lewis's remarkable performance was nominated for an Academy Award in 1989, but everyone expected Tom Cruise to win for *Born on the Fourth of July*. To everyone's amazement, it was Daniel Day Lewis who stepped up on stage at the Dorothy Chandler Pavilion to accept the award for best actor. (Another surprise was the best supporting actress award to Brenda Fricker, who played Christy Brown's mother.) Day Lewis, a charming, entirely likable loner, who often turned up for interviews wearing a worn stetson and torn, faded jeans, his hair flowing to his shoulders, remained skeptical about how the small, highly commercial world of Hollywood regarded him.

"Films tend to be made by formulas, and those are not the kind of films I want to be involved with, ever," he stated. "Most films are made in the belief that some kind of formula has been found, the bottled essence of successful films. Most films tended to be set up by accountants and lawyers it seems to me, men in suits — undertakers I call them . . . But I just think they probably don't quite know whether I'm a bankable prospect or not. And that's what they need to know."

CERTAINLY THERE WAS NO SHORTAGE OF exciting British performers making movies in the eighties, exercising a diversity unknown among American actors. Ben Kingsley came out of nowhere and, in 1982 won an Academy Award for his performance in *Gandhi*, although he was equally good in *Betrayal* and *Pascali's Island*. Gary Oldman dazzled critics with a distinctive performance as the punk rocker Sid Vicious in *Sid and Nancy*, and then as the playwright Joe Orton in *Prick up Your Ears*. The veteran John Hurt won an Oscar nomination for his work as *The Elephant Man* (1980), and stayed busy throughout the decade in everything from *The Hit* to *1984* to *White Mischief* and *Scandal*. Jeremy Irons first attracted international attention in Karel Reisz's *The French Lieutenant's Woman*, and in the TV mini-series, *Brideshead Revisited*. He then appeared in everything from Jerzy Skolimowski's *Moonlighting* to Volker Schlondorff's *Swann in Love* and Roland Joffe's *The Mission*. Julie Walters was irrepressible and almost immediately a star when she repeated her stage success in the film version of *Educating Rita*. Young Emily Lloyd made a dazzling debut in *Wish You Were Here*, then costarred in two lesser American films, *In Country* and *Cookie*. Pauline Collins toiled away anonymously for years before starring in

John Hurt as *The Elephant Man* (1980).

***Above:* Sir John Gielgud, approaching 80, appeared as Dudley Moore's valet in the hit comedy *Arthur* (1981). Although he had been in films since 1924, he won his first Academy Award for the role. He made appearances in *The Elephant Man* (1980), *Chariots of Fire* (1981), *Gandhi* (1982), *The Wicked Lady* (1983), *The Shooting Party* (1984), *Plenty* (1985) and *The Whistle Blower* (1987), to name just a few.**

***Below:* Denholm Elliott was another veteran British character actor who only seemed to get better as the eighties progressed. He appeared in *Raiders of the Lost Ark* (1981), *Trading Places* (1983), *A Room with a View* (1985) and *Indiana Jones and the Last Crusade* (1989).**

Above: Mona Lisa (1986) was a slick, gritty *Beauty and the Beast* gangster story starring Bob Hoskins, *left,* as a petty hood who falls hard for the beautiful London call girl, played by Cathy Tyson, *right*. Michael Caine waded into the middle as one of the decade's smoothest, nastiest villains.

Opposite, above: Kenneth Branagh was hailed as the new Olivier after he filmed a new version of Shakespeare's *Henry V* in 1989. Like Olivier when he did *Henry V* in 1944, Branagh not only starred but directed the film, and adapted Shakespeare's text to the screen.

Opposite, below: Julie Walters graduated from Willy Russell's stage play, *Educating Rita*, into Lewis Gilbert's film version in 1983, and became a British star. None of her subsequent movies — *She'll Be Wearing Pink Pajamas* (1984) and *Personal Services* (1986) were quite so successful.

Shirley Valentine on stage. When Lewis Gilbert, the director of *Educating Rita,* turned *Shirley Valentine* into a movie, he cast her in the title role, and she was nominated for an Academy Award in 1989. Kenneth Branagh found himself favorably compared to the great Laurence Olivier when he brought his version of *Henry V* to the screen in 1989, and, like Olivier in 1944, not only adapted Shakespeare's play, but also directed and starred in it.

If Britain produced an international box office star during the eighties, it was Bob Hoskins. The actor with the Cockney accent was as surprised as anyone by his success. Raised in North London, Hoskins had never even thought of becoming an actor, but when he accidentally read for his first part at the age of 26, he got it. He worked steadily in theater and attracted notice playing the song sheet salesman in Dennis Potter's TV mini-series, *Pennies from Heaven.* The real career breakthrough came in 1980 when he was cast as the beleaguered gangster whose empire is crumbling around him in *The Long Good Friday.* He played tough-guy roles in Francis Coppola's *The Cotton Club* and Neil Jordan's *Mona Lisa.* He was supposed to play Al Capone in Brian De Palma's *The Untouchables,* then Robert De Niro, who previously turned the role down, reconsidered. It was after losing *The Untouchables* that Hoskins landed the biggest, and probably most difficult role of his career — starring opposite the animated Roger Rabbit and friends in Touchstone's *Who Framed Roger Rabbit* (1988). "Other people talk about being on stage with Laurence Olivier," Hoskins said. "I was going to be on film with Bugs Bunny, Donald Duck, Mickey Mouse, everybody — the big boys. I loved it."

IN THE EARLY EIGHTIES, THERE SEEMED TO be no stopping the Australian film industry. Australian movies were admired around the world. Films in the late seventies and early eighties such as *The Chant of Jimmie Blacksmith, My Brilliant Career, Picnic at Hanging Rock, Gallipoli* and *Breaker Morant,* were small, inexpensively made, and they didn't try to hide the fact that they were Australian — and yet they appealed to audiences around the world. In 1981, George Miller's *The Road Warrior,* a futuristic action thriller with Mel Gibson, became Australia's biggest international hit (and, incidentally, the most imitated movie of the eighties). The following year, Peter Weir, again using Gibson, scored another international success with *The Year of Living Dangerously.* At the same time came the release of *The Man from Snowy River,* an outback horse opera which usurped *Road Warrior* as Australia's biggest success.

While other directors packed their bags and headed for Holly-

***The Chant of Jimmie Blacksmith*, made in 1978 by Fred Schepisi, was the highest-budgeted film made in Australia to that date. But its international acclaim drew Schepisi to Hollywood were he languished for a couple of years, making one little-seen western, *Barbarosa* (1981), and becoming involved in a number of projects that never quite came together. Then Norman Jewison hired him in 1984 to direct *Iceman*, about a Neanderthal man (John Lone, *above*), thawed from Arctic ice.**

***Below*: *Phar Lap* (1984), the true story of an Australian champion race horse, did very well with international audiences during the decade.**

No, that's not the American West, but the Southern Alps, although in *The Man From Snowy River* (1983), *opposite*, it was sometimes difficult to tell the difference. Based on a poem by A.B. "Banjo" Paterson, the plot even sounded as though it had been borrowed from an American western: a young man (Tom Burlinson, *below*) sets out to tame a herd of wild horses and falls in love with a cattle-man's daughter. Critics sneered at the movie's corniness but the movie was a huge international success, spawned a much less successful sequel, and helped to fuel the boom in Australian filmmaking.

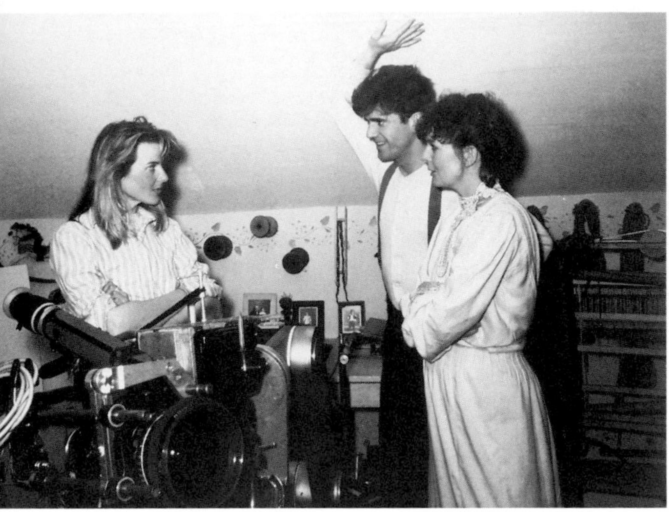

Gillian Armstrong, (*above, left,* with Mel Gibson and Diane Keaton) having directed *My Brilliant Career* (1980) and *Starstruck* (1982), came to Canada in 1984 to make *Mrs. Soffel,* the true story of a prison warden's wife (Keaton) who runs off with the convict (Gibson) she loves. The movie did no business at the box office, and Armstrong returned to Australia.

Below: Yahoo Serious was the unlikely star of an equally unlikely movie titled *Young Einstein.* The movie was a success in Australia, but when it was released in North America in 1989 it was, to put it mildly, no *Crocodile Dundee* at the box office.

wood — among them, Fred Schepisi to do *Barbarosa,* Peter Weir to direct *Witness,* Bruce Beresford to make *Tender Mercies,* and George Miller to take on *The Witches of Eastwick* — Paul Cox, the most personal of the Australian directors to emerge during the decade, decided to stay home and make such unconventional delights as *Lonely Hearts* and *Man of Flowers.* Cox became known, in a country that sniffed at that sort of thing, as its sole creator of so-called "art films."

By the mid-eighties, something had gone terribly wrong with the Australian industry. Lavish tax concessions resulted in a lot of movies being made by producers who merely wanted the benefits of tax-free dollars and could not care less about the quality of movies that were turned out. Ironically, it was during this time that *Crocodile Dundee* (1986), starring Paul Hogan, was released around the world. As *Dundee* amassed more than $300 million in worldwide grosses, the government was growing tired of the tax concessions, investors were backing off, and, by 1987, little more than a year after the release of *Dundee,* there was virtually no Australian movie industry.

The cries for help were quickly heard by a government enjoying Australia's highly visible international profile (*Crocodile Dundee* was certainly a great help). By 1989, a newly created Australian Film Finance Corporation was making $79 million in financing available to producers, and Australia once again had a hit heard around the

Sam Neill and Nicole Kidman in *Dead Calm* (1989).

world — a thriller, *Dead Calm,* starring Sam Neill and newcomer Nicole Kidman.

"Australia has always been a country seeking cultural verification," explained David Williamson, one of the writers of *The Year of Living Dangerously.* "We're stuck down here. We don't have a spectacular economic success like the United States, or cultural success like Europe. We are desperate for recognition because we never had any."

Canadians tended to be immensely proud of the international success of director Norman Jewison. Although he often filmed portions of his films (including *Moonstruck*, 1987) in Canada, the only movie he ever directed that was actually set in his native country was *Agnes of God* (1985), *above*, with Jane Fonda and Meg Tilly.

CANADA, LIKE AUSTRALIA, WAS ALSO A COUNTRY in search of some sort of cultural verification. It was a land where American films and culture so thoroughly dominated that it was hard for anything Canadian to survive. Until the Japanese came along, Canada was the biggest foreign market for American movies. In fact, the Americans considered Canada part of *their* domestic market.

Despite the fact that Canadians, for the most part, looked down on their own movies, there was, for a time in the late seventies and early eighties, support for a film industry propped up largely by government tax incentives. The same thing happened in Canada as happened in Australia: a lot of people who had no business or interest making movies made them and took the 100 percent tax writeoffs then being allowed. The movies produced were largely unreleased — and unreleasable.

In Vancouver, a producer named Peter O'Brian, after trying for years, finally made *The Grey Fox* (1982). It was a turn-of-the-century western about Canada's first train robber — it said something about the country's cultural problems that the first bank robber turned out to be an American (played by former American stuntman Richard Farnsworth). Directed by a young documentary filmmaker named Philip Borsos, *The Grey Fox* attracted international attention, and, even though it was not a box office hit in its own country, it did serve to remind Canadians that it was indeed possible to make worthwhile films.

Still, the industry floundered, and debates flared over the government tax incentives. About the only filmmaker in Canada who didn't care about any of this was a Toronto director named David Cronenberg. Cronenberg had been making low-budget horror movies in Canada since 1975. Movies such as *Rabid* and *Scanners* horrified critics but attracted audiences and — something almost unheard of in Canadian film — profits. Nevertheless, in a country uncertain of either its cultural identity or its ability to make films, Cronenberg and his sometimes producing partner Ivan Reitman, were Canada's most castigated — and successful — filmmakers.

In 1982, Cronenberg finished a new movie titled *Videodrome.* Not only did it do good business but, unusual for a Cronenberg movie, it also received admiring reviews. Producer Dino De Laurentiis saw

***Above*: The remake of *The Fly* (1986), with Jeff Goldblum, was the most successful film of Canadian director David Cronenberg's career.**

***Below*: Director Sandy Wilson filmed a charming coming-of-age movie in 1985 called *My American Cousin*. The cousin was played by Canadian actor John Wildman.**

***Opposite, above*: The ladies of *The Decline of the American Empire* (1986).**

***Opposite, below*: Lothaire Bluteau as *Jesus of Montreal* (1989).**

Videodrome, liked it, and hired Cronenberg to make *The Dead Zone* (1983) based on a novel by Stephen King. As the end of the decade approached, Cronenberg's talents had matured to the point where a 1986 remake of *The Fly* became his most accomplished horror film, and the biggest hit of his career. Cronenberg followed it in 1988 with *Dead Ringers*, his most ambitious and uncompromising movie. The horror story of twin gynecologists (brilliantly portrayed by Jeremy Irons) becoming more and more obsessed with each other was not a big success, but it did confirm Cronenberg as the most original Canadian director working in the English language.

In the latter part of the eighties, government tax incentives mostly dried up, along with private investment. Most Canadian producers could fund their films only through the government's Telefilm Canada. Budgets were small, and audiences for the resulting movies were limited. Nonetheless, a clutch of diverse and interesting filmmakers survived: Francis Mankiewicz (*Les bons Débarras*), Atom Egoyan (*Speaking Parts*), Sandy Wilson (*My American Cousin*), Leon Marr (*Dancing in the Dark*), Patricia Rozema (*I've Heard the Mermaids Singing*), Yves Simoneau (*Pouvoir intime*) and Jean-Claude Lauzon (*Un zoo la nuit*).

The film industry in Quebec generally fared much better than

English-language Canadian cinema. Filmmakers working in French did not seem so concerned with the cultural shadow cast by American movies, and French-speaking Quebec audiences were much more willing to see locally produced films that reflected their lives. "There are Quebec stars that are not interchangeable with American stars," said Stephen J. Roth, the chairman of a Canadian film production company, Cinexus Capital. "There are Quebec jokes, customs and politics which are not interchangeable with what's available in American movies. The differences in English Canada are more subtle and difficult to find, and yet it is those we have to build on."

By far and away the most internationally popular of Canadian filmmakers was a genial, cultured Montrealer named Denys Arcand. Arcand had toiled away for years making other people's films. Finally, he decided to write something that pleased him. The resulting film, *The Decline of the American Empire* pleased just about everyone. In 1986, it became the first Canadian film ever to be nominated for an Academy Award for best foreign film. Three years later, the second Canadian film ever to be nominated for a foreign-language Oscar was *Jesus of Montreal*, also written and directed by Denys Arcand.

If Arcand's success came from making personal films that were

Donald Sutherland, like most Canadian actors, had to leave home in order to become a success. He was living in London when director Robert Aldrich cast him to play a small part in *The Dirty Dozen* in 1967. A couple of years later he was chosen to play Hawkeye Pierce in Robert Altman's *M*A*S*H*. The movie was the runaway surprise hit of 1970. Thereafter, he enjoyed a wildly varied and busy career, making as many as four films a year. He slowed down in the eighties, however, and his son Kiefer Sutherland became the star in the family. Donald Sutherland returned home often to make movies, and in 1987 he was in China filming *Bethune*, the story of the Canadian battlefield surgeon Norman Bethune, a hero of the Chinese revolution. After many delays, the film was finally completed in 1990.

Catherine Mary Stewart was from Edmonton, Alberta. She modeled and landed a role in a television soap, *The Days of Our Lives*, before breaking into feature films. She never broke through to major Hollywood stardom, but she worked a lot during the eighties in such easily forgotten pictures as *The Last Starfighter* (1984), *Mischief* (1985), *Dudes* (1987), *below, and Weekend at Bernie's* (1989). Toward the end of the decade, at the age of 30, Stewart mused: "I think in five years I'll be at a point in my life and career that the performances start showing that I've got the acting experience, and the life experience as well."

local and yet universal at the same time — *Decline* dealt with sex and declining values; *Jesus of Montreal* railed against just about everything — most of the Canadian filmmakers the world heard about during the decade were successful precisely because they didn't stay home and they did not make personal films. Ivan Reitman, Cronenberg's producer, left for Hollywood, where he produced *National Lampoon's Animal House* and directed *Ghostbusters,* which co-starred two other Canadians, Dan Aykroyd and Rick Moranis. Michael J. Fox left Vancouver in order to become a star. Norman Jewison did not leave Canada, but frequently he flew back and forth between Hollywood and Toronto during the decade. James Cameron, who went on to write and direct *Terminator, Aliens* and *The Abyss,* was from Northern Ontario. And Touchstone hired two Canadian writers, Jim Cruickshank and James Orr, to turn a French movie called *Three Men and a Cradle* into an American hit, *Three Men and a Baby.* In the eighties, while the film industry in Canada languished, the most popular American movies were often being made by Canadians.

The French Love Dolphins and Bears; The Germans, Italians and Spanish Keep Laughing

JEAN-JACQUES ANNAUD WAS LUNCHING AT HIS favorite Paris restaurant. He ordered fish and a bottle of Evian water, and began to tear away at the bread while waiters fussed around him. In his forties, he had the sort of wide, disarming smile that not even a movie producer could resist. That smile could be deceptive, however. Annaud was a filmmaker possessed of granite resolve and patience. Since winning an Academy Award for his first film, *Black and White in Color,* he had made three very different and exceedingly difficult movies whose eventual success had made him the most popular French director of the eighties. *Quest for Fire,* a story of Neanderthal man, was shot mostly in the wilderness of Canada's Northern Ontario. *The Name of the Rose* was based on the international bestseller by Umberto Eco. And now there was *L'ours* (*The Bear*), his most difficult and challenging movie — and by far and away his biggest hit.

Annaud's movie, released in Europe in 1988 and written by Gérard Brach, was about an orphaned bear cub that gets involved with an adult grizzly to escape a pair of hunters. What made the story unique was that it was told from the bears' point of view.

The bears themselves could be unpredictable and dangerous, despite years of training — Annaud was mauled during what was supposed to be a friendly photo session. The trainer would have to be hidden, and the chances were very good that if the animal performed a move once, it would not want to repeat it. Bears had never heard of retakes. Sometimes Annaud and his crew would wait two or three days for the bear to decide to do a single move. "If we were fortunate," Annaud said, "we would get 12 seconds of film a day. Many days we would get nothing."

Patience and perseverance were amply rewarded. *The Bear* would gross over $100 million worldwide. In the midst of a period of declining attendance at theaters throughout France, *The Bear* was the number-one hit of 1988, outgrossing American films such as *Who Framed Roger Rabbit* and *Rain Man.* It was difficult to find anyone in France who had not seen the movie, in the same way it was difficult to find anyone in North America in 1982 who had not seen *E.T.*

The public was more and more distracted from French movies by the twin demons of home video and American movies, but even so, France still managed to retain one of the healthiest film industries: an average of 150 movies were produced annually during the eighties for an audience that remained one of the largest in Europe

Director Jean-Jacques Annaud, *below*, cast two unknowns as the leads in his production of *The Bear* (1988). Bart, *left, above*, was a kodiak bear who stood nine feet tall and weighed 1,800 pounds. The little bear cub, *above, right*, was played principally by Douce, who had such consumate charm and personality in front of the camera that the selection committee of the César, the French Academy Awards, was concerned that if Douce was put up as a best actor nominee, not only would the cub be nominated, but there was a very good chance that she would win. Annaud decided not to enter the cub's name for nomination, and one of the great French acting performances of the decade went unrewarded.

Gérard Depardieu, as Rodin in *Camille Claudel* (1989), was France's most popular actor during the eighties. He was born in 1948 in Châteauroux, in the region of France known as Berri, and grew up poor in a two-room house with five siblings. His father was an illiterate sheet metal worker more interested in fishing and drinking than he was in earning a living. Depardieu was a petty thief by the age of eight, and could barely read when he dropped out of school at the age of 12. He held a variety of jobs, before moving to Paris where he drifted into acting in his mid-teens. "I got into acting," he said later, "to try not to be taken for what I looked like — a hoodlum."

— about 122 million tickets were sold. What's more, French films were never in more demand in Hollywood than they were in the eighties, if not in their original versions, then as the raw material for American productions. Often, that raw material was not made good use of. Coline Serreau's hit *Three Men and a Cradle* became Hollywood's *Three Men and a Baby*. Serreau's next film, *Romuald et Juliette* was also a hit, and she came to Hollywood to prepare an American version, *Mama, There's a Man in Your Bed*, with Richard Dreyfuss starring. Francis Veber, the screenwriter who wrote *La cage aux folles* was brought to Hollywood to turn his comedy *Les fugitifs* into *Three Fugitives*, with Nick Nolte done up to look like Gérard Depardieu. *Cousin, Cousine*, a hit from the seventies, became a limp

Hollywood comedy, *Cousins,* in the eighties. And American director Paul Brickman adapted *La vie continue* into a Jessica Lange drama, *Men Don't Leave.*

The most popular French star of the eighties chose not to adapt himself for the American cinema. Gérard Depardieu, a former street tough and high school dropout, said he didn't have to leave home — perhaps because he didn't have time. He was the most prolific actor in the history of French movies, a beefy six-foot-tall blond, "Europe's hunk," possessed, as director Bertrand Blier observed, of "a wonderful inner madness." He made as many as four films a year, drawing on a seemingly inexhaustible supply of energy and a willingness to try just about anything on the screen. Depardieu appeared in more than 50 films — everything from François Truffaut's *The Last Metro,* to the French revolutionary *Danton,* to *The Return of Martin Guerre,* to Jean-Jacques Beineix's *La lune dans le caniveau* (*The Moon in the Gutter*) and *Jean de Florette.* He often had two films in the theaters at the same time, as he did early in 1989 when *Camille Claudel* (in which he played Rodin) and *Trop belle pour toi* (*Too Beautiful for You*) were both hits. Early in 1990, he was back in a lavish retelling of *Cyrano de Bergerac,* and was preparing to finally reinvent himself — a little bit — for the American movies, and make his North American debut in Peter Weir's *Green Card.*

"Acting is a woman's language," he stated. "The desire to be liked, to seduce. So, if I'm an actor at all, I'm a female actor — maybe the most feminine of all."

While Depardieu was the most popular male star to appear during the decade, Isabelle Adjani was the biggest female star. The daughter of an Algerian garage mechanic father and a Bavarian mother, Adjani started attracting attention when she was very young. At the age of 13, she was invited to join the Comédie-Française without an audition, and, at 18, was starring in Truffaut's *The Story of Adèle H.* as the daughter of Victor Hugo who is driven mad by her love for a young soldier. Fourteen years later, she was to play another woman destroyed by love, Camille Claudel, who was the mistress of Auguste Rodin and was finally placed in an insane asylum, where she spent the last 30 years of her life. Adjani initiated the project, worked on the script for three years, and got Bruno Nuytten, a director of photography who was also the father of her child, to direct. *Camille Claudel* was the biggest French hit of 1989, and Adjani received a César, the French equivalent of America's Academy Awards, as well as an Oscar nomi-

American films occasionally made use of European actresses during the eighties, but usually not very well. Isabelle Adjani, *above,* France's most popular actress, was dating Warren Beatty at the time she co-starred with him and Dustin Hoffman in the ill-fated *Ishtar* (1987). Dutch actress Maruschka Detmers became somewhat notorious for performing oral sex on her lover in Marco Bellocchio's *The Devil in the Flesh* (1987). She appeared in an English-language picture, *Hanna's War* (1988), *below,* that caused a great deal less fuss.

Above: Béatrice Dalle played the sensually beautiful-but-crazy young woman in *Betty Blue* (1986), directed by Jean-Jacques Beineix.

Below: Emmanuelle Béart played the title role in *Manon of the Spring* (1987), the conclusion of the Marcel Pagnol story that began with *Jean de Florette* (1986). Directed by Claude Berri and written by Gérard Brach, the two films were immensely popular, not only in France, but around the world as well.

nation for her performance.

New and popular faces appeared during the decade: Christopher Lambert, Valerie Kaprisky, Lambert Wilson, Sandrine Bonnaire, Carole Bouquet, Emmanuelle Béart. Still, the French public tended to stay loyal to its veterans: Catherine Deneuve retained her potent beauty and stardom into her forties. Philippe Noiret, in his late fifties, was second only to Depardieu in screen popularity, particularly in the acclaimed *La vie et rien d'autre*. Jean-Paul Belmondo churned out a series of action-oriented *policiers* during the eighties, although when he tried something different, as he did in Claude Lelouch's *Itinéraire d'un enfant gâté*, audiences still responded. Alain Delon was not so fortunate; the public appeared to grow tired of his tough-guy movies. But Yves Montand, approaching 70, remained a box office star in *Jean de Florette* and in Jacques Demy's musical comedy *Trois places pour le 26*.

DURING THE EIGHTIES, THERE WAS A NEW Socialist government in France, and a Ministry of Culture devoted to the cinema. And French producers kept costs down — all but 41 of the 137 movies produced in 1989 cost under 20 million French francs, or just over 3 million in American dollars. French television was all-important to the financing of feature films.

In the eighties, producers were content, for the most part, to repeat previous commercial successes, in dramatic contrast to the fifties and sixties, when the so-called New Wave rolled across French cinema. In those days, filmmakers such as Truffaut and Jean-Luc Godard breathed fresh air into the stuffy halls of an academic and lifeless cinema — to paraphrase Roman Polanski. They also inadvertently helped kill film for a whole generation of technicians. Lighting cameramen, costume and set designers were no longer needed. As they died, their knowledge died with them. At one point, it appeared every film was set in contemporary times, shot on the streets or in real interiors, with natural lighting and casts made up of friends of the director who wore their own clothes.

By the beginning of the eighties, however, the rebels of the New Wave had become the film establishment. François Truffaut, the darling of North American critics and audiences, had already done his best work and settled in to being cute — it was Godard who pointed out that Truffaut now made the kind of films he used to attack when he was a critic for *Cahiers du Cinéma*. Truffaut died tragically in 1984 of a brain tumor at the age of 52. He had made only three films in the decade, the most popular of which was *The Last Metro* (released in 1980, co-starring Depardieu and Catherine

Deneuve) — his first hit in years. He had come to depend largely on the North American box office for his films, the French audiences not being nearly so enthusiastic.

Claude Chabrol, another of the most prominent New Wave directors, a filmmaker who had few illusions about himself or anyone else, often laughed about his reputation outside France. "They always seem to like my worst films," he said. "Don't they know I can make very dreadful films just like every director? Still, given the way the French feel about me, I'm glad I can be a hero somewhere."

Chabrol specialized in guilt, suspicion, betrayal and romantic love, themes explored in films such as *Fantômes du chapelier* and *Poulet au vinaigre*, a thriller in which it seemed the whole world had a secret. Chabrol's most popular film of the eighties, however, was *Une affaire de femmes*, a huge hit in France that received international distribution and restored his reputation as one of the grand old masters.

Jean-Luc Godard held on to his reputation as one of the most iconoclastic and unpredictable French filmmakers — as well as the most controversial. His modern-day retelling of the story of the Virgin Mary in *Hail Mary* upset the Catholic church and religious groups

Simon de la Brosse and Charlotte Gainsbourg in *The Little Thief* (1988).

in Europe and North America, who tried to have it banned. Controversy caused *Hail Mary* to become one of the few Godard movies that made money in the eighties.

The "New" New Wave of Directors, who came into their own during the seventies, continued to make provocative films through the eighties. Claude Miller (*The Little Thief*, based on an unfinished Truffaut script); Bertrand Tavernier (*Life and Nothing But*); Maurice Pialat (*Under Satan's Sun*), the decade's most controversial winner of the Cannes Film Festival's Palme d'Or.

For all its supposed difficulties, French film continued to find room

It's a good thing Harrison Ford didn't let go of Emmanuelle Seigner's hand in *Frantic* (1988). After finishing the thriller shot in Paris, she married its director, Roman Polanski. Ford met Polanski while he was in Paris with his wife, Melissa Mathison, who was working on a screenplay. The director and star hit it off and decided to make a movie together.

Isabelle Huppert was one of the most respected and prolific French actresses during the decade. She was delightful opposite Philippe Noiret in *Coup de Torchon* (1981), also known as *Clean Slate*, and even in a rather lame comedy such as *My Best Friend's Girl* (1984), her charm and sensuality shone through. However, she did not fare nearly as well when she made *The Trout* (1982) for the late Joseph Losey, *Cactus* (1986) for Australian director Paul Cox and her American movie debut in *Heaven's Gate* (1981). Her second American film was a limp thriller titled *The Bedroom Window* (1987), *above*, in which she co-starred with Steve Guttenberg.

for an amazing number of newcomers. In 1988, for example, 26 directors made their feature film debuts. The two most popular directors to come out of the eighties were Jean-Jacques Beineix and Luc Besson. Both directors were much less interested in stories than they were in images. "I'm trying to express myself with images," Beineix maintained. "It has nothing to do with literature."

Beineix's first film, a stylish thriller titled *Diva,* was originally rejected by the French critics and the public when it was released, in 1981. In North America, however, it was enthusiastically received, and the movie became one of the most popular French-language films released with English subtitles (it eventually was eclipsed by the immense popularity of *Jean de Florette*).

His next film, *La lune dans le caniveau* (*The Moon in the Gutter*) was trashed by critics and ignored by the public, although its almost liquid fluidity and its haunting story of a man (Gérard Depardieu) searching for the rapist/murderer of his sister, attracted a great number of admirers. Depardieu was not one of them; he loudly denounced the film, although his co-star, Nastassia Kinski stood by Beineix.

Jean-Marc Barr and Rosanna Arquette in Luc Besson's *The Big Blue* (1988).

Beineix's third film, *Betty Blue,* was considerably more popular, although he was right back in trouble with both the critics and the public in 1989 when *Roselyne and the Lions* was released.

Luc Besson had considerably more luck. Besson made an auspicious debut with his first film *Le dernier combat* (*The Last Combat*), about a lone survivor in Paris after a nuclear catastrophe. The movie was shot in black and white without dialogue. After that came *Subway,* directed as almost a series of video clips, with a story that made little sense. Teenaged audiences loved it, however, as they did Besson's next film, *Le grand bleu (The Big Blue).*

Hooted off the screen at the Cannes Film Festival, it opened in French theaters in May of 1988, and went on to become the biggest

Next to Depardieu, France's most popular actor at the end of the decade was Philippe Noiret. *Life and Nothing But, above,* Bertrand Tavernier's drama of World War I, was a big hit in 1988, and re-established Noiret's immense popularity. Below: Yves Montand had been a popular singer and actor for four decades, and despite the death of his wife, Simone Signoret, in 1985, Montand's stardom remained intact during the decade thanks to the huge success of *Jean de Florette* (1986).

Opposite: Valerie Kaprisky made her American movie debut in a remake of Godard's *Breathless* in 1983 co-starring with Richard Gere.

Klaus Maria Brandauer, with Faye Dunaway in ***The Burning Secret*** (1988), was a highly respected stage actor in Austria, but he had done little film work before the Hungarian director Istvan Szabo hired him to star in ***Mephisto*** (1981). The film made him something of an international sensation. He played the villain in ***Never Say Never Again*** (1983) and Meryl Streep's philandering husband in ***Out of Africa*** (1985), for which he was nominated for an Academy Award.

Das Boot (1981) or ***The Boat***, concerned life aboard a German U-boat, U-96, as it went after British shipping during World War II. Directed by Wolfgang Petersen, the film provided a graphically claustrophobic view of what it was like to be trapped aboard what amounted to a leaky, crowded tin can. Jürgen Prochnow, ***centre***, was the gimlet-eyed U-boat captain. The film, the most expensive ever produced in Germany at the time, was also the country's biggest international hit.

hit at the French box office during the eighties. *The Big Blue* made Besson a star with the young audience that flocked again and again to see the superb underwater images. They didn't seem to mind the skimpy plot, which revolved around a contest to see who could hold their breath underwater the longest, and contrasted a not-very-happy love affair on the shore with a very happy relationship with the dolphins at sea.

Besson was so incensed by the press response to *The Big Blue*, that, when he completed his next film, *Nikita*, he refused to press screen it. The film, about a condemned murderess/drug addict turned into a professional assassin by some secret French agency, was a hit when it was released early in 1990 — and even some critics liked it.

THE GERMANS WERE ABLE TO BRING DOWN THE wall, but they could not save their film industry from the doldrums in the eighties. Ironically, the wall fell just as the German cinema — having reached new heights of artistic achievement and commercial success earlier in the decade — now seemed without direction and in crisis.

The "New German Cinema" began in the early seventies with young directors like Werner Herzog, Alexander Kluge, Wim Wenders and Rainer Werner Fassbinder making personal films on a low budget backed, for the most part, by government subsidies derived from taxes on television sets and theater tickets. By 1979, German films and directors were winning nearly every prize at every major film festival. Leading them all was Fassbinder, the Bavarian-born former actor who was influenced by the American melodramas of Douglas Sirk. Immensely prolific — no major director cranked out as many films — his melodramas were fast-moving, technically brilliant, often darkly comic, featuring characters destroying themselves through self-delusion or by accepting society's usually twisted values. Audiences around the world flocked to see *The Marriage of Maria Braun*, made in 1979; and on German television, *Berlin-Alexanderplatz*, about pre-war Germany's slide into hell, was a big hit. Fassbinder was at the height of his creative and technical prowess when he made *Veronika Voss*, the tale of an ex-film star in the clutches of corrupt doctors, done as a kind of remake of *Sunset Boulevard*. Fassbinder made one more film, *Querelle*, before he died suddenly from a drug overdose in 1982 at the age of 36. His death seemed to traumatize the German film industry. It was as though the train had lost its locomotive. Other directors continued to make films, but the energy and inspiration had disappeared. Wim

Wenders was perhaps the one exception. His 1976 *Kings of the Road* was considered a masterpiece of the German cinema, and he continued into the eighties, making films such as *Paris, Texas* and *Wings of Desire* that were often highly praised among critics, and applauded at film festivals.

By the end of the eighties, however, audiences had turned increasingly to comedy, not a genre for which the German cinema previously had been noted. Doris Dörrie's *Men* was a surprise hit in 1986, as was *Me and Him*, a comedy shot in English in New York about a man with a talking penis. And Percy Adlon's *Bagdad Cafe* was an international success.

Above: **Wim Wenders, whose reputation was second only to Fassbinder's, attracted international audiences to his films. *Paris, Texas* (1984), featured Dean Stockwell, *left*, and Harry Dean Stanton, *right*.**

Insert: **Director Percy Adlon (*Celeste*, 1981 and *Sugarbaby*, 1985) set his first English-language film, *Bagdad Cafe* (1988) on the edge of the Mojave Desert. Veteran American actor Jack Palance, *above,* played a former Hollywood set painter.**

Italian director Francesco Rosi produced a lavish and surprisingly cinematic version of *Carmen* in 1984. If Placido Domingo seemed a trifle old and plump portraying the naive army corporal, one overlooked it as soon as he opened his mouth to sing. American singer Julia Migenes-Johnson was superb in the title role.

Audiences all over the world embraced Pedro Almodóvar's delightful social comedy, *Women on the Verge of a Nervous Breakdown* (1988). However, his next comedy, *Tie Me Up! Tie Me Down!* (1990) was much more controversial, and much less successful. It concerned a porn actress (Victoria Abril, *above*) who is kidnapped by a young admirer, who eventually succeeds in making her fall in love with him.

Opposite: Maurizio Nichetti, *centre,* was known as Italy's Woody Allen, and directed and starred in *The Icicle Thief* (1989).

THE ITALIANS ALSO PREFERRED LAUGHTER. The biggest hit of the 1988-89 season was a modestly budgeted comedy, *The Little Devil* (*Il piccolo diavolo*), starring the most popular new Italian star of the decade, Roberto Benigni (best known to North American audiences from Jim Jarmusch's *Down by Law*). Internationally, Maurizio Nichetti created a stir with *The Icicle Thief* (*Ladri di saponette*), a sly reference to De Sica's *The Bicycle Thief,* and a gentle spoof of television and the way it handles movies. Giuseppe Tornatore's *Cinema Paradiso* also dealt with a love of the cinema, and went on to win the Oscar for best foreign film in 1989. It, along with the success of *Icicle Thief* in the same year, hinted at a long-awaited resurgence of an industry that languished through most of the eighties.

Italy continued to turn out about 100 films a year, throughout the eighties, but few of those movies received wide release. The Taviani brothers, Paolo and Vittorio, made at least one masterpiece, *Night of the Shooting Stars,* and one not-quite masterpiece, *Good Morning, Babylon.* The Russian Nikita Mikhalkov made the very Italian romantic melodrama *Dark Eyes* with the very Italian Marcello Mastroianni, who gave one of the decade's great performances.

The exterior of Giuseppe Tornatore's *Cinema Paradiso* (1989).

Bernardo Bertolucci, the most internationally renowned Italian filmmaker, made *The Tragedy of a Ridiculous Man* in Italy. But his most ambitious achievement, *The Last Emperor,* was shot on location in China. The great Federico Fellini stayed home during the eighties and made *City of Women* and *The Voice of the Moon.*

In Spain during the eighties, Carlos Saura made *Blood Wedding* and a great flamenco dance version of *Carmen.* But otherwise, just about the only Spanish filmmaker who could attract international

Mishima: A Life in Four Chapters **(1985) was one of the most audaciously ambitious films attempted during the eighties. The American screenwriter and director Paul Schrader undertook to bring to the screen the life of Yukio Mishima: soldier, philosopher, right-wing fanatic, Japan's most popular and controversial novelist, and, eventually, a suicide victim who committed *hara-kiri* at the age of 45. The Japanese were often hostile toward the idea, and the major American studios were uninterested, until Francis Coppola and George Lucas stepped in to lend a hand. Ken Ogata, *above*, played the title role. The movie was bold and lovely, and if it did not always work, it was never less than fascinating. Mishima was released only briefly in North America and was not seen at all in Japan, such was the touchiness about the subject. Schrader, who previously had directed *Blue Collar* (1978) and *American Gigolo* (1980), had to go back to screenwriting-for-hire for a time in order to pay off the debts incurred by his decision to do *Mishima*.**

distribution was a young director named Pedro Almodóvar. A former pop singer, who once appeared on stage in fishnet stockings singing "I Want to Be a Mother," Almodóvar made his feature film debut in 1984, and, within four years, was finishing *Women on the Verge of a Nervous Breakdown,* about what happens when a woman discovers her husband is having an affair. It grossed an astronomical $9 million in Spain alone — the most successful film in the country's history. It then went on to become a worldwide success, and established Almodóvar as one of the major European filmmakers to emerge during the decade. Had success changed him? Not as far as he was concerned, he advised the Spanish public in *El País,* the country's most prestigious newspaper. However, he was having this terrible problem with constipation . . .

IN THE EASTERN BLOC COUNTRIES, THE ONE great discovery of the decade was the Polish filmmaker Krzysztof Kieślowski. He made short films and several features in the seventies. But it was his *A Short Film about Killing* that attracted raves at the Cannes Film Festival in 1987. It dealt with what happens when a taxi driver is senselessly killed by a young man, who, in turn, is senselessly killed by the state. The other major film figure who emerged out of Eastern Europe, Andrei Tarkovsky, was exiled from his native Russia. Tarkovsky's was a meditative cinema in which an extremely personal world was created in long takes full of precise details. His final films *Nostalghia* and *The Sacrifice* were made in exile in Italy and Sweden respectively. *The Sacrifice* was a rumination about the director's own impending death.

On the other side of the world, the films of Lino Brocka showed, with unflinching authenticity, the poverty, political repression and corruption in the Philippines under Marcos. Brocka had started out making popular entertainment, but increasingly his movies — the most popular shown in the Philippines — focused on criticisms of the Marcos regime. Films such as *Jaguar* and *Bona* ran into problems being shown at home, but were screened at festivals around the world, and were a major reason why the world began to focus on the fight for democracy in the Philippines.

Audiences in Hong Kong loved action and martial arts pictures, although increasingly, during the eighties, young directors began to make films that had something to say. Most notable was Ann Hui, who began by making ghost comedies, but then turned up with two emotionally wrenching films about the problem of refugees, *Woo Viet* and *Boat People.* In Taiwan, the government both supported and interfered with the local cinema. Still, Edward Yang was able to make *Taipei Story*, and Hou Hsiao-hsien was able to produce *City of Sadness*, a masterpiece that was to the history of Taiwan what *Gone with the Wind* was to the history of the American South.

The Japanese loved films about animals during the eighties — the biggest Japanese-produced hit of the decade was 1983's *Nankyoku Monogatari* (called *Antarctica* abroad), about faithful sled dogs and their Japanese hunter masters. Otherwise, if they went to Japanese movies at all, it was to see samurai dramas, low-budget comedies featuring pop music stars, and sequels such as the popular "Tora San" adventures.

The good news was that two of Japan's great masters of cinema continued to work. Shohei Imamura made *The Ballad of Narayama*, winner of the Palme d'Or at the Cannes Film Festival in 1983, and *Black Rain* in 1989. The legendary Akira Kurosawa made two films, *Kagemusha* and *Ran*, although both of them had to be financed with the help of Francis Coppola and George Lucas. At the end of the decade, at the age of 79, he was preparing yet another movie, the autobiographical *Dreams*, with help, this time, from Steven Spielberg. He remained as outspoken as ever, and, when he talked about the state of Japanese film, he might have been summing up much of the movie world beyond Hollywood: "The films they show are hardly worth seeing anyway; it's by and large the same stuff you see on TV, and why pay for what you can see at home for nothing?"

Akira Kurosawa, the great Japanese master of the cinema was 75 years old when he filmed *Ran* in 1985. Based on Shakespeare's *King Lear*, the film told the story of an aging and confused warlord, and the family struggle that breaks out when he gives control of his empire to one of his three sons. *Ran* was a throwback to the epic movie-making of Kurosawa's *The Seven Samurai* (1955) and *Yojimbo* (1962). It was not the first time the director put Shakespeare to good use. *Throne of Blood*, made in 1957, was based on *Macbeth*.

EPILOGUE
BACKWARD INTO THE FUTURE

Above: **The only surprise in the sequel *Another 48 HRS* (1990), was that it took Eddie Murphy and co-star Nick Nolte along with director Walter Hill the better part of a decade to do it.**

At the beginning of the nineties, Hollywood was once again circling the wagons. The cost of making a movie had more than doubled from the beginning of the eighties to an average of $23 million, and audiences dipped just enough to give pause to the always-sensitive industry. The number of motion pictures being made was down 30 percent, and even the video boom appeared to be quieting, as the novelty of watching movies on VCRs began to wear off. Accord-

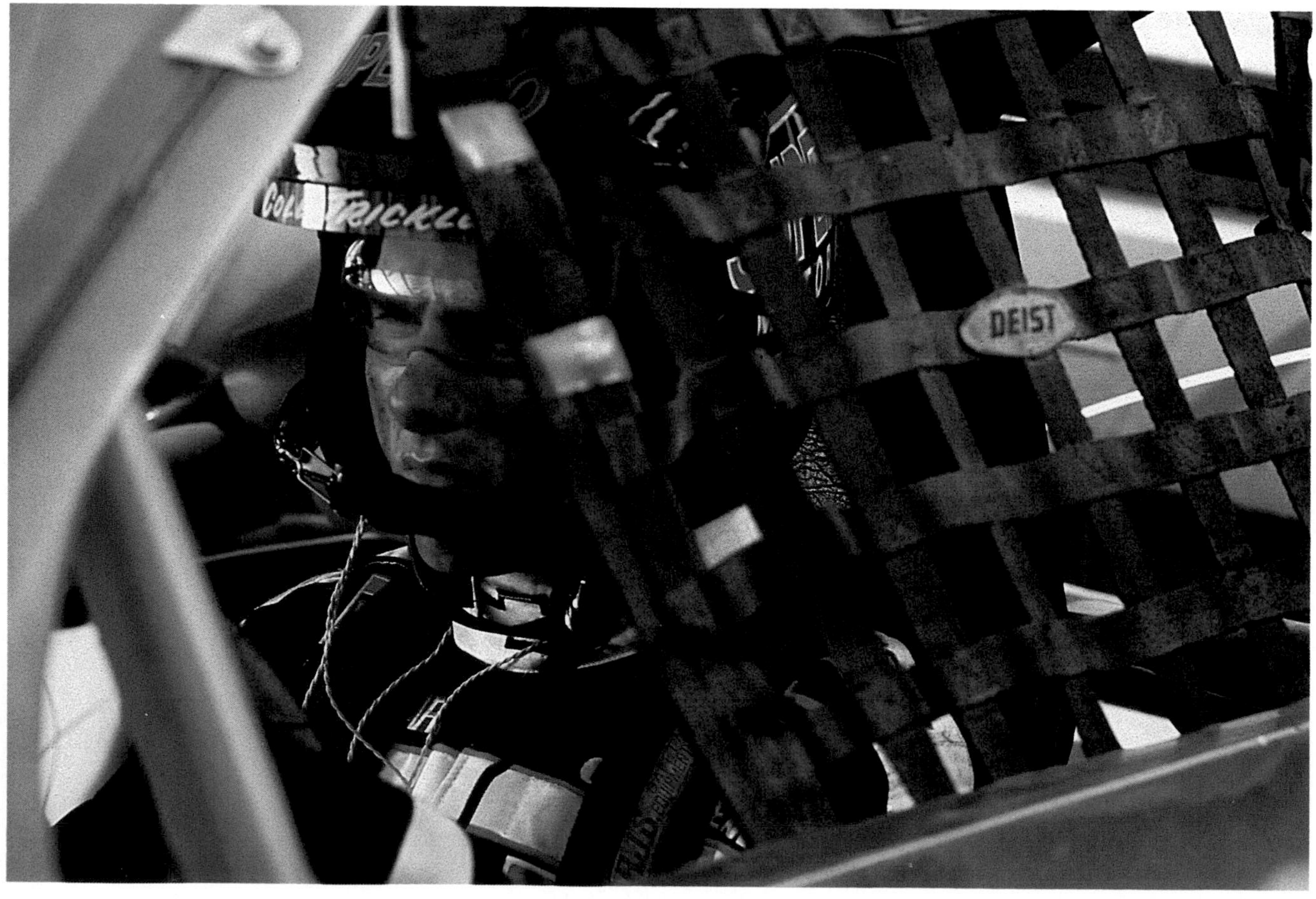

***Days of Thunder*, starring Tom Cruise, *below*, was not the big blockbuster summer hit that everyone expected it to be. Audiences could care less about their hero as a stock car racer named Cole Trickle.**

ing to A.C. Nielsen Media Research, Americans were renting a monthly average of 3.26 movies per household in 1986. By 1990, the figure had fallen to 2.07.

As the summer of 1990 approached, there was yet another shock wave of revelations about the cost of doing business in Hollywood. Tom Cruise was said to be getting $10 million to appear in the stock car racing adventure, *Days of Thunder*, and the movie itself was rumored to be costing Paramount Pictures as much as $55 million. *Total Recall*, the new Arnold Schwarzenegger science fiction action movie was said to have cost anywhere from $55 to $60 million, but that included the cost of recreating the planet Mars. *Another 48 HRS*, the sequel to the movie that made Eddie Murphy famous, was budgeted at $50 million, and the situation had changed a bit since Eddie did the first picture. This time, instead of $200,000, he was paid $10 million. He was getting top billing over Nick Nolte, and he didn't worry that he could not sustain a scene. In fact he wouldn't even come to work until one o'clock in the afternoon. The costs of turning out the big summer action pictures had grown so enormous that some sequels cost more than the original pictures had earned in profits. There was concern that, even if the summer movies were hits, they could never make enough to recoup their

Above: Harrison Ford (with Raul Julia) got some of the best notices of his career when he starred in _Presumed Innocent_ in the summer of 1990. Ford said his short haircut was one way to let the audience know that, for the moment at least, he had given up the whips and quips and action scenes in order to make a serious drama.

Below: Arnold Schwarzenegger's _Total Recall_ became a hit in the summer of 1990.

Tom Selleck, *top,* co-starred with Laura San Giacomo in *Quigley Down Under* (1990), about an American cowboy and his adventures in Australia.

While Selleck moved Down Under, Mel Gibson, *above,* chased around the U.S. eluding bad guys in *Bird on a Wire,* with Goldie Hawn. Despite the presence of two major stars, the movie did not fare well at the box office.

Richard Gere and Julia Roberts, *opposite,* became the year's favorite couple, co-starring in *Pretty Woman.* The movie, made for a fraction of the cost of the blockbuster movies, looked as though it would become the biggest hit of 1990.

Above: The most hyped movie of the summer of 1990 was *Dick Tracy,* directed by and starring Warren Beatty. It was no *Batman* at the box office, but then neither was it the disaster many observers predicted. *Dick Tracy* was regarded as wonderful summer entertainment and something of a comeback for Beatty both as a director and as a box office attraction.

Insert: Patrick Swayze and Demi Moore co-starred in *Ghost* (1990), a romantic comedy about a man who is killed, then comes back as a ghost to save the woman he loves. It became something of a sleeper hit and its success along with that of *Pretty Woman* may have signaled a return to less expensive movies starring witty people who don't shoot at each other.

production and marketing costs. "What's going on is insane," *Variety* reported one studio executive as yelling. "These people are making movies literally as if nothing else mattered. They have completely lost sight of reality." In other words it was pretty much business — and pessimism — as usual.

Worthy movies were still getting made, but as always, it was a struggle. At the beginning of 1990, the story of how *Driving Miss Daisy* almost didn't come to the screen was already taking its place in the lore of Hollywood. Producer Richard Zanuck, and his wife, Lili Fini Zanuck, were turned down by every studio in town, and were about to give up, when the Canadian financier Jake Eberts appeared on the scene. Eberts lived in London and had helped find money for films such as *Chariots of Fire* and *Gandhi*. He liked the script for *Driving Miss Daisy* and agreed to put up $3.5 million. Warner Bros., seeing Eberts' willingness to take a risk, finally anted up the remaining $4.5 million needed to make the movie. *Driving Miss Daisy*, financed by a Canadian, directed by an Australian (Bruce Beresford), became a bona fide American hit during the Christmas of 1989. It went on to win the Academy Award for best picture (as well as Oscars for the 80-year-old Tandy, and screenwriter Alfred Uhry), and gross over $100 million in North America.

Kowabunga! *Teenage Mutant Ninja Turtles* was a surprise hit in 1990.

"One observation I could make about European filmmaking is that people tend to make films which *they* want to make," Eberts said, "whereas in America people seem to make films that they think other people want to see."

Those were the kind of movies that continued to dominate the business, and, it must be admitted, draw audiences around the world. It may say something about the kind of movie that would be made in the future to note that the first major hit of the new decade was a movie based on a cartoon show. In early 1990, *Teenage Mutant Ninja Turtles* were eating pizza and conquering the world. Hollywood, as usual, was worried. After all, every studio in town turned down *that* movie, too.

Above: Bill Murray was back on the screen in 1990 in _Quick Change,_ but audiences were indifferent to it.

Opposite: Laura Dern and Nicolas Cage starred as a hot-headed, hot-blooded young couple in David Lynch's _Wild at Heart_ (1990).

Below: Jack Nicholson finally returned to the screen as private detective Jake Gittes in a sequel to _Chinatown_ (1974) titled _The Two Jakes_ (1990), that Nicholson also directed from Robert Towne's screenplay.

ACKNOWLEDGMENTS AND CREDITS

It was the *Toronto Star* who sent Ron Base all over the world throughout the eighties in pursuit of movies and the people who make them. The paper never grumbled *too* much about expense accounts from Los Angeles, New York, Paris, Cannes, Cairo or even China, and for that, the author is forever grateful. Editor Sandra Tooze did a wonderful job of seeing the forest when the authors were only seeing the trees; Alexandra Lenhoff made untold contributions both as an editor and a fact checker; Duncan McKenzie and Diane Talbot, as line editors, made endless changes and improvements to the copy. At the offices of *Marquee* magazine Angela Lawrence, Josette Luyckx and Susan Saccucci were constantly patient, helpful and understanding. We were guided through the vagaries of book publishing by Jack Stoddart and Bill Hanna of Stoddart Publishing of Toronto, and we received helpful advice and encouragement from Malcolm Lester of Lester and Orpen Dennys. Bruno Monti of Canada's Coles Book Stores made all the difference, and in London we went looking for a publisher at The Macdonald Group and with Alan Samson came away not only with a publisher, but a friend. Finally, Judi Schwam has been a friend for years, never more so than in the preparation of this book. Without the efforts of these people, there would not have been a book, *The Movies of the Eighties*, and we are eternally grateful.

Peter Goddard, an author and *Toronto Star* movie critic, acted as consultant and editor.

David Overbey, Paris-based writer and critic, acted as contributing editor to the *Beyond Hollywood* section.

Cover: *Top film strip #1, left to right: The War of the Roses*, Copyright © 20th Century-Fox Film Corporation; *Who Framed Roger Rabbit*, © 1988 Touchstone Pictures and Amblin Entertainment, Inc.; *Commando*, © 20th Century-Fox Film Corporation; **Cover:** *film strip #2, left to right: The Empire Strikes Back*, © 1980 Lucasfilm Ltd.; *Top Gun*, © 1986 Paramount Pictures Corp.; *E.T. The Extra-Terrestrial*, © 1982 Universal City Studios, Inc.; **Cover:** *film strip #3, left to right: Mad Max Beyond Thunderdome*, © 1985 Warner Bros. Inc.; *Rocky*, Copyright © MCMLXXXII United Artists Corporation; **Cover:** *film strip #4, left to right: Beetlejuice*, © 1988 The Geffen Film Co.; *My Left Foot*, A Miramax Films Release © 1989; *Batman*, TMs & © 1989 DC Comics Inc.; *Silkwood*, © Copyright 1983 American Broadcasting Companies, Inc.; *Beverly Hills Cop*, © 1987 Paramount Pictures Corp.; *Ghostbusters*, Copyright © 1984, Columbia Pictures Industries, Inc.; *Indiana Jones and the Temple of Doom*, © 1983 Lucasfilm Ltd.;

4: *Who Framed Roger Rabbit*, © 1988 Touchstone Pictures and Amblin Entertainment, Inc.;
6: *E.T. The Extra-Terrestrial*, Copyright © 1982 Universal City Studios, Inc.;
8: *left: Cocoon*, Copyright © 1985 20th Century-Fox Film Corporation; *centre: Brainstorm*, Copyright © 1983 MGM/UA Entertainment Co.;
9: *above: E.T. The Extra-Terrestrial*, Copyright © 1982 Universal City Studios, Inc.; *below: E.T. The Extra-Terrestrial*, © 1986 Universal City Studios, Inc.;
10: *left: Tron*, © MCMLXXXII Walt Disney Productions; *centre: Close Encounters of the Third Kind*, Copyright © 1976 Columbia Pictures Industries, Inc.;
11: *Indiana Jones and the Temple of Doom*, © 1983 Lucasfilm Ltd;
12: *Starman*, Copyright © 1984 Columbia Pictures Industries, Inc.;
13: *above: The Last Starfighter*, © 1984 Universal City Studios, Inc.; *below: Heartbeeps*, © 1981 Universal City Studios, Inc.;
14: *The Color Purple*, © 1985 Warner Bros. Inc.;
15: *above: Always*, © 1989 Universal City Studios, Inc.; *below: Empire of the Sun*, © 1987 Warner Bros. Inc.;
16: *above: The Goonies*, © 1985 Warner Bros. Inc.; *below: Cat's Eye*, © 1985 Famous Films Productions, N.V.;
17: *above: Superman*, TMs © DC Comics Inc. 1978, 1980; *below: Superman IV: The Quest for Peace*, Copyright © 1987 Cannon Films Inc. and Warner Bros. Inc. TM & © 1987 DC Comics Inc.;
18: *above: Yes, Giorgio*, © 1982 MGM/UA Entertainment Co.; *below: Santa Claus: The Movie*, © 1985 Tri-Star Pictures;
19: *centre: Heaven's Gate*, Copyright © 1981 United Artists Corporation; *right: Twilight Zone - The Movie*, Copyright © 1983 Warner Bros. Inc.;
20-21: *Rambo First Blood Part II*, © 1985 Tri-Star Pictures;
22: *above: Return to Oz*, © MCMLXXXIV Walt Disney Productions; *below: WarGames*, © 1983 MGM/UA Entertainment Co.;
22-23: *centre: Heaven's Gate*, Copyright © 1981 United Artists Corporation;
23: *above: Jewel of the Nile*, Copyright © 20th Century-Fox Film Corporation; *below: Cloak and Dagger*, © 1984 Universal City Studios, Inc.;
24: *left: Short Circuit II*, © 1988 Tri-Star Pictures, Inc.; *centre: Gremlins*, © 1990 Warner Bros. Inc.;
25: *Back to the Future*, © 1985 Universal City Studios, Inc.;
26: *above: Amadeus*, The Saul Zaentz Co. Copyright 1984 Orion Pictures Corp.; *below: Body Heat*, © 1981 Ladd Company;
26-27: *centre: The Big Chill*, Copyright © 1983, Columbia Pictures Industries, Inc.;
27: *A Soldier's Story*, Copyright © 1984, Columbia Pictures Industries, Inc.;
28: *above: Year of the Dragon*, © 1985 Dino De Laurentiis Corp.; *below: The Sicilian*, Copyright © 1987 Gladden Entertainment Corp.;
29: *The Killing Fields*, © 1984 Warner Bros. Inc.;
30-31: *Indiana Jones and the Last Crusade*, © 1989 Lucasfilm Ltd.;
32: *left: Never Say Never Again*, © Taliafilm, Inc. 1983; *centre: The Living Daylights*, © 1987 Danjaq, S.A.;
33: *above: Five Days One Summer*, © 1982 The Ladd Co.; *below: License to Kill*, © 1988 Danjaq, S.A.;
34: *above: Octopussy*, © 1982 Danjaq, S.A.; *below: Octopussy*, © Danjaq, S.A. 1982;
35: *above: For Your Eyes Only*, Copyright © 1979 United Artists Corporation; *below: Never Say Never Again*, © Taliafilm, Inc. 1983;
36: *Ffolkes*, © 1979 Universal City Studios, Inc.;
37: *above: The Untouchables*, © 1987 Paramount Pictures Corp.; *below: Outland*, Copyright © 1981 The Ladd Company;
38: *above: Dead-Bang*, Copyright © 1989 Warner Bros. Inc.; *below: The Hunter*, Copyright © MCMLXXX Paramount Pictures Corporation; *centre: Die Hard*, Copyright © 1988 20th Century-Fox Film Corporation;
39: *Heartbreak Ridge*, © 1986 Warner Bros. Inc.;
40: *Lone Wolf McQuade*, © 1982 Orion Pictures Corporation; *centre: Pale Rider*, © 1985 Warner Bros. Inc.;
41: *Death Hunt*, Copyright © 20th Century-Fox Film Corporation; *centre: Bronco Billy*, Copyright © 1980 Warner Bros. Inc.;
42: *above: Rambo III*, © 1988 Tri-Star Pictures, Inc.; *below, left: Nighthawks*, Copyright © 1981 Universal City Studios, Inc.; *below, right: Lock Up*, Copyright © 1989 Tri-Star Pictures, Inc.; *insert: Victory*, Copyright © 1980 Lorimar Productions Inc.;
43: *above: Above the Law*, Copyright © 1988 Warner Bros. Inc.; *below: High Road to China*, © 1983 Warner Bros. Inc.;
44: *above: Stick*, © 1984 Universal City Studios, Inc.; *below: Stroker Ace*, Copyright © 1983 Universal Studios, Inc. - Warner Bros.;
45: *above: National Lampoon's European Vacation*, © 1985 Warner Bros. Inc.; *below: National Lampoon's Vacation*, © 1983 Warner Bros. Inc.; *centre: Tango & Cash*, Copyright © 1989 Warner Bros. Inc.;
46: *Conan the Barbarian*, © 1981 Copyright Dino DeLaurentiis Corporation;
47: *Conan the Destroyer*, © 1983 Copyright Dino DeLaurentiis Corporation;
48: *above: Red Sonja*, © 1985 MGM/UA Entertainment Co.; *below: Twins*, © 1988 Universal City Studios, Inc.; *centre: The Terminator*, Orion Pictures Corp. Copyright 1984;
49: *above: Greystoke: The Legend of Tarzan, Lord of the Apes*, Copyright © 1983 Warner Bros. Inc.; *below: Ladyhawke*, © 1985 Warner Bros. Inc. and Twentieth Century-Fox Corp.;
50: *Blade Runner*, © 1982 Ladd Company;
51: *Spaceballs: The Movie*, © 1987 Metro-Goldwyn-Mayer Pictures, Inc.; *centre: Witness*, Copyright © MCMLXXXV Paramount Pictures Corporation;
52: *top: Lifeforce*, © 1985 Tri-Star Pictures; *middle: Enemy Mine*, Copyright © 20th Century-Fox Film Corporation; *bottom: Saturn Three*, © 1979 Associated Film Distribution;
53: *Return of the Jedi*, TM & © Lucasfilm Ltd. 1983;

54: *above*: *Aliens*, 1986 Copyright © 20th Century-Fox Film Corporation; *below*: *The Abyss*, 1989 Copyright © 20th Century-Fox Film Corporation;
55: *above*: *2010*, © 1984 MGM/UA Entertainment Co.; *below*: *Poltergeist*, © 1982 Metro-Goldwyn-Mayer Film Co.;
56: *above*: *The Empire Strikes Back*, © 1980 Lucasfilm, Ltd.; *below*: *RoboCop*, Orion Pictures Corp., © Copyright 1990;
57: *Return of the Jedi*, © 1983 Lucasfilm Ltd.;
58-59: *The Right Stuff*, © 1982 Ladd Company;
60: *Crocodile Dundee*, Copyright © 1986 Rimfire Films Limited;
61: *above*: *Star Trek: The Search for Spock*, © 1984 Paramount Pictures Corp.; *insert*: *Star Trek 2*, © 1982 Paramount Pictures Corporation; *below*: *Karate Kid*, Copyright © 1984 Columbia Pictures Industries, Inc.;
62: *above*: *Police Academy*, © 1984 Ladd Company; *below*: *K-9*, © 1988 Universal City Studios, Inc.;
63: *above*: *Batman*, TMs & © 1989 DC Comics Inc.; *below*: *Batman*, TM and © 1964 DC Comics Inc.;
64: *above*: *Beetlejuice*, © 1988 The Geffen Film Co.; *below*: *Pee-wee's Big Adventure*, © 1985 Warner Bros. Inc.;
65: *above*: *Big Trouble in Little China*, 1986 Copyright © 20th Century-Fox Film Corporation; *below*: *Flash Gordon*, Copyright 1980 Famous Films, B.V.; *centre*: *Batman*, TMs & © 1989 DC Comics Inc.;
66: *Nightmare on Elm Street*, © MCMLXXXVIII New Line Cinema Corp.; *insert, above*: *Fright Night*, Copyright © 1985 Columbia Pictures Industries, Inc.; *insert, below*: *Halloween 4*, © 1988 Trancas International Films Inc. and Halloween 4 Partnership;
67: *Hellbound: Hellraiser II*, New World Pictures © 1988; *insert*: *Friday the 13th: Part VIII*, © 1989 Paramount Pictures Corp.;
68-69: *Bull Durham*, Orion Pictures Corp. © Copyright 1988;
70: *above*: *No Man's Land*, Orion Pictures Corp. © Copyright 1987; *below*: *Rumble Fish*, © 1983 Universal City Studios, Inc.; *centre*: *Taps*, 1981 Copyright © 20th Century-Fox Film Corporation;
71: *Cocktail*, © 1988 Touchstone Pictures;
72-73: *Year of the Dragon*, © 1985 MGM/UA Entertainment Co.;
74: *above*: *Vision Quest*, © 1984 Warner Bros. Inc.; *below*: *Best Seller*, Orion Pictures Corp. Copyright 1986; *centre*: *The Outsiders*, © Pony Boy, Inc. 1982;
75: *Haunted Honeymoon*, Orion Pictures Corp. Copyright 1985; *centre*: *Risky Business*, Copyright © 1983 Warner Bros. Inc.;
76: *above*: *Dirty Dancing*, Copyright © 1987 Vestron Pictures; *below*: *Staying Alive*, © 1983 Paramount Pictures Corporation;
77: *Top Gun*, © 1986 Paramount Pictures Corp.;
78: *above*: *Someone to Watch over Me*, Copyright © 1987 Columbia Pictures Industries, Inc.; *below*: *Always*, © 1989 Universal City Studios, Inc.;
79: *The Verdict*, 1982 Copyright © 20th Century-Fox Film Corporation;
80-81: *The Natural*, © 1984 Tri-Star Pictures;
82: *above*: *The Fiendish Plot of Dr. Fu Manchu*, © 1980 Orion Pictures Company; *below*: *The Formula*, © 1980 Metro-Goldywn-Mayer Inc.; *centre*: *The Verdict*, Copyright © 1982 Twentieth Century-Fox Film Corp.;
83: *Terms of Endearment*, © 1983 Paramount Pictures Corporation;
84: *The Shining*, © Warner Bros. 1980;
85: *above*: *La Bamba*, Copyright © 1985 Columbia Pictures Industries, Inc.; *below*: *Walk Like a Man*, © 1986 MGM Entertainment Co.; *centre*: *Lethal Weapon 2*, Copyright © 1989 Warner Bros. Inc.;
86: *So Fine*, Copyright © 1981 Warner Bros. Inc.; *centre*: *Ferris Bueller's Day Off*, Copyright © 1986 Paramount Pictures Corporation;
87: *Mississippi Burning*, Orion Pictures Corp. © Copyright 1988;
88: *above*: *Cry Freedom*, Copyright © 1987 Universal City Studios Inc.; *below*: *Against All Odds*, Copyright © 1984 Columbia Pictures Industries, Inc.;
89: *Tootsie*, Copyright © 1982 Columbia Pictures Industries, Inc.;
90: *above*: *Great Balls of Fire*, Orion Pictures Corp. © Copyright 1989; *below*: *Arthur 2: On the Rocks*, © 1988 Warner Bros. Inc.; *centre*: *No Way Out*, © 1987 Orion Pictures Corporation;
91: *Silverado*, Copyright © 1985 Columbia Pictures Industries, Inc.;
92: *above*: *White Nights*, Copyright © 1985 Columbia Pictures Industries, Inc.; *below*: *Footloose*, Copyright © MCMLXXXIV Paramount Pictures Corporation;
93: *Mad Max Beyond Thunderdome*, © 1985 Warner Bros. Inc.;
94: *Raising Arizona*, Copyright © 1987 Circle Films, Inc.; *centre*: *The Year of Living Dangerously*, © 1983 MGM/UA Entertainment Co.;
95: *above*: *Shoot to Kill*, © 1987 Touchstone Pictures; *below*: *Dangerous Liaisons*, © 1989 Warner Bros. Inc.;
96: *Beverly Hills Cop*, Copyright © 1984 Paramount Pictures Corporation;
97: *above*: *Tough Guys*, © 1986 Touchstone Pictures; *below*: *The Black Marble*, Avco Embassy Pictures; *centre*: *Cannery Row*, Copyright © 1981 Metro-Goldywn-Mayer Film Co.;
98: *above*: *Wisdom*, 1987 Copyright © 20th Century-Fox Film Corporation; *below*: *Colors*, Orion Pictures Corp. © Copyright 1988;
99: *above*: *Coming to America*, © 1987 Paramount Pictures Corp.; *below*: *Trading Places*, © 1982 Paramount Pictures Corp.;
100: *above*: *Cocoon: The Return*, 1988 Copyright © 20th Century-Fox Film Corporation; *below*: *Better Late Than Never*, © 1983 Warner Bros. Inc.; *centre*: *Uncle Buck*, Copyright © 1989 Universal City Studios Inc.;
101: *The Three Amigos*, © 1986 Orion Pictures Corporation;
102: *above*: *Planes, Trains and Automobiles*, © 1987 Paramount Pictures Corp.; *below*: *Honey, I Shrunk the Kids*, © 1989 Buena Vista Pictures Distribution, Inc.;
103: *Three Men and a Baby*, © 1987 Touchstone Pictures;
104: *Mannequin*, Copyright © 1986 Twentieth Century-Fox Film Corporation; *centre*: *Ghostbusters*, Copyright © 1984, Columbia Pictures Industries, Inc.;
105: *above*: *Tribute*, 1980 Copyright © 20th Century-Fox Film Corporation; *below*: *Little Miss Marker*, © 1979 Universal City Studios, Inc.;
106: *above*: *Easy Money*, © 1983 Orion Pictures Corporation; *below*: *Zorro, the Gay Blade*, 1981, Copyright © 20th Century-Fox Film Corporation; *centre*: *Caddyshack*, © 1980 Orion Pictures Company;
107: *The Razor's Edge*, Copyright © 1984 Columbia Pictures Industries, Inc.;
108: *above*: *Cannonball Run II*, © 1984 Arcafin B.V./Claridge Pictures Inc.; *below*: *Tender Mercies*, © 1982 Universal City Studios, Inc.; *centre*: *Big*, 1988 Copyright © 20th Century-Fox Film Corporation;
109: *Splash*, © MCMLXXXIII Buena Vista Distribution Co., Inc.;
110: *Evil Under the Sun*, Copyright © 1982 Universal City Studios Inc.; *centre*: *Back to the Future*, © 1985 Universal City Studios, Inc.;
111: *The Secret of My Success*, © 1987 Universal City Studios, Inc.; *insert*: *Casualties of War*, Copyright © 1988 Columbia Pictures Industries, Inc.;
112: *above*: *Running Scared*, © 1986 MGM/UA Entertainment Co.; *below*: *Stir Crazy*, Copyright © 1980 Columbia Pictures Industries, Inc.;
113: *Moscow on the Hudson*, Copyright © 1984 Columbia Pictures Industries, Inc.;
114: *above*: *Dead Poets Society*, © 1989 Touchstone Pictures; *below*: *Good Morning, Vietnam*, © 1987 Touchstone Pictures;
115: *Sea of Love*, © 1988 Universal City Studios Inc.; *centre*: *Roxanne*, Copyright © 1986 Columbia Pictures Industries, Inc.;
116: *above*: *Continental Divide*, © 1981 Universal City Studios, Inc.; *below*: *Stand by Me*, Copyright © 1986 Columbia Pictures Industries, Inc.; *centre*: *Dead Men Don't Wear Plaid*, © 1982 Universal City Studios, Inc.;
117: *Married to the Mob*, Orion Pictures Corp. © Copyright 1988;
118-119: *Fat Man and Little Boy*, © 1989 Paramount Pictures Corp.;
120-121: *Steel Magnolias*, © 1989 Tri-Star Pictures, Inc.;
122: *above*: *Last Flight of Noah's Ark*, © Walt Disney Productions MCMLXXX; *below*: *Crimes and Misdemeanors*, © 1989 Orion Pictures Corporation; *centre*: *Sophie's Choice*, Copyright © 1982 Universal City Studios, Inc.;
123: *Sophie's Choice*, Copyright © 1982 Universal City Studios;
124: *Silkwood*, Copyright © 1983 ABC Motion Pictures, Inc.;
125: *above*: *Crossing Delancey*, © 1988 Warner Bros. Inc.; *below*: *Mad Max Beyond Thunderdome*, © 1985 Warner Bros. Inc.;
126-127: *Crimes of the Heart*, © 1986 De Laurentiis Entertainment Group;
128: *above*: *Coal Miner's Daughter*, © 1979 Universal City Studios, Inc.; *below*: *Who's That Girl*, © 1987 Warner Bros. Inc.;

129: *above*: *Nine to Five*, 1980 Copyright © 20th Century-Fox Film Corporation; *below*: *Broadcast News*, 1987 Copyright © 20th Century-Fox Film Corporation; *centre*: *Mrs. Soffel*, © 1984 MGM/UA Entertainment Co.;
130: *above*: *The Bride*, Copyright © 1985 Columbia Pictures Industries, Inc.; *below*: *Carny*, Copyright © 1980 Lorimar Productions, Inc.; *centre*: *Mask*, Copyright © 1984 Universal City Studios, Inc.;
131: *Clan of the Cave Bear*, © 1986 Warner Bros. Inc. and Jonesfilm;
132: *above*: *Dreamscape*, Copyright © 20th Century-Fox Film Corporation; *below*: *Back to the Future*, © 1985 Universal City Studios, Inc.; *centre*: *Nuts*, Copyright © 1987 Warner Bros. Inc.;
133: *Yentl*, © MCMLXXXIII Ladbroke Entertainments Limited;
134: *The Natural*, © 1984 Tri-Star Pictures; *centre*: *The Morning After*, © 1986 Lorimar Motion Pictures Management, Inc., as Trustee for Lorimar Film Partners, L.P.;
135: *above*: *The Blue Lagoon*, Copyright © MCMLXXX, Columbia Pictures Industries, Inc.; *below*: *Cotton Club*, Orion Pictures Corp. Copyright 1984; *centre*: *On Golden Pond*, © 1981 Universal City Studios, Inc.;
136: *above*: *Impulse*, © Copyright 1983 American Broadcasting Companies, Inc.; *below*: *Old Gringo*, Copyright © 1989 Columbia Pictures Industries, Inc.;
137: *above*: *Eight Million Ways to Die*, © 1985 Tri-Star Pictures; *below*: *Hard Bodies*, Copyright © 1984, Columbia Pictures Industries, Inc.; *centre*: *Absence of Malice*, Copyright © 1981, Columbia Pictures Industries, Inc.;
138: *above*: *Just Tell Me What You Want*, Copyright © Warner Bros. Inc.; *below*: *Stick*, © 1983 Universal City Studios, Inc.; *centre*: *Places in the Heart*, © 1984 Tri-Star Pictures;
139: *above*: *See You in the Morning*, © 1989 Warner Bros. Inc.; *below*: *Flamingo Kid*, © Copyright 1983 American Broadcasting Companies, Inc.;
140: *above*: *Cross Creek*, © 1983 Universal City Studios, Inc.; *below*, *The Legend of Billie Jean*, © 1985 Tri-Star Pictures, Inc.; *centre*: *King Kong*, © MCMLXXVI Dino De Laurentiis Corporation;
141: *Frances*, © 1982 Universal City Studios, Inc.;
142: *above*: *Tempest*, Copyright © 1982, Columbia Pictures Industries, Inc.; *below*: *Witness*, © 1984 Paramount Pictures Corporation;
143: *above*: *Moscow on the Hudson*, Copyright © 1984, Columbia Pictures Industries, Inc.; *below*: *Cat People*, © 1982 Universal City Studios, Inc.;
144: *above, left*: *Star 80*, © 1983 Ladd Company; *above, right*: *The Lonely Lady*, © 1983 Universal City Studios, Inc.; *below*: *Tarzan, The Ape Man*, © 1981 Metro-Goldwyn-Mayer Film Co.;
145: *Perfect*, Copyright © 1985, Columbia Pictures Industries, Inc.;
146: *above*: *Blame It on Rio*, 1983 Copyright © 20th Century-Fox Film Corporation; *below*: *Victor/Victoria*, © 1982 Metro-Goldwyn-Mayer Film Co.; *centre*: *Prizzi's Honor*, © Copyright 1985 American Broadcasting Companies, Inc.;
147: *The Woman in Red*, Orion Pictures Corp. Copyright 1984;
148: *Fatal Attraction*, © 1987 Paramount Pictures Corp.;
149: *Barfly*, © 1987 Cannon Films, Inc.;
150: *above*: *Against All Odds*, Copyright © 1984, Columbia Pictures Industries, Inc.; *below*: *Dune*, Copyright © 1984 Universal City Studios, Inc. and Dino De Laurentiis Corporation;
151: *9 1/2 Weeks*, © 1985 Jonesfilm;
152: *The Fabulous Baker Boys*, Copyright © 20th Century-Fox Film Corporation;
153: *above*: *All of Me*, © 1984 Universal City Studios, Inc.; *below*: *Fast Times at Ridgemont High*, Copyright © 1982 Universal City Studios, Inc.; *centre*: *Seems Like Old Times*, Copyright © 1980, Columbia Pictures Industries, Inc.;
154: *Private Benjamin*, Copyright © 1980 Warner Bros. Inc.;
155: *above*: *The Color Purple*, © 1985 Warner Bros. Inc.; *below*: *Commando*, 1985 Copyright © 20th Century-Fox Film Corporation;
156: *above*: *About Last Night*, © 1985 Tri-Star Pictures; *below*: *Caveman*, Copyright © 1981 United Artists Corporation;
157: *Working Girl*, Copyright © 20th Century-Fox Film Corporation;
158: *above*: *Bukaroo Banzai*, Copyright © 20th Century-Fox Film Corporation; *below*: *Oxford Blues*, © 1984 MGM/UA Entertainment Co.; *centre*: *Down and out in Beverly Hills*, © MCMLXXXV Touchstone Films;
159: *Lovesick*, Copyright © 1982 The Ladd Company;
160: *When Harry Met Sally . . .* Copyright © 1989 Castle Rock Entertainment;
161: *above*: *Mike's Murder*, © 1982 Ladd Company; *below*: *Sixteen Candles*, © 1983 Universal City Studios, Inc.; *centre*: *Steel Magnolias*, © 1989 Tri-Star Pictures, Inc.;
162-163: *Milagro Beanfield War*, © 1988 Universal City Studios, Inc.;
164: *above*: *Hannah and Her Sisters*, © 1985 Orion Pictures Corporation; *below*: *Crimes and Misdemeanors*, © 1989 Orion Pictures Corporation;
165: *above*: *Another Woman*, Orion Pictures Corp. © Copyright 1988; *below*: *New York Stories*, © MCMLXXXIX Touchstone Pictures;
166: *above*: *Another Woman*, © 1988 Orion Pictures Corporation; *below*: *Rain Man*, © 1988 United Artists Pictures, Inc.;
167: *above*: *Mike's Murder*, © 1982 Ladd Company; *below*: *Stakeout*, © 1987 Touchstone Pictures; *centre*: *Crimes and Misdemeanors*, © 1989 Orion Pictures Corporation;
168: *above*: *Fatso*, Copyright © 1980 20th Century-Fox Film Corporation; *centre*: *Jumpin Jack Flash*, Copyright © 20th Century-Fox Film Corporation; *below*: *Yentl*, © 1983 MGM/UA Entertainment Co.;
169: *She-Devil*, Orion Pictures Corp. © Copyright 1989;
170: *above*: *Smorgasbord — Cracking Up*, © 1983 Warner Bros. Inc.; *below*: *Nothing in Common*, © 1986 Tri-Star Pictures, Inc.; *centre*: *Down and out in Beverly Hills*, © MCMLXXXV Touchstone Films;
171: *above*: *The King of Comedy*, Copyright © 1982 20th Century-Fox Film Corporation; *below*: *Suspect*, © 1987 Tri-Star Pictures, Inc.;
172: *above*: *Scrooged*, Copyright © 1988 Paramount Pictures Corporation; *below*: *Ghostbusters*, Copyright © 1984, Columbia Pictures Industries, Inc.;
173: *Raging Bull*, Copyright © 1980 United Artists Corporation;
174: *above*: *Rich and Famous*, © 1981 Metro-Goldwyn-Mayer Film Co.; *below*: *Big Red One*, Copyright © 1980 Lorimar Productions, Inc.;
175: *above*: *Buddy, Buddy*, © 1981 Metro-Goldwyn-Mayer Film Co.; *below*: *The King of Comedy*, Copyright © 1982 20th Century-Fox Film Corporation;
176: *above*: *Sweet Liberty*, © 1985 Universal City Studios, Inc.; *below*: *Stir Crazy*, Copyright 1980, Columbia Pictures Industries, Inc.;
177: *The Last Temptation of Christ*, Copyright © 1988 Universal City Studios, Inc.;
178: *The Outsiders*, © Pony Boy, Inc. 1982;
179: *above*: *Star Trek: The Final Frontier*, Copyright © 1989 Paramount Pictures Corporation; *below*: *The Good Mother*, © 1988 Touchstone Pictures;
180: *above*: *An American Tail*, © 1986 Universal City Studios, Inc.; *below*: *Who Framed Roger Rabbit*, © 1988 Touchstone Pictures and Amblin Entertainment, Inc.; *centre*: *One from the Heart*, © Zoetrope Studios 1982;
181: *Star 80*, Copyright © 1983 The Ladd Company; *centre*: *Scarface*, © 1983 Universal City Studios, Inc.;
182: *above*: *Casulaties of War*, Copyright © 1989 Columbia Pictures Industries, Inc.; *below*: *Predator*, Copyright © 1987 Twentieth Century-Fox Film Corp.;
183: *above*: *Weird Science*, Copyright © 1984 Universal City Studios, Inc.; *below*: *The World According to Garp*, Copyright © 1981 Warner Bros. Inc.; *centre*: *Victor/Victoria*, © 1982 Metro-Goldwyn-Mayer Film Co.;
184: *above*: *Black Rain*, Copyright © 1989 Paramount Pictures Corporation; *below*: *Target*, © 1985 CBS, Inc.; *centre*: *Lawrence of Arabia*, © 1962 Horizon Pictures (GB);
185: *A Passage to India*, Copyright © 1984 Columbia Pictures Industries, Inc.;
186: *above*: *Out of Africa*, © 1985 Universal City Studios, Inc; *below*: *Once upon a Time in America*, Copyright © 1984 The Ladd Company;
187: *above*: *On Golden Pond*, Copyright © 1981 Universal City Studios Inc.; *below*: *Murphy's Romance*, Copyright © 1985 Columbia Pictures Industries, Inc.;
188-189: *The War of the Roses*, Copyright © 20th Century-Fox Film Corporation;
190: *above*: *Colors*, Orion Pictures Corp. Copyright 1987; *below*: *Platoon*, © 1986 Orion Pictures Corporation;
191: *above*: *Under the Volcano*, © 1984 Universal City Studios, Inc.; *below*: *Mr. North*, © 1988 The Samuel Goldwyn Company;
192: *Hairspray*, © New Line Cinema Corp. MCMLXXXVIII; *centre*: *Talk Radio*, © 1988 Cineplex Odeon Films, Inc.;
193: *above*: *Dune*, © 1984 Copyright Dino Delaurentiis Corporation; *below*: *Raising Arizona*, Copyright © 20th Century-Fox Film Corporation;
194: *above*: *Willow*, © 1988 Lucasfilm Ltd.; *below*: *My Favorite Year*, © 1982 Metro-Goldwyn-Mayer Film Co.; *centre*: *Blue Velvet*, © 1986 De Laurentiis Entertainment Group;
195: *above*: *The Great Muppet Caper*, Copyright 1981 Henson Associates, Inc.; *below*: *Five Days One Summer*, © 1982 The Ladd Co.;
196: *Do the Right Thing*, © 1989 Universal City Studios, Inc.;
197: *above*: *Roger & Me*, Copyright © 1989 Warner Bros. Inc.; *below*: *Harry and Son*, Orion Pictures Corp. Copyright 1983; *centre*: *sex, lies, and videotape*, A Miramax Films Release © 1989;
198-199: *Wall Street*, Copyright © 20th Century-Fox Film Corporation;
200: *Sudden Impact*, Copyright © 1983 Warner Bros. Inc.; *centre*: *The Killing Fields*, Copyright © 1984 Warner Bros. Inc.;
201: *The Mission*, © 1986 Warner Bros. Inc.;
202-203: *Chariots of Fire*, © 1981 Ladd Company;

204: *above*: *Family Business*, Copyright © 1989 Tri-Star Pictures, Inc.; *below*: *Tucker: The Man and His Dream*, TM & Copyright © 1988 by Lucasfilm Ltd. (LFL); *centre*: *Everybody's All-American*, © 1988 Warner Bros. Inc.;
205: *above*: *Over the Top*, © 1987 Cannon Films Inc. and Warner Bros. Inc.; *below*: *Thief of Hearts*, © 1984 Paramount Pictures Corporation;
206: *Stanley & Iris*, © 1990 MGM Pictures, Inc.;
207: *above*: *52 Pick-up*, Copyright © 1986 Cannon Films, Inc. and Canon International B.V.; *below*: *Ishtar*, Copyright © 1986 Columbia Pictures Industries, Inc.;
208: *Out of Africa*, © 1985 Universal City Studios, Inc.;
209: *above*: *Stakeout*, © MCMLXXXVII Touchstone Pictures; *below*: *Blaze*, © 1989 Touchstone Pictures; *centre, above*: *Uncle Buck*, Copyright © 1989 Universal City Studios, Inc.; *centre, below*: *Howard the Duck*, © 1986 Universal City Studios, Inc.;
210: *The Bounty*, © 1983 Orion Pictures Corporation; *centre*: *The Karate Kid*, Copyright © 1984, Columbia Pictures Industries, Inc.;
211: *Sheena, Queen of the Jungle*, Copyright © 1983 Columbia Pictures Industries, Inc.;
212: *above*: *The Jazz Singer*, © 1980 Associated Film Distribution; *below*: *Raise the Titanic*, © 1980 Associated Film Distribution;
213: *Can't Stop the Music*, © 1980 Associated Film Distribution; *insert*: *The Legend of the Lone Ranger*, © 1981 Associated Film Distribution;
214: *Pennies from Heaven*, © 1981 Metro-Goldwyn-Mayer Film Co.;
215: *above*: *Pirates*, © 1986 Cannon Films, Inc. and Canon International B.V.; *below*: *Tai-Pan*, TM © 1986 De Laurentiis Entertainment Group;
216: *above*: *Something Wicked This Way*, © MCMLXXXII Walt Disney Productions; *below, left*: *An Officer and a Gentleman*, © 1982 Paramount Pictures Corporation; *below, right*: *Flashdance*, © 1983 Paramount Pictures Corporation;
217: *above*: *Porky's*, Copyright © 20th Century-Fox Film Corporation; *below*: *Ironweed*, © 1987 Taft Entertainment Pictures/Keith Barish Productions;
218: *above*: *Never Cry Wolf*, © Walt Disney Productions MCMLXXXII;
218-219: *Splash*, © MCMLXXXIII Buena Vista Distribution Co., Inc.;
220: *above*: *Look Who's Talking*, © 1989 Tri-Star Pictures, Inc.; *below*: *Glory*, © 1989 Tri-Star Pictures, Inc.; *centre*: *Tempest*, Copyright © 1982, Columbia Pictures Industries, Inc.;
221: *Down and out in Beverly Hills*, © MCMLXXXV Touchstone Films;
222: *below*: *The Great Mouse Detective*, © 1986 The Walt Disney Company;
222-223: *The Black Cauldron*, © MCMLXXXV Walt Disney Productions;
223: *above*: *Hand writing on the Walt*, © 1987 Greg Shelton; *below*: *The Little Mermaid*, © The Walt Disney Company;
224: *Moonstruck*, © 1987 Metro-Goldwyn-Mayer Pictures, Inc.;
225: *Ghostbusters*, Copyright © 1988 Columbia Pictures Industries, Inc.;
226: *above*: *Dune*, © 1983 Universal City Studios, Inc.; *below*: *The Last Emperor*, Copyright © 1987 Columbia Pictures Industries, Inc.; *centre*: *Leonard Part VI*, Copyright © 1986 Columbia Pictures Industries, Inc.;
227: *Somewhere in Time*, © 1980 Universal City Studios, Inc.;
228: *above*: *Highlander*, Copyright © 20th Century-Fox Film Corporation; *below*: *Hunt for Red October*, © 1989 Paramount Pictures Corp.; *centre*: *The Witches of Eastwick*, © 1987 Warner Bros. Inc.;
229: *Rain Man*, © 1988 United Artists Pictures, Inc.;
230: *above*: *Annie*, Copyright © 1982, Columbia Pictures Industries, Inc.; *below*: *True Believer*, Copyright © 198 Columbia Pictures Industries, Inc.;
231: *above*: *My Stepmother Is an Alien*, Weintraub Entertainment Group © 1989; *below, left*: *Driving Miss Daisy*, © 1989 Warner Bros. Inc.; *below, right*: *Lethal Weapon II*, © 1989 Warner Bros. Inc.;
232: *above*: *Turner and Hooch*, © 1989 Touchstone Pictures; *below*: *Young Guns*, Copyright © 1988 Morgan Creek Productions, Inc.;
233: *above*: *Valmont*, © Copyright 1989 Renn Productions/Orion Pictures Corp.; *below*: *The Princess Bride*, Copyright © 20th Century-Fox Film Corporation; *centre*: *The Memphis Belle*, © 1990 Warner Bros. Inc.;
234-234: *Brazil*, Copyright 1983 © Brazil Production Company Ltd.;
236: *above*: *Scandal*, © 1989 Miramax Films; *below*: *Club Paradise*, © 1985 Warner Bros. Inc.; *centre*: *Revolution*, © 1985 Warner Bros. Inc.;
237: *Gandhi*, Copyright © 1982 Columbia Pictures Industries, Inc.;
238: *A Fish Called Wanda*, © 1988 Metro-Goldwyn-Mayer Pictures, Inc.;
239: *above*: *Clash of the Titans*, © 1981 Metro-Goldwyn-Mayer Film Co.; *below*: *Without a Clue*, © 1988 Orion Pictures Corporation; *centre*: *A Room with a View*, © 1986 Cinecom International Films Inc.;
240: *above and below*: *Dangerous Liaisons*, © 1989 Warner Bros. Inc.; *insert*: *Sammy and Rosie Get Laid*, © 1987 Cinecom Entertainment Group;
241 *above*: *Shirley Valentine*, © 1989 Paramount Pictures Corp.; *below*: *Miss Mary*, © 1986 New World Pictures;
242: *above*: *The Dresser*, Copyright © 1983, Columbia Pictures Industries, Inc.; *below*: *Little Dorrit*, © 1988 Cannon Films, Inc.; *centre*: *Local Hero*, © 1983 Warner Bros. Inc./Golden Comm.Co.Ltd.;
243: *above and insert*: *My Left Foot*, A Miramax Films Release © 1989;
244: *Give My Regards to Broad Street*, Copyright © 20th Century-Fox Film Corporation; *insert*: *Buster*, Hemdale Film Corp. © Copyright 1988;
245: *Pink Floyd: The Wall*, © 1982 Metro-Goldwyn-Mayer Film Co.; *insert*: *Merry Christmas, Mr. Lawrence*, © 1983 Universal City Studios, Inc.;
246: *above*: *Excalibur*, © 1980 Orion Pictures Company; *below*: *Hope and Glory*, Copyright © 1986 Columbia Pictures Industries, Inc.; *centre*: *The Unbearable Lightness of Being*, © 1987 The Saul Zaentz Company;
247: *above*: *Arthur*, Copyright © 1981 Orion Pictures Company; *below*: *Razor's Edge*, Copyright © 1984 Columbia Pictures Industries, Inc.; *centre*: *The Elephant Man*, Copyright © MCMLXXX Brooksfilms Limited;
248: *above*: *Mona Lisa*, © 1986 Handmade Films; *insert, above*: *Henry V*, © 1989 The Samuel Goldwyn Company; *insert, below*: *Educating Rita*, Copyright © 1983, Columbia Pictures Industries, Inc.;
249: *above*: *Iceman*, © 1984 Universal City Studios, Inc.; *below*: *Phar Lap*, Copyright © 20th Century-Fox Film Corporation;
250-251: *The Man From Snowy River*, © MCMLXXXII The Burrowes Film Group;
251: *insert*: *Return to Snowy River, Part II*, © 1988 The Burrowes Film Group;
252: *above*: *Mrs. Soffel*, © 1984 MGM/UA Entertainment Co.; *below*: *Young Einstein*, © 1989 Warner Bros. Inc.; *centre*: *Dead Calm*, Copyright © 1989 Warner Bros. Inc.;
253: *above and below*: *Agnes of God*, Copyright © 1985 Columbia Pictures Industries, Inc.;
254: *above*: *The Fly*, Copyright © 20th Century-Fox Film Corporation; *below*: *My American Cousin*, © 1986 Spectrafilm Inc.;
255: *Eye of the Needle*, Copyright © MCMLXXXI United Artists Corporation; *centre, above*: *The Decline of the American Empire*, © 1986 Malo Film Group and the National Film Board of Canada; *centre, below*: *Jesus of Montreal*, © Max Films Productions Inc. 1989 Gerard Mital Productions;
256: *Dudes*, © 1987 The Vista Organization Partnership, L.P.;
257: *The Bear*, © 1989 Tri-Star Pictures, Inc.;
258: *Camille Claudel*, © 1989 Orion Pictures Corp.;
259: *above*: *Camille Claudel*, © 1989 Orion Pictures Corp.; *below*: *Hanna's War*, Copyright © 1988 Cannon Films, Inc.;
260: *above*: *Betty Blue*, © 1986 Alive Films; *below*: *Date with an Angel*, © 1987 De Laurentiis Entertainment Group Inc.;
261: *above*: *Frantic*, © 1988 Warner Bros. Inc.; *below*: *The Bedroom Window*, © 1986 De Laurentiis Entertainment Group; *centre*: *The Little Thief*, A Miramax Films Release © 1989;
262: *Breathless*, Copyright 1983 Orion Pictures Corp.;
263: *above*: *Life and Nothing But*, © 1989 Hachette Premiere Groupe Europe 1 Communication – AB Films, Littlebear – A2; *below*: *Manon of the Spring*, © Copyright 1987 Orion Pictures Corporation; *centre*: *The Big Blue*, © 1988 Weintraub;
264: *above*: *Burning Secret*, Copyright © 1988 Vestron Pictures; *below*: *Das Boot*, © 1982 Columbia Pictures Industries, Inc.;
265: *Paris, Texas*, Copyright © 20th Century-Fox Film Corporation; *insert*: *Bagdad Cafe*, Copyright © 1988 Island Pictures;
266: *above*: *Carmen*, © 1984, International Spectrafilm Distribution, Inc.; *below*: *Tie Me Up! Tie Me Down!*, A Miramax Films Release © 1990; *centre*: *Cinema Paradiso*, © 1989 Sovereign Pictures, Inc.;
267: *The Icicle Thief*, © 1989 Bambu Cinema e TV;
268: *Mishima: A Life in Four Chapters*, © 1985 The M Film Company;
269: *Ran*, Copyright 1985 Orion Classics;
270: *above*: *Another 48 HRS*, © 1990 Paramount Pictures Corp.; *below*: *Days of Thunder*, © 1990 Paramount Pictures Corp.;
271: *above*: *Presumed Innocent*, Copyright © 1990 Warner Bros. Inc.; *below*: *Total Recall*, © 1990 Tri-Star Pictures, Inc.;
272: *above*: *Quigley Down Under*, © 1990 Pathé Entertainment, Inc.; *below*: *Bird on a Wire*, © 1990 Universal City Studios, Inc.; *centre*: *Pretty Woman*, © Touchstone Pictures;
273: *above*: *Dick Tracy*, © The Walt Disney Company; *insert*: *Ghost*, © 1990 Paramount Pictures Corp.;
274: *Wild at Heart*, © 1990 PolyGram Filmprodukton GmbH;
275: *above*: *Quick Change*, Copyright © 1990 Warner Bros. Inc.; *below*: *The Two Jakes*, © 1990 Paramount Pictures Corp.; *centre*: *Teenage Mutant Ninja Turtles*, © 1990 New Line Cinema;
288: *E.T. The Extra-Terrestrial*, Copyright © 1982 Universal City Studios, Inc.

INDEX

Bolded numbers indicate photo captions.

BIBLIOGRAPHY

The majority of interviews in this book were conducted by the author, Ron Base. However, other sources were consulted, in particular, *Variety*, regarded as "the bible" of the movie industry.

Allen, Jennifer. "Cher and Altman on Broadway." *New York* magazine. February 1, 1982.

Auty, Martyn. Roddick, Nick. *British Cinema Now*. British Film Institute Publishing. London, 1985.

Bach, Steven. *Final Cut: Dreams and Disaster in the Making of Heaven's Gate*. William Morrow and Co., Inc. New York, 1985.

Bruck, Connie. "Deal of the Year." *New Yorker* magazine. January, 1990.

Bygrove, Mike. Goodman, Joan. "Meet Me in Las Vegas." *American Film* magazine. October, 1981.

Chatkow, Paul. "The Private War of Tom Cruise." *New York Times*. December 17, 1989.

Collins, Glenn. "For Oliver Stone, It's Time to Move on From Vietnam." *New York Times*. January 2, 1990.

Connaughton, Shane. Sheridan, Jim. *My Left Foot*. Faber and Faber Ltd. London, 1989.

Corliss, Richard. "Tom Terrific." *Time* magazine. December 25, 1989.

Corliss, Richard. "What Makes Meryl Magic." *Time* magazine. September 7, 1981.

Cowie, Peter. *Variety International Film Guide*. Andre Deutch. London, 1990.

Dermody, Susan. Jacka, Elizabeth. *The Screening of Australia: Anatomy of a Film Industry*. Currency Press. Sidney, 1987.

Dormoney, Bruce. "Puttnam's Revenge." *M* magazine. April, 1990.

Dunne, John Gregory. *The Studio*. Farrar, Strauss and Giroux. New York, 1968-69.

Eastman, John. *Retakes: Behind the Scenes of 500 Classic Movies*. Ballentine Books. New York, 1989.

Easton, Nina J. "Behind the Scenes of the Big Deal." *Los Angeles Times/Calendar* magazine. December 31, 1989.

Fabrikant, Geraldine. "Hollywood's Next Hot Property?" *New York Times*. December 3, 1989.

Fayard, Judy. "The World's Favorite Movie Star Is — No Kidding — Clint Eastwood." *Life* magazine. July 23, 1971.

Feldman, Seth. *Take Two: A Tribute to Film in Canada*. Irwin Publishing. Toronto, 1984.

Field, Syd. *Selling a Screenplay: The Screenwriters' Guide to Hollywood*. Dell Publishing. New York, 1989.

Finler, Joel W. *The Hollywood Story*. Octopus Books. London, 1988.

Gabler, Neal. *An Empire of Their Own: How the Jews Invented Hollywood*. Crown Publishers, Inc. New York, 1988.

Giffin, Nancy. Masters, Kim. "Columbia's New King Pins." *Premiere* magazine. March, 1990.

Goldman William. *Adventures in the Screen Trade: A Personal View of Hollywood and Screenwriting*. Warner Books. New York, 1983.

Goldman, William. *Hype and Glory*. Villard Books. New York, 1990.

Grobel, Lawrence. "Playboy Interview: Goldie Hawn." *Playboy* magazine. January, 1985.

Halliwell, Leslie. *Halliwells' Film Guide — 7th Edition*. Grafton Books. London, 1989.

Hampton, Christopher. *Dangerous Liaisons: The Film*. Faber and Faber. London, 1989.

Harmetz, Aljean. "With Salaries Soaring, It's Time out for Films Made on the Cheap." *New York Times*. December 7, 1989.

Hibbin, Sally. *The Official James Bond Movie Book*. Crown Publishers. New York, 1987.

Hinson, Hal. "Mysteries of the Orgasm." *Smart* magazine. January-February, 1990.

Hoffman, Jan. "Why You Can't Laugh at Cher Anymore." *Premiere* magazine. February, 1988.

Jaehne, Karen. "Casualty of War." *Film Comment* magazine. January-February, 1990.

Johnstone, Iain. "Dark Knight in the City of Dreams." *Empire* magazine. August, 1989.

Kaplan, James. "Golden Lady." *Premiere* magazine. September, 1988.

Kaplan, James. "Star Turner." *Vanity Fair* magazine. March, 1990.

Kipps, Charles. *Out of Focus: Power Pride and Prejudice — David Puttnam in Hollywood.* Silver Arrow Books/William Morrow and Co., Inc. New York, 1989.

Kolson, Anne. "Cher Has Last Laugh on Hollywood." *Knight-Ridder* newspapers. March, 1985.

Kornbluth, Jesse. "A Cool Breeze — Kevin Costner." *Vanity Fair* magazine. May 1989.

Kornbluth, Jesse. "Kevin Costner, a Cool Breeze." *Premiere* magazine. May 1989.

Kureishi, Hanif. *My Beautiful Launderette.* Faber and Faber. London, 1986.

Lindsay, Robert. "The New Wave of Film Makers." *New York Times* magazine. May 28, 1978.

Litwak, Mark. *Reel Power: The Struggle for Influence and Success in Hollywood.* William Morrow and Co., Inc. New York, 1986.

MacPherson, Malcolm. "Kathleen Turner: The Single-Minded Cinderella." *Premiere* magazine. November, 1989.

Maibaum, Richard. "My Word is Bond: A View from the Back Room." *Esquire* magazine. June, 1965.

Mailer, Norman. "Clint Eastwood." *Parade* magazine. October 23, 1983.

Marriott, John. *Batman, The Official Book of the Movie.* Hamlyn Publishing Group. London, 1989.

McClintick David. *Indecent Exposure: A True Story of Hollywood and Wall Street.* William Morrow and Co., Inc. New York, 1982.

Midler, Bette. *A View from A Broad.* Simon and Schuster. New York, 1980.

Miller, Russell. "No One Says No to Sean Connery." *Sunday Times* magazine. November 5, 1989.

Newcomb, Peter. "The Magic Kingdom." *Forbes* magazine. October 7, 1989.

Nolitzer, Meg. "Bette on It." *Fame* magazine. December, 1989.

Orleans, Susan. "Dandy Andie." *Rolling Stone* magazine. October 19, 1989.

Orth, Maureen. "The New Hollywood." *Newsweek* magazine. November 25, 1974.

Pollock, Dale. *Skywalking: The Life and Films of George Lucas.* Harmony Books. New York, 1983.

Quinlan, David. *Quinlan's Illustrated Directory of Film Stars.* R.T. Batsford. London, 1986.

Rensin, David. "Playboy Interview: Eddie Murphy." *Playboy* magazine. February, 1990.

Rich, Frank. "Woody Allen." *Time* magazine. July 2, 1972.

Ritts, Herb. "Goldie's Second Takeoff." *Vanity Fair* magazine. September, 1989.

Rosenfield, Paul. "The Inside Man." *Los Angeles Times/Calendar* magazine. December 7, 1989.

Rubin, Steven Jay. *The James Bond Films.* Arlington House. New York, 1981, 1983.

Scheer, Robert. "Playboy Interview: Tom Cruise." *Playboy* magazine. January, 1990.

Schwartz, Tony. "Comedy's New Face." *Newsweek* magazine. April 3, 1978.

Schwarzenegger, Arnold. *Arnold: Education of a Body Builder.* Simon and Schuster. New York, 1977.

Silverman, Stephen M. *David Lean.* Harry N. Abrams Inc. New York, 1989.

Silverman, Stephen M. *The Fox That Got Away: The Last Days of the Zanuck Dynasty at Twentieth Century Fox.* Lyle Stuart Inc. Secaucus, 1988.

Soderbergh, Steven. *sex, lies, and videotape.* Harper and Row Publishers. New York, 1990.

Stivers, Cyndi. "Blond Ambition." *Premiere* magazine. September, 1989.

Stone, Oliver. *Platoon and Salvador: The Original Screenplays.* Vintage Books. New York, 1987.

Taylor, John. *Storming the Magic Kingdom: Wall Street, the Raiders, and the Battle for Disney.* Alfred A. Knopf. New York, 1987.

"The Man with the Golden Bond." *Time* magazine. August 21, 1965.

Vincour, John. "Clint Eastwood Seriously." *New York Times* magazine. February 24, 1985.

Yule, Andrew. *Hollywood a Go-Go: The True Story of Cannon Film Empire.* Sphere Books Ltd. London, 1987.

Zebme, Bill. "Eddy Murphy." *Rolling Stone* magazine. August 24, 1989.

Zimmerman, Paul. "The Godfather: Triumph for Brando." *Newsweek* magazine. March 13, 1972.

DESIGN AND ART DIRECTION:

Gordon Sibley
Katharine Webb

EDITORS:

Sandra Tooze
Alexandra Lenhoff

EDITORIAL ASSISTANCE:

Duncan McKenzie
Diane Talbot

INDEXING:

Heather L. Ebbs

TYPOGRAPHY:

On-line Graphics

FILM SEPARATIONS:

Colour Technologies

PRINTING AND BINDING:

R. R. Donnelley & Sons Company
Willard, Ohio USA

PRODUCED BY:

Marquee Communications Incorporated
77 Mowat Avenue, Suite 621
Toronto, Ontario
Canada
M6K 3E3